must *write*
Edna Staebler's Diaries

must *write*
Edna Staebler's Diaries

edited by Christl Verduyn

Wilfrid Laurier University Press
WLU

We acknowledge the support of the Canada Council for the Arts for our publishing program. We acknowledge the financial support of the Government of Canada through the Book Publishing Industry Development Program for our publishing activities. We acknowledge the financial support of the Waterloo Regional Heritage Foundation. heritage

ONTARIO ARTS COUNCIL
CONSEIL DES ARTS DE L'ONTARIO

Library and Archives Canada Cataloguing in Publication

Staebler, Edna, 1906–
    Must write : Edna Staebler's diaries / edited by Christl Verduyn.

(Life writing series)
ISBN 0-88920-481-0

    1. Staebler, Edna, 1906– —Diaries. 2. Authors, Canadian (English)—20th century—Diaries. I. Verduyn, Christl, 1953– II. Title. III. Series.

FC601.S69A3 2005   C818'.5403   C2005-903941-8

© 2005 Wilfrid Laurier University Press
Waterloo, Ontario, Canada
www.wlupress.wlu.ca

Cover photograph courtesy of Edna Staebler.
Cover and interior design by P.J. Woodland.

"To Youth," from *In American* by John V.A. Weaver, 1939. Used by permission of Alfred A. Knopf, a division of Random House.

Every reasonable effort has been made to acquire permission for copyright material used in this text, and to acknowledge all such indebtedness accurately. Any errors and omissions called to the publisher's attention will be corrected in future printings.

∞

Printed in Canada

Contents

Acknowledgments

I WOULD LIKE TO ACKNOWLEDGE and thank a number of individuals and institutions for their support of this project.

First and foremost, thanks to Edna Staebler, whose diary writing is at the heart of this book. I am extremely grateful for her permission to publish material from her archives and for her generous cooperation throughout. Thanks to Sandra Woolfrey, former director of Wilfrid Laurier University Press, who introduced me to Edna and who encouraged my conception of the project. Thanks as well to Brian Henderson, current director of Wilfrid Laurier University Press, and to his staff at WLUP, in particular Jacqueline Larson, Carroll Klein, and Pamela Woodland, for seeing the book through production to publication.

An agreement between the University of Guelph and Wilfrid Laurier University, approved by Edna Staebler, enabled the transfer of her diaries from the University of Guelph Library Archives to Wilfrid Laurier University Archives during the summer of 2001. This arrangement allowed for much easier access to the materials for transcription by two student assistants, Lisa Butler and Sally Heath. For facilitating the agreement, thanks to Lorne Bruce, Head of Archival and Special Collections at the University of Guelph, as well as Tim Sauer, Head of Collections Services, University of Guelph Library, and at Wilfrid Laurier University, Virginia Gillham, former University Librarian. For their helpful and friendly assistance in the archives, thanks to Ellen Morrison and Darlene Wiltsie at the University of Guelph and to Joan Mitchell and Cindy Preece at Wilfrid Laurier University.

For conversations about Edna's diaries and for her help with photographs for the book, thanks to Kathryn Wardropper. Thanks as well as to Sally Heath, who stayed on as a research assistant for the duration of the project and to whose trusty transcription work I am enormously indebted. Sylvia Hoang helpfully scanned Staebler's journalism articles for the volume and Kerry Cannon lent a welcome hand with some elusive footnote material. Ann Wood and Sheila Bauman of the Kitchener Public Library tracked down an obituary notice for Yvonne Craig. Early on in the project, I spoke with Judith Miller, who excerpted a passage from Edna's diaries for the collection *The Small Details of Life: Twenty Diaries by Women in Canada 1830–1996*, edited by Kathryn Carter (2002). Last but not least, I would like to acknowledge Veronica Ross, whose biography of Staebler appeared as I was nearing the end of my work and presents a wonderful companion volume to this one.

A Wilfrid Laurier University short-term grant was helpful at the outset of this project and a Social Sciences and Humanities Research Council grant supported the completion of the work. I am grateful to the council for its support of my work over the years and I sincerely hope it will continue to fund research in the humanities for many years to come. Throughout this and other research projects, I have had the steady, good-humoured support of my family, and my final thanks and deepest appreciation belong as always to Robert Campbell and our four children.

Introduction

Life as Writing
Edna Staebler's Diaries

L ONG BEFORE SHE BECAME a renowned author of best-selling cookbooks, an award-winning journalist, a published author, and a mentor of creative non-fiction, Edna Staebler was a writer of a different sort. She was a prodigious diarist. Staebler began serious diary writing at the age of sixteen in 1922 and continued for over eighty years until she suffered a mild stroke in 2003.[1] Approaching her centenary in 2006, Edna Staebler is the author of a voluminous body of diary writing. Housed in Archival and Special Collections at the University of Guelph, the Staebler diaries comprise thousands of handwritten, single-spaced, double-sided pages. This book presents excerpts from that substantial literary corpus, creating a portrait of Edna Staebler as a writer and the author of this volume of life writing.

It is tempting to see the Staebler diaries as biography, and indeed the diaries contain a great deal of information about Edna's life.[2] However, they do not provide an uninterrupted record and this volume is not presented as biography in the traditional sense of the genre. When Staebler travelled to Europe, for instance, letters home replaced diary writing. And when she was in the throes of her cookbook work and journalism, her diary writing slowed down noticeably. Rather than biography, this book proposes that the Staebler diaries constitute a compelling example of life writing as well as the literary work that the author longed to achieve throughout her life. This introduction briefly situates Staebler's diaries in the context of her published work and also within the genre and practice of life writing as well as the larger related frame of autobiographical writing. It provides an overview of the material and the structure of the book and addresses the question of the literary value of diary writing. It is followed by a chronology of Staebler's life that includes a segment of family tree relevant to the diaries.

The Public Writer

Cookbook readers readily recognize Edna Staebler as the author of the enormously successful series that began with *Food That Really Schmecks*.³ The series offers readers not only recipes but also stories and anecdotes about the people and places linked to the recipes. Described by Edith Fowke as folklore literature, Staebler's cookbooks have earned her national acclaim and local fame.⁴ Although it is as a cookbook author that she is best known today, Edna Staebler initially made her mark as a writer through journalism. Her first published piece, "Duellists of the Deep," appeared in *Maclean's* magazine in 1948. Based on a fishing expedition on which Staebler joined Cape Bretoners fishing for swordfish, it caught the attention of Scott Young, *Maclean's* magazine editor at the time. Journalism put Staebler in touch with a host of Canadian writers, starting with W.O. Mitchell, who introduced her to another *Maclean's* editor, Pierre Berton. Berton invited Staebler to write an article about Mennonites. The resulting "How to Live without Wars and Wedding Rings," published in July 1950, earned her the Canadian Women's Press Award for Outstanding Journalism. To prepare this piece, Edna took her journalism into the field. She stayed with a Mennonite family and prepared meals alongside the community women who became lifelong friends. This experience later inspired and shaped the unique nature of Staebler's cookbooks.

The opportunities presented by journalism, and later by the success of her cookbooks, took Staebler from one side of the country to the other. This was an exceptional experience for her in an era when 1950s middle-class women in North America lived fairly house-bound existences. Still, Staebler's writing ambitions lay elsewhere. Although she longed to write fiction, she had little idea of how to proceed, for as she told the audience at Queen's University in May 1997 in her Margaret Laurence Memorial Address to the Writers' Union of Canada, growing up in southwestern Ontario during the Depression, she "knew no writers, there were no local colleges or universities where writing was taught."⁵ Staebler eventually published creative non-fiction, a genre that she pioneered through her own book about the small, east-coast fishing community of Neil's Harbour—*Cape Breton Harbour* (1972). Inspired by a three-week sojourn in August 1945, CBH, as Staebler would refer to it in her diaries, explores a part of the country since celebrated by writers such as Anne-Marie MacDonald and Alistair MacLeod. Staebler later helped win recognition for creative non-fiction through the establishment and funding of an annual award for the best of the genre.[6]

Staebler took an active interest in literary form, though she struggled with it throughout her writing life. She wanted to "just simply and easily write about things that I see and people without the need of giving form to my work. I'd like just to show life and love and beauty as I find them—as anyone could find them if their eyes are open and their hearts are listening" (September 2, 1954). Time and again, however, writing about her world proved to be anything but simple. In 1962, Staebler enrolled in a course on writing. The instructor, Evelyn Boyd, examined various forms of writing and discussed the creative process of writing in various genres—prose, poetry, essays, and journalism.[7] While she tried, and indeed succeeded, at different genres, Staebler came to feel most at ease in her diary writing.[8] "I am happy sitting here writing. I must never stop writing. I've done none, none for a very long time. And I hate myself for not doing it. It is a sort of denial of life, as if nothing is important enough, or exciting or interesting or beautiful enough to be recorded. Every day, every minute should have something in it that should be written down. To keep it alive, to give it survival, eternity" (January 6, 1973).

A strong sense of the value in daily recording and the deep pleasure derived from it combined to make writing a must for Edna Staebler. "I must write," she observed matter-of-factly years later; "The passion is not spent" (March 10, 1984). "Every day has had something in it that I should have recorded" (July 15, 1984). Quite simply, for Staebler not writing was *"a sort of denial of life"* (emphasis added). "I always feel better having written," she remarked, "as if a day hasn't passed unrecorded into oblivion" (January 26–27, 1992). "If I don't write, I am dead" (February 21, 1992). Even more than a must, writing was life. As a record for over eighty years of the determination, drive, and desire to be and succeed as a writer, Staebler's diaries stand as a significant life-writing achievement.

Life Writing

In the 1992 collection *Essays on Life Writing*, editor Marlene Kadar and contributors to the volume established life writing as both a genre and a critical practice encompassing many kinds of texts, from autobiography to letters, diaries, and journals, as well as the *Bildungsroman* and fragments of self writing in confessional novels and autofiction.[9] Expansive and unconventional, life writing has been characterized as a "genre of documents or fragments of documents written out of a life, or unabashedly out of a personal experience of the writer" (Kadar, *Essays in Life Writing*, 5). This liberating genre and critical practice opened the doors of literature and literary criticism to many texts and authors previously overlooked by the academy. Foremost among these have been the journals and diaries of women.[10]

Recent years have seen a sharp increase in scholarship on diaries and journal writing, a discussion in which feminist literary criticism in particular has argued the value of these writing forms as practised by women. A long-standing view held that diary writing, like autobiographical writing in general, involves less skill than fictional works, which require greater mastery of language and are more complex and rewarding to study. This view began to change in the early 1980s. An explosion of scholarship in the field challenged the "sub-literary" status of autobiographical writing in general, and women's diary writing in particular.[11] Sidonie Smith and Julia Watson, taking stock of autobiographical studies at the end of the twentieth century in their introduction to *Women, Autobiography, Theory*, observe:

> Women's autobiography is now a privileged site for thinking about issues of writing at the intersection of feminist, postcolonial, and postmodern critical theories. Processes of subject formation and agency occupy theorists of narrative and, indeed, of culture as never before. If feminism has revolutionized literary and social theory, the texts and theory of women's autobiography have been pivotal for revising our concepts of women's life issues—growing up female, coming to voice, affiliation, sexuality and textuality, the life cycle. (5)

Women's autobiographical writing remains at the critical forefront and is increasingly discussed as sets of discourses rather than in terms of genre. In *Mirror Talk: Genres of Crisis in Contemporary Autobiography*, Susanna Egan employs the concept of "mirror talk" to discuss autobiography in drama and documentary film as well as in the written text. As Egan and other analysts in the field observe, electronic media make up one of the newest areas for autobiographical studies as personal home pages proliferate on the World Wide Web.

At such an intensely theoretical juncture in autobiographical studies and at a point when the critical scene is so deeply engaged with discourse analysis, postcolonial critique, and globalization and diaspora studies, what place can the diaries of Edna Staebler take? In the first instance, the answer to this question calls upon earlier feminist work on the recovery of "ordinary" women's voices. Notwithstanding her accomplishments as a journalist and a cookbook author, in her diaries Staebler writes as an "ordinary" woman. It is still the case that the majority of women's diaries published to date are those of celebrated novelists and professional fiction writers such as Virginia Woolf, Elizabeth Smart, and Anaïs Nin. Similarly, critical studies of women's diaries have tended to focus on writers whose work has been recognized by the literary establishment. Thus, for example, Barbara Frey Waxman chooses literary autobiographers of aging—Maya Angelou, Maxine Hong Kingston, Audre Lorde, and May Sarton, among others—in her book *To Live in the Center of the Moment*. Staebler's diaries offer the opportunity to explore and understand the "ordinary" woman's struggle. In the second instance, the place Staebler's diaries take on the contemporary critical stage centres on the organizing theme of the collection—writing. Staebler's diary excerpts chronicle the struggle to write, to express the self in writing, an act which, if it comes more easily to women novelists or poets, can be extremely challenging to the "ordinary woman." Her diaries show how that struggle still produces text and how the theoretical, cultural, historical, and literary value of that text emerges through the acts of editing. As Smith and Watson observe: "Autobiography has been employed by many women writers to write themselves into history. Not only feminism but also literary and cultural theory have felt the impact of women's autobiography as a previously unacknowledged mode of making visible formerly invisible subjects" (5).

In a field of study so vibrantly theoretical and international in scope, Edna Staebler's diaries also point readers and scholars toward the wealth of life writing and critical work available within the Canadian context. In their introduction to a special issue of *Canadian Literature* on autobiography, Susanna Egan and Gabriele Helms note a lack of international interest in Canadian autobiography. If there was limited Canadian activity in the field of autobiographical studies during the 1980s, as Shirley Neuman remarked in 1996, the situation has changed significantly since and will continue to change as new publications appear. In *The Small Details of Life: Twenty Diaries by Women in Canada, 1830–1996*, editor Kathryn Carter focuses on the diary practices of twenty Canadian women, including Edna Staebler, who is presented in the collection by Judith Miller.[12] Working from the premise that the details of individual women's lives deepen the understanding of history, Carter notes how individual writings heighten the importance of historical and geographic contexts (6–7). She argues for both the historical and cultural significance of Canadian women's personal writing, from Anna Jameson, Susanna Moodie, and Catharine Parr Traill in the nineteenth century to Edna Staebler today. Not only do their writings "illuminate the unevenness of historical developments" (6), they also illustrate the "perennial and plastic" nature of diary writing and its span of styles "from reportage to confession, polemic to introspection" (6). Scholars today recognize that diaries are far more multifaceted in form and function than is suggested by the popular image of them as a private record characterized by spontaneity and secrecy. In fact, this image is fairly recent and considerably more limited than the actual practices of diary writing have been over the years. The history of the diary reveals that it has evolved through various stages and forms.[13] The early travel diary was intended to be read by individuals at home as well as by the traveller. The diary as "public journal" was also intended for reading by others. The "journal of conscience" served as a record of one's moral obedience, notably girls' and women's obedience to their fathers and husbands. The diary of personal memoranda, the "record of things done and seen and heard" (Fothergill 19), paved the way for the personal diary that is familiar today, commonly associated with girls and women, as distinct from the diary's origins as a predominantly male practice. To these different forms and functions of diary writing may be added the diary as modernist literary text.

Diary qua Book

In *Daily Modernism: The Literary Diaries of Virginia Woolf, Antonia White, Elizabeth Smart, and Anaïs Nin*, Elizabeth Podnieks makes the case for the validity and value of the diary—in particular women's diaries—as modernist literary texts. Podnieks examines the journals of the well-known novelists Woolf, White, Smart, and Nin, producing ample evidence of their diaries' status as literary works (35). She shows how diary writing can use the techniques and themes of modernism that have been associated with the novel, in particular modernism's displacement of the unified self by the concept of the multiple, polyvocal self, and the disruption or fragmentation of narrative line that reflects this concept.[14] Women's diaries are seen anew as sites for modern struggles with human identity and its artistic representation.

The ferment of activity concerning autobiographical scholarship in recent years coincided with a "historical moment," Shirley Neuman has pointed out, "when the dominant understanding of an internally coherent and stable 'self' was called into question by theories of the subject as constructed in and by discourses" (1). Reconceptualizing human identity revitalized cultural analysis during the last decades of the twentieth century, and women's writing emerged as exemplifying many of the new concepts. Women's diary writing in particular appeared attuned to new theories of identity conceived as more multiple than singular, more relational than autonomous, more subject to change than stable. The open-ended, cyclical, cumulative nature of much diary writing resonated with the powerful French feminist concept of "écriture au féminin"—writing characterized as unfinished, fluid, exploded, fragmented, polysemic, and subversive of the structures, logic, and syntax of masculine language. Like the new writing discussed and developed by theorists such as Hélène Cixous, Luce Irigaray, and Julia Kristeva, diary writing blurred boundaries between genres, between writer and reader, between reality and fiction. As Diane P. Freedman stated, "for women, borders—of ego, genre, discipline, geography—are made to be crossed" (80).

The diary, then, has offered women a viable written form with which to re-present and to challenge self and literature. At one level conventional and "traditionally female," the diary can convert into a space for literary experimentation and expression. This is how Woolf, White, Smart, and Nin used their diaries, Podnieks demonstrates, "to both mime and undermine modernist principles, creating texts which are at once aesthetically autonomous and historically honest" (96). Their diaries are major literary achievements, Podnieks argues. Antonia White's diary is "her most important work" (224), she asserts, testifying to "the life that has been lived, both inside and outside the text. The diary had always been there to console her, to absorb her neuroses, and to reconcile her fractured selves.... It alone was sustained for a period of more than fifty years and without inhibition" (224). Elizabeth Smart's diary writing likewise sustained her throughout adult life. "It was so clearly her 'work,'" Podnieks asserts, "that towards the end of her life she set about having its extensive volumes published" (225).

Edna Staebler's diaries have functioned in a similar fashion. Referring to the author's total body of work, Judith Miller describes Staebler's writing as

> a clear example of postmodernist writing, long before it was fashionable. She grounds her work in her local area, but creates a national and international audience. She makes room for voices from the margins. She works with fragments drawn together into a pleasing whole.

Her writing has a clear voice. She works in genres that have been mar-
ginalized—personal essays, journalism, cookbooks, and, more recently,
women's letters, with the publication of her sister's letters from the
fifties, *Haven't Any News: Ruby's Letters from the '50s*.[15]

Staebler's thousands of diary pages confirm their central position in all
this writing. Staebler felt nothing less than "compelled to record" ("My
Writing Life"). Writing was "an enthusiasm for something that had to be
expressed and the need to learn how best to express it" (January 25,
1999). Form remained a constant concern. After reading Henry Miller's
Tropic of Cancer, Staebler wanted to "tell my story, my life—to express me,
in the same way, but differently—my way, with different experiences &
motivation & faith & fulfilment & defeat & success & my own indul-
gences & guilt & ideals & failures—& life all around me & people I've
known & loved—or not loved" (March 26, 1973). If she frequently felt dissatisfied with her diary writing (July 12, 1988), Staebler also found her
journals "fascinating" (September 4, 1992), "dramatic" (September 7,
1992), "well written," and "straight from the heart" (October 15, 1988);
"there is much good writing and feeling and philosophizing there" (September 12, 1997). Staebler's diaries transgress the law of her generation
that women "should not call attention to their accomplishments and
that their lives have meaning only in relation to others as wives or care-
givers" (Brownley and Kimmich 95).

Staebler also conceived of her journals in book form, even as she spec-
ulated that "no one would publish my journal entries ... transcribing is
difficult ... it's so hard to read my writing" (September 12, 1997). "If anyone worked on my papers, used them and perhaps had the journals
published," Staebler considered, "I'd live forever. Or would I? But I hope
in that way my life would not have been in vain" (December 20, 1992).
Aware of the interest and importance of the journals, Staebler calculated
that "the most interesting and uninhibited part begins in 1945 after my
visit to Neil's Harbour and my determination to write about it" (May 1,
1989). Her determination to write was matched by the struggle to write.
In this, the diaries played a key role:

The journals also show my struggle with my writing. Had a wife a
right to spend her time indulging herself or should I be a proper wife
who plays bridge in the afternoons and does all the entertaining and
petty things that other men's wives seem to enjoy.... Also in the journals there is revealed my determination to keep up my spirits, to not
let K[eith] destroy me, to keep loving and appreciating the world
around me, the beauty and the joy.[16]... Frustration with myself because

I didn't write. I really had plenty of time to do all I needed to and to write as well, but I didn't write except in my journal. (May 14, 1989)

The struggle to write is intense and pervasive throughout the pages that follow, magnified by the sheer volume of Staebler's diaries. "All my life I have talked about writing and kept scribbling in my notebook," Staebler acknowledged on November 12, 1986, "as if that makes me a writer." The argument of this volume is that Staebler's diaries have indeed made her a writer.

Spanning nearly the entire twentieth century and extending into the twenty-first century, the diaries are extraordinary in their breadth and volume. Vividly illuminating both the intensely personal and the wider social scene, they proceed from the 1920s through the Depression years and into the postwar period and contemporary Canada. Written throughout a time of major social, political, and cultural change, they offer a window onto an evolving world as experienced by a girl growing up in southwestern Ontario. Rich in uninhibited and insightful observations of both personal and public events, they address such wide-ranging topics as love, friendship, faith, depression, betrayal, divorce, travels, politics, war, poverty, prejudice, nationalism, and Canadian versus American characteristics. In this, they exhibit all the qualities of a great diary, as characterized by Alan Bishop writing about Vera Brittain's diaries: a wide range of interests and experiences, sharp observation, the determination to record honestly, and a personality vigorously transmitted in the process (16).[17] To these, contemporary scholars have insisted on the addition of literary value.

Diaries are now widely recognized for their interest as psychological documents that enhance our understanding of human behaviour, for their importance as socio-historical documents that broaden our understanding of human experience, and for their value as philosophical or spiritual documents that deepen our understanding of human nature. The literary value of diaries, however, remains subject to scrutiny. In addition to the techniques and themes of modernism associated with the novel—in particular modernism's multiple, polyvocal self and the disruption or fragmentation of narrative line reflecting this concept (Podnieks)—women's diaries and other autobiographical writing display many of the literary techniques typically analyzed in fiction. Helen Buss examines the use of hyperbole and meiosis in the autobiographies of Maya Angelou, Maxine Hong Kingston, and Mary McCarthy.[18] Barbara Frey Waxman emphasizes the literariness of the works she selects for examination in *To Live in the Center of the Moment: Literary Autobiographies of Aging.*[19] "Sophisticated narrative methods, depth of characterizations, and rich descriptive powers" count among the literary experiences such writing offers readers (Waxman 17). When it comes to the language, content, and narrative structure of women's diaries in general, Judy Nolte Lensink nevertheless warns against critical insistence upon "an obviously literary design" (153). In "Expanding the Boundaries of Criticism," Lensink suggests that the initial sense of incoherence that may be experienced when reading an ordinary woman's diary, such as comments on the weather, health, and tomato canning, for example, followed by a stanza of sentimental poetry (153), occurs because we are used to constructed books (154). A coherent world does exist within the text of the diary, but it is one formed by the writer's perceptions, Lensink maintains, as well as by changes that transpire over time to create the natural "plot" of the diary (154). In Staebler's diaries, the struggle to write lends coherence—arguably even plot—to the sprawl of writing over an eighty-year period in which comments abound about the weather, the condition of the lake surrounding her home, the squirrels and birds that feed outside her window, visitors she entertains, food she enjoys, and so on. "Intensity of experience is usually signalled by quantity of language," Lensink points out (153), language that may sometimes seem tedious because it is both more repetitive and more literal than metaphoric in style.

Quantity is decidedly a striking feature of the Staebler diaries and the struggle to write is a recurring, almost overwhelming topic. Quantity and repetition may be viewed positively in women's diary writing, however, as effective techniques with which women diarists lend coherence to their experiential lives (Lensink 154). This functions even in the face of self-doubt or denigration, a frequent note in Staebler's diaries:

> Why am I writing all this? Who will read it? Why have I always written written written—in the dark hours of the night all my life, when I'm disturbed or lonely—or happy—I've always written, and the pages have piled up and will never be read. I'm sure no one could read them. I couldn't read them myself. I write so quickly…and who would be interested anyway? It's just scribbling, getting the skeleton of my thoughts down on paper.[20]

Whether with doubt or not, Staebler's diaries record an unrelenting desire to write. As the theme underlying all others in the diaries, it is the guiding thread of the selections in this volume.

Selection and Presentation

In an entry on December 20, 1997, Edna Staebler estimated that her journals were "probably millions of pages" long.[21] The Staebler diaries are indeed daunting in length and clearly invite more than one volume of selections. The collection presented here has been guided and shaped by the salient theme of writing itself. Given complete freedom in the editorial process by the author, this decision emerged quickly upon my first forays into the diaries, where the central importance of writing leapt to the fore. Editorial selections were made in relation to the key subject of Staebler's interest in and development as a writer. Readers will encounter a writer struggling to master a range of writing challenges, from form to topic. Sometimes the writer prefers simply to observe life; other times, she becomes a philosopher of life. At all times, writing is the medium chosen to express her thoughts and reflections.

The selections are presented chronologically by decade, beginning with the 1920s when Staebler first became serious about diary writing and proceeding into the twenty-first century. Chapters vary in length according to the prominence of the foundation theme of writing within each ten-year period. Thus, for example, the 1920s and 1930s are short compared to the 1950s and 1960s, since a good deal of diary space during the early years of writing was devoted to romantic recollections of dates with boyfriends and social life in general. Already present amidst the youthful sentiments, however, is the interest in writing and the search for the voice that develops during the ensuing decades.

Each section is introduced by a brief overview of key events in Staebler's life during the ten-year period in question as well as sample highlights from the decade's diaries. Because Staebler's diary writing is likely to find readership outside as well as inside the world of scholarship, I have used endnotes only where most needed to assist readers' understanding. Whenever the addition of a few words between square brackets could fulfill that same function, I adopted the latter approach; thus, for example: Ruby [Edna's sister]. Endnotes also provide details of the archive location for each diary excerpt. At present, the Staebler diaries are stored in boxes, but not fully in files. The boxes contain a non-chronological selection of diaries. Thus for example, Box R3–1 contains, among other journals, "Diary from age 16 to 1936," "Diary 1927-28," and "Diary 1948," but the diaries for the period "January 7, 1946–September 5, 1954," are in Box R3–6 and the "Diary Trip to Florida 1952" is in Box R3–4, and so on. In future, the Staebler diaries will most likely be archived in both box and file manner. Until then, given a variety of diaries within a box,

I adopted the following approach to reduce otherwise unavoidably excessive repetition in identifying individual entry archive location. An endnote accompanying a diary entry date indicates the archive box location for all the entries that follow until a new endnote on a diary date signals a change of box or a change of diary within a box.

Staebler's handwriting is difficult to decipher; indeed, it often defies its own author. In cases where neither I nor Staebler herself could make out a word, square brackets appear as follows: [illegible]. Punctuation presented a particularly difficult editorial decision. I was partial to Staebler's extensive use of the dash in place of punctuation as well as her recourse to the ampersand (&) for the word "and." Sample pages from the diaries included herein depict these usages and convey a sense of the speed, even the urgency, with which Staebler wrote. In the only previously published excerpt from Staebler's diaries, in *The Small Details of Life: Twenty Diaries by Women in Canada,* Judith Miller has preserved the use of the dash and the ampersand.[22] This is very effective in a short excerpt. In longer excerpts, however, especially when collected in a full volume, the recurrent use of the dash would have encumbered the presentation of the text. The decision to regularize punctuation and most abbreviations, as well as to italicize titles, was finalized by the overall argument of this volume that Staebler's diary writing be considered the literary text to which she aspired throughout her life of writing.[23] In this regard, Staebler's diary writing takes its place alongside the publications of Staebler the journalist and cookbook writer. Accordingly, four examples of Staebler's more public writing are included in this volume. "Duellists of the Deep" (1948), Staebler's first published article, appears between the 1940s and the 1950s back-to-back with her award-winning article about Mennonite life, "How to Live without Wars and Wedding Rings" (1950). Similarly, the opening chapter of Staebler's *Cape Breton Harbour* (1972) is included between the 1970s and the 1980s, followed by her lively account of "The Great Cookie War." The latter, originally published in *Saturday Night* magazine (May 1987), was reprinted in *Schmecks Appeal* (1987) and so offers a sense of the unique approach Edna took in her cookbooks as well as the professional journalist behind them.

In structure and organization, *Must Write: Edna Staebler's Diaries* thus integrates the private and public nature of her writing. What it cannot fully capture is the striking physical materiality of Staebler's diaries. Diary scholar Lawrence Rosenwald has established the importance of the physical nature of the diarist's chosen vehicle (18). Beyond their incredible volume, the special format of Staebler's diaries dates back to her high school science notebook—a hard-covered, seven-by-ten-inch, loose-leaf affair to which additional pages were added by threading them on to the laces binding the whole into a block. In the 1950s, fearing her favourite looseleaf sheets might go out of print, Staebler purchased a two-foot-high supply from the Merchant Printing Company in Kitchener.[24] She used this supply for her diary writing over the years, as well as manufactured diaries of the kind sold by department stores, travel diaries, and loose pages. Since her stroke in May 2003, Staebler's diary is the monthly calendar page, onto which she squeezes an incredible amount of information about visitors received and plans for the future as she proceeds toward her centenary.

Finally, throughout this introduction, I have referred to Edna Staebler by her first name, by her last name, and by her full name. This pattern continues in the pages to follow, the more personal use of the first name sitting comfortably alongside the more professional use of the last name in a blend of private and public that seems aptly to describe Edna Staebler's life and writing.

Notes

1 To widespread relief, Staebler recovered quickly and well. Since her extensive diary writing ceased after the stroke, its discussion in this volume is in the past tense.

2 A first biography of Staebler, *To Experience Wonder: Edna Staebler, A Life* was published by Veronica Ross in the fall of 2003. Ross draws primarily on personal interviews with Staebler and on Staebler's considerable collection of correspondence, as well as on some diary material.

3 *Food That Really Schmecks: Mennonite Country Cooking as Prepared by My Mennonite Friend, Bevvy Martin, My Mother, and Other Fine Cooks* (Toronto: Ryerson Press, 1968); *More Food That Really Schmecks* (Toronto: McClelland and Stewart, 1979); *Schmecks Appeal: More Mennonite Cooking* (Toronto: McClelland and Stewart, 1988). See bibliography for more details and information about Staebler's publications.

4 Edith Fowke, *Canadian Folklore* (Toronto: Oxford UP, 1988), 100, 110.

5 "My Writing Life," The Margaret Laurence Memorial Address. Writers' Union of Canada annual meeting, Queen's University, Kingston, Ontario, May 24–26, 1997. Hereafter "My Writing Life."

6 The Edna Staebler Award for Creative Non-Fiction has been won by writers such as Denise Chong, Charlotte Gray, Elizabeth Hay, and Wayson Choy.

7 Staebler told Boyd that she "suffered from not knowing what kind I should do" (February 16, 1962).

8 "The only writing that's easy is what I write here [in my journals], or writing letters—undisciplined" (February 5, 1964).

9 Marlene Kadar, ed. *Essays on Life Writing: From Genre to Critical Practice* (Toronto: U of Toronto P, 1992).

10 Given ambiguities in the history and evolution of the terms and practices of the diary and the journal, many scholars (see note 11) use the terms interchangeably, as do I throughout this volume.

11 The list of scholars and books is long and still growing as the critical examination of autobiography continues. Some key references, in alphabetical order, include: Shari Benstock (1988), Harriet Blodgett (1988), Suzanne L. Bunkers and Cynthia A. Huff (1996), Helen Buss (1993, 1999), Margo Culley (1985, 1992), Robert Fothergill (1974), Gail Godwin (1988), Elizabeth Hamsten (1982), Carolyn Heilbrun (1988), Estelle Jelinek (1980, 1986), Marlene Kadar (1989, 1992), Philippe Lejeune (1989, 1993), Judy Nolte Lensink (1987), Nancy Miller (1991), Shirley Neuman (1991), James Olney (1988), Elizabeth Podnieks (2000), Lawrence Rosenwald (1988), Judy Simons (1990) and Sidonie Smith (1987).

12 Miller chose an excerpt in which Staebler writes about receiving the Order of Canada in 1995. See Carter, 454–67.

13 For more information, see Robert Fothergill, *Private Chronicles: A Study of English Diaries* and Verduyn, *Marian Engel's Notebooks*.

14 As well as with male practitioners, Podnieks notes, an observation she explores and qualifies (64–65).

15 Judith Miller, "Edna Staebler," in Carter, 455.

16 Keith Staebler, Edna's husband. Diary entries and introductions that follow provide more information about this relationship.

17 Vera Brittain (1893–1970) pacifist, feminist, and author of *Testament of Youth* (1933) and *Testament of Friendship* (1940). Of her diary writing, Brittain commented that her "intimate, undisciplined outpourings were forced from my immaturity by the urgent need for self-expression" (qtd. in Bishop, 13).

18 Hyperbole, or overstatement, exaggeration; meiosis, understatement or belittling.

19 Among other writers, Waxman includes Maya Angelou, Maxine Hong Kingston, Audre Lorde, and May Sarton.

20 Box R3–4. Diary of February 9, 1985–October 12, 1985 (p. 62).

21 In later decades, Staebler sometimes numbered the pages of the particular diary she was writing in, the total count often creeping into the thousands. When available in the excerpts that follow, pagination is included in brackets at the end of the entry to give a sense of the volume of some of the diaries and to help direct and orient any intrepid readers who might wish to delve in the originals and find themselves confronted with upward of 5,000 pages in a single diary.

22 Carter, 454–67.

23 Including use of capital letters and periods for the beginnings and ends of sentences, replacing "&" with "and," and silent correction of obvious spelling mis-

takes. Some idiosyncrasies have been retained as reminders of the diarist's personal touch. Examples include: tho' for though; thru' or thro for through; nite for night; aft. for afternoon; Cdn for Canadian.

24 Staebler recounted this story to various friends, including Judith Miller, who mentions it in her presentation of the excerpt from Edna's diaries in *The Small Details of Life* (Carter 455).

Edna's Chronology

1906	(January 15) Born in Berlin (present-day Kitchener), Ontario
1921	(age 16) Begins regular journal writing
1926	Graduates from Kitchener Collegiate Institute
1929	Graduates from University of Toronto (BA)
1930	Hired by the *Kitchener News Record* in collections
1931	Attends Ontario College of Education
1932	Teaches at Ingersoll Collegiate
1932	(October 23) Father (John Geib Cress) dies
1933	Manages her deceased father's Waterloo Spring Company
1933	(October 14) Marriage to Keith Staebler
1943–1945	President of the Canadian Federation of University Women
1945	First trip to Neil's Harbour (summer)
1945	Meets Dr. John D. Robins at a Women's Canadian Club meeting
1947	Return trip to Neil's Harbour (summer)
1948	(July 15) "Duellists of the Deep," first magazine article published in *Maclean's*
1949	Return trip to Neil's Harbour (summer)
1950	(April 1) "How to Live without Wars and Wedding Rings" published in *Maclean's*
1950	Canadian Women's Press Club Award for Outstanding Literary Journalism (for "How to Live without Wars and Wedding Rings" in *Maclean's*)
1950	(November 1) "Isles of Codfish and Champagne" published in *Maclean's*
1951	Return trip to Neil's Harbour (summer)
1951	Becomes a member of the Canadian Authors Association
1951	(July 1) "Boats That Sail a Warpath" published in *Maclean's*
1951	(November 1) "Maggie's Leaving Home" published in *Maclean's*
1952	(March 15) "The Lord Will Take Care of Us" published in *Maclean's*

1952   (October 1) "Happily Married Cities" published in *Maclean's*

1954   First trip to Europe by herself (3 months)

1954   (April 1) "Those Mouth-watering Mennonite Meals" published in *Maclean's*

1955   (November 12) "Unconquered Warriors of the Oshweken (Six Nations)" published in *Maclean's*

1956   (May 12) "Would You Change the Lives of These People?" published in *Maclean's*

1958   (September 17) "Why the Amish Want No Part of Progress" published in *Maclean's*

1961   (December) "The Village That Lives One Day at a Time" published in *Chatelaine*

1962   Marriage ends

1962   (March) "Miner's Wife" published in *Chatelaine*

1963   (June) "We're Happy Being Slaves of Jehovah" published in *Toronto Star Weekly*

1965   (March) "Italian Canadians" published in *Chatelaine*

1967   *Sauerkraut and Enterprise* published

1967   Ryerson Press asks Edna to write a book on Mennonite cooking

1968   *Food That Really Schmecks* published

1969   *Sauerkraut and Enterprise* reissued

1972   *Cape Breton Harbour* published

1972   (March 8) Mother (Louise Rose Cress née Sattler) dies

1975   George, a *Cape Breton Harbour* fan, appears on her doorstep and stays with her

1979   *More Food That Really Schmecks* published

1980   Named Kitchener-Waterloo Woman of the Year

1983   *Whatever Happened to Maggie and Other People I've Known* published

1984   "The Great Cookie War" between Procter & Gamble and Nabisco

1984   Honorary Doctor of Letters degree from Wilfrid Laurier University

1987   Edna's account of the Great Cookie War published in *Saturday Night* ("Cooking the Evidence")

1987   Cookie War article wins Canadian National Magazine Award

1987   *Schmecks Appeal* published

1988   Waterloo-Wellington Hospitality Award

1989   Province of Ontario Senior Achievement Award

1989   Kitchener-Waterloo Arts Award

1990   Establishes Edna Staebler Award for Creative Non-Fiction
1990   *Places I've Been, People I've Known* published (*Whatever Happened to Maggie* reissued with new title)
1991   Silver Ladle Award for Outstanding Contribution to the Culinary Arts
1991   (April 28) Proclaimed "Edna Staebler Day" by Kitchener mayor Dom Cardillo
1993   Governor General's Commemorative Medal
1994   Joseph Schneider Haus establishes the Edna Staebler Research Fellowship
1994   Regional Municipality of Waterloo Volunteer Award
1995   *Haven't Any News: Ruby's Letters from the '50s* published
1995   Donates literary papers to University of Guelph archives
1996   (January 4) Order of Canada
1996   Lifetime Achievement Award of Cuisine Canada, to be called "The Edna" in perpetuity
1996   Endows the Edna Staebler Writer-in-Residence Program at the Kitchener Public Library
1997   (May) Delivers the Margaret Laurence Memorial Lecture at the Writers' Union of Canada Conference
1998   Inducted into the Waterloo Region Hall of Fame (only living writer)
2002   (October) Declines invitation to appear on Jay Leno's *The Tonight Show*
2003   (April) Honoured at Kitchener-Waterloo Mayors' Dinner
2005   Looking forward to her 100th birthday, January 15, 2006.

Family Lines

Cress

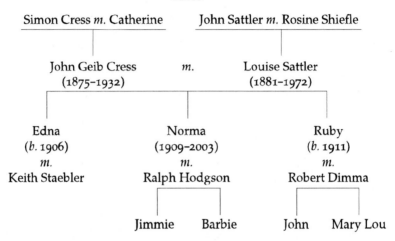

Simon Cress *m.* Catherine | John Sattler *m.* Rosine Shiefle

John Geib Cress   *m.*   Louise Sattler
(1875–1932)   (1881–1972)

Edna   Norma   Ruby
(*b.* 1906)   (1909–2003)   (*b.* 1911)
m.   *m.*   *m.*
Keith Staebler   Ralph Hodgson   Robert Dimma

Jimmie   Barbie   John   Mary Lou

Staebler

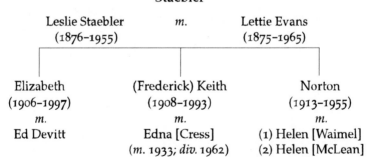

Leslie Staebler   *m.*   Lettie Evans
(1876–1955)   (1875–1965)

Elizabeth   (Frederick) Keith   Norton
(1906–1997)   (1908–1993)   (1913–1955)
m.   *m.*   *m.*
Ed Devitt   Edna [Cress]   (1) Helen [Waimel]
            (*m.* 1933; *div.* 1962)   (2) Helen [McLean]

1900s

⬚ *top left* Louise and John Cress, Edna's parents; *top right* Edna as a toddler; *lower left* the Cress sisters, 1919: Norma (*l*) Edna (*c*) Ruby (*r*)

the
1920s
Words to Express

THIS VOLUME OF EXCERPTS from Edna Staebler's diaries begins
with the young diarist drawing a line between the "foolish" entries
of her fifteen-year-old self and the more serious writing to which,
already at age sixteen, Staebler aspired.[1]

The brevity of chapter 1, "the 1920s," belies the significance of this
period in Edna Staebler's life. The decade coincides with her teenage
and high school years as well as her years at university and, finally, her
entry into the adult world of work. For many, this is a period of major
change and intense experience, and in this regard Staebler was no ex-
ception. Her diaries reveal a distinct personality well in the making.
Clearly aware of the social mores and societal expectations for young
women of her time and place, Staebler was also conscious of an individual need and desire to be a little different, to stray somewhat from the
path laid out before her and other girls and women of her generation.
"At eighteen," Staebler wrote on her birthday, January 15, 1924, "I think
one is expected to stop fooling and settle down a little. Not get married
or anything, Mother certainly didn't mean that," she hastens to add.
What it did mean, Staebler knew, was that she was expected to stop
playing about like her younger sisters, Norma and Ruby. As for marriage,
Staebler realized that most of her peers thought about it "more than
anything else" (March 7, 1925). Unlike them, however, she was not sure
marriage was for her. "I don't know if I want to be [married] after all.
It'd be kinda nice, I guess, having a bunch of kids when you're sort of
old. But the monotony of it" (March 7, 1925). "Maybe I'll learn to sew,"

Staebler mused. "But what for?" she then queried. Edna's ambitions lay elsewhere: "travel and see everything" (March 7, 1925). Her diaries capture a keen desire to read and learn. She especially wanted to learn how to express herself. She explored the possibility of painting, but it was writing that drew her most.

Staebler's struggle to write, to express her thoughts and feelings, reverberates throughout her high school and university years. Graduing from Kitchener Collegiate Institute (KCI) in 1926, Staebler proceeded to the University of Toronto, where she completed her BA in 1929. She was not a stellar student. She wrestled with essay assignments (November 17, 1927) and with the demands of "thinking" rather than "doing" (March 16, 1928). She was, however, an observant student (March 15, 1928), highly appreciative of the opportunity to "learn more and feel more and live more" (March 29, 1928). Moreover, though writing was difficult (July 24, 1928), it was also glorious when words managed to express feelings (August 21, 1928). Those moments were still all too rare, however, and Staebler had not yet found them in diary writing. Indeed, at times she had to force herself to write in her diary "to express things that I think I might like to know my views on later" (April 5, 1928) or to catch up on missed entries (November 3, 1928). "I feel awful doing that," she admitted (November 3, 1928), but these were busy teenage years that did not necessarily lend themselves to the regular entries of traditional diary writing. Staebler was reading more than she was writing and, as might be expected of a teenager and young adult, she was learning about herself (May 19, 1924) and about life beyond childhood.

By all accounts Staebler's childhood was pleasant and fulfilling. Her parents, Louise Rose (née Sattler) and John Cress, had three daughters, Edna (1906), Norma (1910), and Ruby (1911). John Cress was a successful supplier of springs to the many furniture companies that thrived in the Kitchener-Waterloo area at the outset of the 1900s and was able to provide his family with a comfortable home. Staebler has fond memories of family life on Scott Street, Berlin (Kitchener), Ontario. "Candlelight, horse-drawn sleigh rides, tobogganing on wooden sidewalks and the advent of telephones and motor cars" (qtd. in Rafferty 189); streetcar rides along King Street to KCI, her high school; strolls home with friends after school; weekend dances in the Crystal Ballroom at the Walper Hotel: these are experiences she recalls from the years she lived at home. Especially vivid are her memories of trips to the Kitchener Public Library, located two short blocks away. Beyond a condensed set of *The Books of Knowledge* and *The Harvard Classics*, the Cress household did not boast a huge collection of books, and Staebler visited the library two and three times a week to select books of her own choosing. Her reading developed largely unguided and, as a result, she later told members of the Writers' Union in her 1977 address, she missed many mainstream titles such as *Robinson Crusoe* and *Alice's Adventures in Wonderland*, for example. Instead, she read about "Jimmy Skunk, the little cousins who lived around the world, mild mysteries, and adventures" ("My Writing Life"). As soon as she was allowed to borrow books from the adult library, Staebler's reading habits evolved and she became a lifelong reader with eclectic interests.

Accounts of an entirely agreeable and untroubled childhood are modified in adult recollections recorded in subsequent Staebler diaries. In a long entry on March 6, 1975, she portrayed the social stratifications of early and mid-twentieth-century Kitchener and their impact on her life:

> As I grew older, I was ashamed of my parents. They weren't in society, didn't dance or play golf, or read books. I corrected their grammar. They came of local stock. Daddy's people were Mennonite pioneers. I didn't want my friends to know that. During the First World War, I suspected they were pro-German and I was scared of that too. I was thoroughly British in all my sentiments. Mother kept saying they weren't pro-German, they were simply against the war, hating, and destroying. I listened to all the war propaganda and thought that whatever the British did was great or inevitable. I wanted to be British. I resented my Mennonite-German local mixed ancestry. I rejoiced when I found out that one of my great grandmothers was Irish. I spoke of it often. I almost developed an Irish accent. I loved everything Irish. Then French. Daddy's people, way back, came from Alsace. Aunt Rachel told us. I like that too, though I know nothing of Alsace. But it was French and the French were allies of the British and romantic, marvellous, artistic, sophisticated people. As I grew older, I liked to identify with them. So, my guilt? I suppose I was always afraid I'd be found out, that my background would not be acceptable to my friends, my WASP friends, and they'd drop me, ridicule me. They were such snobs, and I was the worst snob of all because I had to work so hard at doing the right thing. I made many mistakes, which humiliated me, showed my ignorance and my lack of breeding—God—*breeding*. (March 6, 1975)

This entry depicts another Edna Staebler, a young woman striving to fit in, secretly ashamed of her family's German connections, and painfully aware of the privilege of a British background.

Staebler had dismissed her earlier diaries as foolish and "full of trashy stuff about boys" (January 15, 1922). Like many young women of her milieu, Edna enjoyed dancing and parties. She was popular and did not lack for invitations. The man she eventually would marry, Keith Staebler, makes his entry in this chapter (January 12, 1927). Life with Keith, as chapters to follow reveal, would not be what Edna and women like her were led to expect of marriage. But nor was life what she might have hoped for with a university degree in hand when she graduated from the University of Toronto in June 1929. Though she would later tell amusing stories about her failure to secure work after graduating, Edna's diaries tell a different story of life—hers and that of her community—at the end of the 1920s.[2] The Great Depression was about to unfold. Work of any kind was scarce, and Staebler returned to live with her parents. "Every day I heard people talk about hard times and unemployment. Away from the prescribed and stimulating environment of the university, I was bewildered and scared," she recalled ("Convocation Address"). "I was often depressed. I worried that I'd never get a job, or be married.... Every day I wrote miserable entries in my journal" ("My Writing Life"). The final diary selections in this chapter attest to this unhappy phase of Staebler's life. "I didn't want to write all the terrible low thoughts I had," she recorded on December 9, 1929, "and often I'd not written for so long.... All thro' September I sat around afraid of living—afraid to think, afraid to talk, afraid to do anything, thinking always of myself and my personality—afraid I'[d] lose it" (December 9, 1929). The 1920s ended on a fearful note for Staebler and for her world. On October 29, 1929, the New York stock market crashed, plunging millions into financial ruin and hardship.

Notes

1 In June 1921, for example, during a trip to Toledo, Ohio, to visit her mother's friends, the Gilberts, Edna observed in her travel diary and in letters home that "Things are so different here. We're so polite and I'm sure they think I am a society belle (I'm so polite, tee hee). Here they say Ha (meaning what) and they say yeah (meaning yes). Golly, but it's queer. Golly, Gosh, Darn. Damn is a *very* common expression" (Travel Diary Toledo 1921 Box R1). In her comments on the differences between Canadians and Americans, it is possible to glimpse the observant eye of the future journalist, even at fifteen:

June 26, 1921
Differences
They eat ice cream with a spoon.
They have dinner at night.
The girls flirt with boys.
...
They knit on Sunday.
—Travel Diary, Toledo 1921 Box R1

2 "I wanted to be a writer but knew I couldn't make a living that way. I went
down to Simpson's big store in Toronto and somehow got an interview with
C.L. Burton, the president of the company. I told him I'd heard that Simpson's
was opening a store in Kitchener and thought I'd be a good manager for it.
Mr. Burton asked me if I'd had any merchandising experience. I said, no, but
I'd lived in Kitchener all my life and I thought I knew what Kitchener people like. He seemed rather puzzled before he said, 'Edna, I think you'd better start in one of the store departments as a clerk.' A clerk!—no way, I was
a university graduate. I was prepared for something BIG" ("Convocation
Address").

Staebler was then "taken on by the *Kitchener Record* at ten dollars a week!
I wanted to be a reporter of course, but they put me in the circulation department where my job was to take the money the little newsboys had collected,
then add it up and get a balance. I tried hard but I never did get a balance,
not once. The two heads of the department kept muttering about it and sometimes they said quite emphatically, 'What's the good of a university education if you can't even add nickels and dimes and coppers'" ("Convocation
Address").

"A month later an old bachelor friend got me a job as a ledger keeper at
Waterloo Trust. Because they couldn't read my writing they made me sit on
a stool and fill pages of foolscap from 1 to 1,000. Clients came in to the bank
to deposit or withdraw their money and I had to enter the amounts in their
pass books and hand them back with a smile and sometimes chat. One day
I was asked to go to the President's office.... I thought he'd fire me but he
smiled and said, 'You have too much imagination for the job you're doing;
you're more interested in the people you serve than you are in figures. But
do try to concentrate on the work until you find something better suited to
your talents'" ("Convocation Address").

∾

🁢 *top left* 1920s. Edna and Lib Eastman (née Ruddell); *top right* 1924. The Cress sisters, from the left, Ruby, Edna, and Norma; *bottom* 1920s. Edna, Oliphant, Ontario.

From the Diaries

January 15, 1922[1]
Sixteen! Jove, it seems queer. I wonder if this diary will terminate the way my others did (in the furnace). All my other diarys [*sic*] were rather foolish and full of trashy stuff about boys. However, I am older now and although I can't say the "never been kissed" part of the clause (for I have been, dozens of times I guess), I can say never while sixteen, and I hope that on January 14, 1923, I'll be able to say the same then without a prickly conscience.

February 15, 1922
Here it is, almost another week since I've written here. I haven't time to write oftener or I would. Some of the girls are keeping "thought books." How on earth they ever have time to record their thoughts is more than I can tell.

(undated)[2]
Resolutions for 1924
1 Not say catty things about girls.
2 Study *hard*.
3 Not eat for the pleasure of eating (broke on 7th).
4 Read 2 words in the dictionary every day.
5 Not be mean or play dirty tricks on boys.
6 Go to church as often as possible (missed choir on 4th).
7 Not let boys kiss me.
8 Not go to shows that aren't worthwhile.
9 Not be late (broke on 3rd).
10 Brush my teeth *four* times a day.
11 Not to be selfish.

January 14, 1924
This is the last day I'll be seventeen. I dread the thought of being eighteen. It scares me. It seems so old and I am so very ignorant. I've no sense at all hardly. I s'pose now I'll start "filling out" as people said I would when I was eighteen. I only weigh 106 now and I'm quite comfortable. At eighteen I think one is expected to stop fooling and settle down a

little. Not get married or anything, mother certainly didn't mean that, but just act sensibly and not go running and jumping and acting like Norm and Ruby [Edna's sisters]. Maybe I'll learn to sew. But what for? Oh well, we'll let eighteen take care of itself. I feel just the same every year and I never change much anyway.

March 30, 1924
I don't think nearly enough about serious things. I'm beginning to believe that I'm not quite so deep and thoughtful as I thought I was. Oh well, I guess it will develop in time.

May 19, 1924
I wonder what people really think of me. I know what I think of myself. I'll write it down so that in later years when I look this over I'll know what sort of a fool I was. First of all—my looks. Well, I'm not altogether ill pleased with them altho' sometimes I hate myself. I like my mouth but not my teeth, and my eyes and hair are greatly flattered by other people. I'm thin and straight, thank goodness. I'm fearfully conceited, I know, but it doesn't show since no one else thinks so. I think I'm pretty smart and have a fairly good insight into other people's characters. I read a lot of good books, not trashy modern novels, and I think it helps just loads. Oh yes, I think I'm fairly well liked and am extremely witty at times, sometimes even clever. I think, too, that I can make boys like me. Now, what other people say—I'm s'posed to be very attractive, wear nice clothes and wear them well, have lovely hair, eyes, and pretty mouth and nice white skin and long slender hands. I dance, oh, just wonderfully and I am very different from the rest of the girls. Have, quote, "a personality of my own." I don't believe all this, of course, it's mostly nonsense because I'm not all that extraordinary. They say that both the boys and girls like me rather well. I hope that's true because I love nothing better than good friends and I think I have some. 'Nough said of myself for just about six months and then we'll see if I've changed any.

June 9, 1924
At last I really believe I'm developing a character. I hope so. Lately, tho', I've been very, very thoughtful and queer. Perhaps it's excessive study but I really believe I'm getting some sense. I hope it lasts.

September 9, 1924
I've been very worried all day. I must take nine upper school subjects in

order to take the English and History courses at Varsity. That's almost too hard and Mother won't let me do it so I guess I'll have to go two more years. I'd love to go to college tho'. One meets so many people and gets such a better insight into things and broader interests. The only objection is the number of years it takes. If I stopped school now and worked I'd be earning money, of course, but I couldn't be learning anything. I'd probably slide into a rut and think of only my work and the fun I could get after office hours and I don't want that. I want to read a lot and learn about things and people. Rather hazy all this, but that's another thing I lack—expression.

March 7, 1925
Funny, too, we always do seem to think about getting married more than anything else. Yet I don't know if I want to be after all. It'd be kinda nice, I guess, having a bunch of kids when you're sort of old. But the monotony of it. If I'd be an old maid, I'd want to travel all the time, only then I wouldn't have enough money and I'd really need an awful lot. My ambition has always been to travel and see everything. I must do it somehow. I'd like to do something awfully good and beneficial to mankind; only that way I wouldn't have anything, I guess. Then, too, I'd like to get married for awhile also. Darn, there's so much to do and here I have to stick in school all my life, it seems, and I'm so foolish and never study or get ahead. I'd like to stop, only I'm afraid then I wouldn't get anywhere at all and if I keep on, it will take so long and even then it's uncertain. Oh damn.

June 28, 1925
Felt like writing Murray [Snyder, a friend] and congratulating him, but I guessed I'd better not or he might think me too keen. Darn, I wish I could do just as I wished and not have any actions or words misinterpreted. That happens so very often and it is that which restrains a person so much and keeps one from being really individual and free-like.

May 26, 1926
O dear, I must learn to express myself. I just can't say things concisely and in a way that anyone might understand. Expression is what I absolutely lack. I'm sure I can appreciate it in others. I think art is really just expression and I can't express myself any way at all. I never will. I s'pose I'm not artistic—oh damn, what the devil am I anyway?

January 12, 1927
Just had a nice talk with Keith [Staebler]. Not a bit sentimental. We really are getting away from that physical sort of stuff and I like it so much more because I really do like him so much, but not that way. Worked hard all day. We were talking about Heaven tonite. I wonder what it is like and yet I never think about it when I'm by myself. I know it'll be lovely and peaceful and feel like I do when I'm listening to lovely music or feeling gentle breezes on a blue and white cloudy day or on a moonlight nite in the summer at the lake.

July 25, 1927
All alone. Don't like it much. In a book today I read that sorrow was made for one alone and happiness was made for two. It's so darn hard not to think of anyone, but I'm just not going to.

August 22, 1927[3]
Things I want to remember.[4] Camp fire, the forget-me-nots in the swamp, the crows in the morning, service at sunset rock … the lake with the sky so blue and the clouds so white and billowy and all about the Ultimate Reality, it seemed so very simple then, and the big willow by the dock and the shore with the sunlight on it and the black clouds behind the glorious misty sunny morning early.

October 19, 1927
The new Parliament building in the spot light.
The trees like lace against the sky from my window at the Hall, with a tiny crescent moon above it all at sunset time.
The night at Ward's Island with Keith and the stars.
Stars on a misty night.
The College buildings on a cool, clear, sunny morning.
The Centenary Ball, the quadrangle, the swimming pool and everything.
Canoeing on the lake with Helen—the silvery blueness of it.
The Carillon and the Memorial Tower.
Trinity College and Hart House in the spotlight.
Communion Service at St Thomas Anglican Church—the priests, choir boys and the windows and census and candles.
Portraits at the Art Gallery—"A Young Breton," "Mrs. Chaci," "The Insult."

Crispy cold night in Innis Park when the moon is bright and the sky very blue with clear twinkly stars and the trees look big and old silhouetted against the blueness.

The lyre pine tree near Galt.

The misty night in the park with Keith.

The girl who danced like a flame in "White Eagle"—her eyes.

The feathery, snowy night in the park with Keith.

The oriental dancer and the background at the Uptown with Wilf.

The tinsel trees.

Holy night.

Auditorium, Masonic Temple, Detroit.

Rachmaninoff.

The English Church nun on the street car.

The spider making his web.

Mac MacLean.[5]

The picnic by the river in St Jacobs.

The capricious moon in the wheat field—June 30 [1927].

[…]

Things I don't like

People—young ones—dragging their feet and slipslopping in bedroom slippers.

November 17, 1927[6]

Wrote essay. I hate writing rotten essays.[7] It makes me feel so terrible and guilty. I get all sorts of beautiful thoughts and I know exactly what should be there and can always tell what doesn't sound right, but somehow I never can write what I'd like to. It's an awful feeling, so darn hopeless and feeble. There just never are words to express that feeling of inspiration that comes.

(undated)[8]

"go on writing and stop being a damned young fool. That all living is hunger, and that without hunger we perish. That each man's city of refuge must be built within himself of broken toys. That the only people who truly live are those who are always beginning again. That it was not I, or Cicely, who mattered, but love itself: not my suffering that must be eased, but love that must be served. That only by love do we come to understanding the truth. That the mocking magic that comes and goes is the lamp that's lighting us to beauty. That this beauty is the happiness of God, and is not in clouds or on hilltops, but everywhere about us."   —Thomas Burke "The Wind and the Rain"[9]

March 15, 1928
There is a Jewish girl at college who fascinates me. I can't take my eyes away from her. She is beautiful. She wears a heavenly blue dress, her hair is golden and wavy like a Lorelei's and her dress cut low in front shows the fair whiteness of her throat way down.[10] It is glorious. I could look forever, even her face is lovely, grave and always interested. She knows so much. I wish I could talk to her and ask her what she thinks of all the time, but I'd never dare, she's too big for me. I wonder what she'll do or be.

March 16, 1928
I want to be doing things. I hate only thinking about them but if I keep thinking and believing, perhaps some day I shall be doing them, I will do them, perchance.

March 29, 1928
Another day that has made me feel like living a thousand years so that I can learn more and feel more and live more.

April 5, 1928
I think people who are privileged to feel things more keenly than other people ought to try to remember and be worthy of them, to make all their actions burning with the greatest thoughts and emotions they have, and a person isn't doing that if they act deceitfully or weakly, and Keith does in a way because he makes every girl he's with think she's the one he likes best and it's darned unfair. I'm not really jealous a bit. I'm sure I don't want to like a person who won't conform with my ideas about things like that. I can't write about it tho'. It's too deep inside me to be put boldly in paper like this. I rather hate this book. I so often force myself to express things that I think I might like to know my views on later and they aren't a bit natural, really, and would be better left unsaid.

May 9, 1928
Art to me is interest, interest in life. In what you do, there should always be that inspiring interest—even to the most uninteresting line or thought.
    Curiosity is the most obvious of sentiments.[11]
    My ideas should be my own—do not let other people influence me in the least.

One can do anything if they [*sic*] make up their mind.

The creative power in mankind is the building of a nation—it is necessary in all walks of life. Without it the people become smug, satisfied, and from this comes decadence.

Why can't I use any colour so long as I get the form?

To be free from all traditions is a wonderful thing or the only thing for an artist. In one's make-up there comes up that *doubt* about doing things. If this could only be overcome by…the arts, say. I am free from everything. I can use any colour, any line value, providing these things are harmonious in a picture.

The thing in painting is seeing and *putting down*. One is lost without the *other*.

An object in art, to me, is to make every little detail of a picture interesting, which all the time these are to play a part in the construction of the picture as a whole expression of life.

I have got to develop a strong character—not a pretentious one but a true, genuine one.

Everything I do must be careful—or it should be that wonderful thing: interest. Interest is *everything*.

Watch your *imagination—it plays hell* with one.

Opposition in life makes things more intense—it is the building of a life. Patience is the virtue of mankind. My life up to the present has been interesting from my point of view—but I still have the greatest things to get out of life—when I put them into practice.

Get the main masses.

Don't get unenthusiastic. Keep it up.

Everybody in the world means good—but there is that ever-subconscious mind working behind one's whole body. I don't want to be a person who sits back and lets circumstances make my environment. *I want* to make my own environment and *live it*.

Here is where the creative value comes in—at present I have lost my zest to carry the drawing through. What has caused this? Is it laziness? Is it because the thing looks hopeless? Is it because it doesn't look like what someone else has done? Is it because I have lost the creative spirit which has carried me so far? Or have I lost the interest which is essential to carry on? Or is it because my mind has not the capacity to, as yet, run at that zest for any longer than an hour? Curse satisfaction. I get myself out of many ruts but I always fall back again. Watch it—never become satisfied whatever.

One has to make oneself do things sometimes.

The thing is to keep that great enthusiasm and also have complete control of oneself.

A thing should be put down with clear conception. To actively create I have to keep my mind actively awake all the time.

I have a tendency to only improve on my drawings from what I know other artists have done. Instead I should be continually looking for new ways of presentation.

I want my life to be a life of great rolling and tumbling—rhythm of life.

Everything should be interesting. Life should be lived.

It has taken me a long time to realize what has kept me back in the world and for God's sake, don't let it go.

I get the idea of what I want out, [but] when I come to put it down, it requires so much force to hold it and the 101 other things, that I forget it.

Never let your mind think a thing is impossible.

One reason I can't stand a lot of painters is because they have acquired a way of painting and continue to paint in that same way. This uninterest in ever creating, or becoming satisfied, has the greatest tendency to make your work uninteresting.

One should be a person looking for new ways to present things and new things to present.

The trouble with me is that I see nature through other people's eyes. Instead I should be continually looking for how to present something new that I haven't seen in nature and to re-create from something in nature.

I have got to fight and push all the time.

In work, the thing is to get one's mind settled.

If I keep that forever curious attitude in life I think my work should be interesting and not get stale....

If I can only realize that whatever I do, it should be free in execution. The idea is that, in my early life, if I don't get what I want by free execution and very careful thought, then it will take years to get anything if I am tight in thought and execution.

The thing about making rules for oneself is to know when to break them—if one only lives on rules in this world, they [sic] would perhaps get somewhere in the end, but if they had that human touch of knowing when to break them, I think that a person would be a hundred times better.

The strong character of a person, or the will power, will prevent him from letting his mind be carried away.

Everything—a beauty if looked at in the right way.

Too much thought and not enough practice and not enough thought when at practice. When your mind is turned against anything or anybody, it is the greatest hindrance and menace to one's life. The only thing to do is to put it right out of your mind and say that it will turn out sometime.

The thing in life is to keep one's mind alive. When it gets tired, lie down for a while.

In my thoughts, do I have a tendency to analyze the minute things in life and sometimes lose sight of the large things? Can one explain the pleasure one gets out of a book to anyone? But will they get the same benefit of it? This, I think, depends on the other person's attitude—whether or not they are in the right mood. The thing is that people will believe you and have far more respect for you if they can also see in it your life. Love is held up by the great creative power behind it. In my life I find that the things that interest me most are the things which build up our understanding of life. Consequently, when other things that have not got that value come along, then I am not interested. Is this right? The thing is to have the love for the small parts and also to keep that same love for them when they are organized into larger parts.

The conception is the important thing and the student must be encouraged to rely on his own idea, to have faith enough in it to sustain him through the period of probation, to the medium of his art.

If a student is able to free himself of preconceptions, begin to work in a spirit of play, of honest experiment with the sincerity of a child, he will find not only a source of refreshment for his imagination, but added technical training and a widened field of vision.

I want to get the feeling in art of the large planes fitting into one another and creating a relationship.

As I mentioned before, it is the balance of the seeing and the putting down which makes the artist. One can sit back and see but he will never put it down if he is hardly ever painting or drawing. It is necessary to be continually putting into practice what you see, just like the musician—he has to practise for hours at a time before he can expect to do anything. If a man looked at himself—his mind self—as if he were looking into a mirror, I think that is the only way for me to get on—providing when looking at oneself, one is very critical and alive.

Painting, music, and literature sometimes overpower me so that I feel useless to try to create anything more. This has got to be pushed away.

Look at the interest in colour, line, time value, etc. that very few artists have gone through—interest in character.

It is the obvious romantic which I want to get away from.

I want to have every object giving a reaction of love, care, and fascination.

And on top of that, I want simplicity.

Art is hopeless to me unless I am striving for that abstract mystic vision.

Art is essentially an abstract thing.

A mental attitude is at the basis of all art that is any good.[12]

July 24, 1928

Work again and writing this up. I seem rather winded now. I hope I can keep on with this again. I'd like to write down thoughts as they come to me—guess I'll need a special section. Mr. Lowe asked me today if I'd consider working on *The Record* after I graduate—gosh—after that I'm scared stiff.[13] If I only knew things. I'm scared to death I'll just keep drifting from one thing to another and never do anything. I get myself into so many moods sometimes I wonder how to reach old age without having had some period of insanity. It terrifies me. I feel as if the whole world were pressing down on me, forcing me, squashing me, then other times I feel like spreading myself over all the world. If I could only write things, things that could invoke people to feel and think as I feel. But I feel too much. All my life is that, just feeling my way thro' all sorts of things and not thinking at all. I can't think.

August 21, 1928

Happiest gloriousest day. I feel as if I'd been thrown into a new world. Wrote a story today and when it was finished, Mr. Donohoe, editor, said I should be a Free Lancer [*sic*], write things to make people feel, because I felt so much myself that I had to make them feel.[14] The only way, he said, is to read, and read good books, and know people and be interested in book characters and relate them to people I see and know, think about them and feel for them and so write about them and not to be afraid, as he was, to have absolute confidence in myself and not force myself to write. Colour and rhythm and beauty of form or words mean nothing if there isn't any feeling, something that will make your heart glow. And

not to imitate, have personality plus keep it, write as I feel, not as someone else has done, not as I think it should be, but as I feel it should be.

November 3, 1928
Wrote up my diary all day—thirty days back. I feel awful doing that, so
darn dishonest with myself, and missing so much. Trying to record so
many moods. I'm in the same one all the time. I hope I won't ever have
to do that again.

December 9, 1929
The last three months have been the most awful I've ever lived. Perhaps
they've been good for me too. I've learned so many things. I wish I'd kept
on writing but I hadn't enough courage at the start. I didn't want to
write all the terrible low thoughts I had and often I'd not written for so
long. I just kept putting things off and it does seem silly now, but I'm
afraid that if I don't write things I'll forget them and there are always
some things I don't want to forget. All thro' September I sat around
afraid of living—afraid to think, afraid to talk, afraid to do anything,
thinking always of myself and my personality, afraid I'll lose it.

Notes

1 Box R3-1. Diary from age 16 to 1936. This diary is incorrectly identified in date;
  it ends in 1930.
2 Box R3-1. Diary from age 16 to 1936.
3 Box R3-1. Diary 1927-28.
4 From her summer at CGIT (Canadian Girls in Training) camp.
5 MacLean was studying with artist Arthur Lismer. Edna enjoyed discussing
  art with MacLean, and while she valued his friendship, she declined his proposal of marriage (Ross, 50).
6 Box R3-1. Diary from age 16 to 1936.
7 Staebler was a student at the University of Toronto from 1926 to graduation
  in 1929.
8 Box R3-1. Diary 1927-28.
9 Thomas Burke (1887-1945), *The Wind and the Rain: A Book of Confessions* (New
  York: George H. Doran [1924]); London, UK: Thornton Butterworth, 1924.
10 Lorelei or Loreley. Reference to the German legend about a beautiful woman
  with long blond hair who would sit on a rock along the Rhine River and
  sing, distracting boatmen whose vessels would founder on the rocks.
11 This marks the beginning of a series of brief reflections and musings about
  art and creativity that Edna included in this diary as she explored the world
  of painting.

12 The series of reflections ends here.

13 Editor at the local newspaper for Kitchener-Waterloo, known from 1916–1947 as the *Kitchener News Record*.

14 The *Kitchener News Record*, where Edna was working in the accounts office.

the
1930s

*Longing to Make
Something*

L IKE THE PRECEDING DECADE, the 1930s were eventful, busy years
for Edna Staebler and regular diary entries eluded her. The slim
volume of selections comprising the 1930s reflects this irregular-
ity. At the same time, diary writing retained its place of importance in
Edna's life. "I love writing in it," she declared on New Year's Day, 1931.
"A fresh start in this old, old diary.... I must keep writing, it makes me
feel that I am living with more purpose" (January 1, 1931).

Despite the dismal employment prospects of the times, Edna found
work at the *Kitchener News Record* during the first year of the decade, not
as a reporter, as she had hoped, but as a clerk in the circulation department. For ten dollars a week, her job was to tally the money collected by
the newspaper boys who delivered door to door. "I never did get a balance, not once," she recalled ("Convocation Address"). From there, Staebler landed a job as a ledger keeper at Waterloo Trust. "Clients came
into the bank to deposit or withdraw their money and I had to enter the
amounts in their pass books and hand them back with a smile and sometimes a chat," Edna described her work (ibid.). Her skills of addition
and subtraction proved to be no stronger in her new job. Edna was gently advised to find work "better suited to [her] talents" (ibid.). Her talents were an ongoing discovery for Edna. Foreshadowing developments
much later in her life, she discovered pleasure in cooking. "I used to
think cooking so prosaic and ordinary," she confessed in her diary January 2, 1931, "but now I think it may be my nearest approach to being
artistic." The desire to be creative surfaces throughout the entries of the
1930s. At times, the "longing to touch something and make something"

(January 12, 1931) seemed overwhelming, and at one point, Edna tried her hand at painting. But the times lent themselves to practical decisions, and following the lead of a school friend earning $1,700 as a high school teacher ("My Writing Life"), Staebler enrolled at the Ontario College of Education in Toronto. Entries from January to November 1931 provide a glimpse of Staebler's experience at the college and as a teacher in Ingersoll, Ontario. Her employer at Waterloo Trust had characterized Edna as a "people person" ("Convocation Address"), the kind of individual who could enjoy the company of colleagues and children, and this proved to be the case. Edna loved being with the students and worked hard at preparing lessons (ibid.). Her future did not lie in the teaching profession, however. When her teaching contract was not renewed, Edna returned to Kitchener in the summer of 1932.[1] That autumn, her father fell seriously ill, and, on October 23, 1932, John Cress died of Hodgkin's disease.

As the eldest Cress daughter, Edna was called upon to oversee her father's Waterloo Spring Company until its sale. This consumed much of her attention and energy during the year following his death. Together with another major event in her life—marriage to Keith Staebler on October 14, 1933—John Cress's death accounts for an extended gap in Edna's diary writing between September 1932 and June 1934. Upon returning to her diary, she reflected on the impact of her father's death on her life:

> I've just read over my last entry in this book—I remember so often I wanted to write more about Daddie but I just couldn't at that time. He was so marvellous I only wish I could have been with him more.... But I must stop thinking of it [her father's death] now—I hope I'll keep on writing here faithfully as I did when I was at school. It seemed a great help then. Days didn't fly into nothingness and utter forgetfulness. They're too precious to let go forever, without one word being said for them. (June 4, 1934)

This entry articulates the role played by writing—in particular diary writing—in Staebler's life. Writing was a way of staving off "nothingness" and "utter forgetfulness." This was no guarantee against more difficult days ahead, however, or another year-and-a-half writing lapse (June 1934 to January 1936). If it was initially fulfilling, married life for Edna soon was filled with anxiety and dissatisfaction. She quickly grew tired of the social obligations that attended her new status in life (April 7, 1937). She fell despondent about the loss of ideals she observed among her peers (August 11, 1938). She worried about her husband's mood swings and late nights. She felt lonely and "on the outside of things other people [were] doing and saying" (August 2, 1939). Last but not least, she struggled with writing. Stories she attempted seemed "pedantic, didactic, stilted, stupid, no use" (January 27, 1936), even if she won first prize for a play she wrote and submitted to a competition sponsored by Kitchener's Little Theatre in June 1937.[2] As the decade neared its end, Staebler renewed her resolution to write in her diary more regularly. "This diary used to be a great satisfaction to me," she wrote, "a place to air my innermost thoughts and for so long now I've neglected it and kept my thoughts to myself or spilled them in places that I shouldn't have; so I'd like to try and keep this up again every day" (August 22, 1939). The 1930s, like the 1920s before it, featured "many stages" for Edna Staebler. Writing in her diary towards the end of summer 1939, she realized this. A new decade was beginning with the world at war.

Notes

1 Ross's biography suggests that this was because Edna "seemed too young to be a teacher, she was told; the principal didn't like her doing somersaults in front of the students" (57)—her only athletic accomplishment, Staebler wryly observed.

2 Entitled "The White Waistcoat," the play was set in Kitchener's music society. Its plot is as follows: At a party in his honour following his Kitchener performance, celebrated violinist Frantz Neumann meets Margaret Craig, a friend from the past. Now a widow, Craig is raising a son who turns out to be Neumann's. Craig had kept this secret so that Neumann might not be impeded from success, which is symbolized by the white waistcoat. See Ross 67–69 for more on the play and its production.

～

🔲 *top* 1930s. Edna (seated, 2nd from right) with friends, including Lib Eastman (née Ruddell) (far left) and the Reidel sisters, Margaret and Catherine—reclining figure not identified; *bottom left* 1930s. Edna at Rand Lake; *bottom right* 1932. Edna with chicks bought at market.

top left and right 1932. Edna and Keith at the Breithaupt's cottage; *bottom* 1939. Edna with mother (Louise Cress), Norma, and Ruby, en route to Florida.

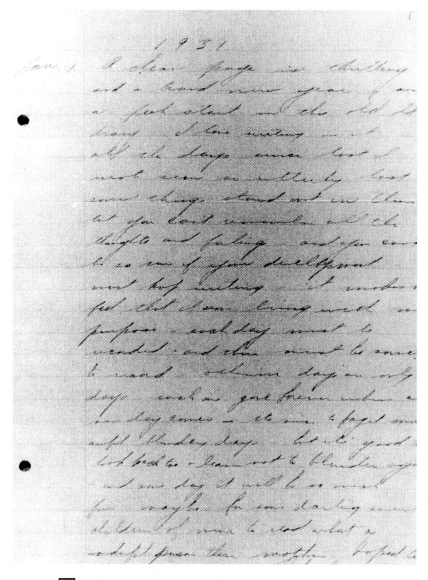

January 1, 1931. Edna Staebler Collection. (Archival and Special Collections, University of Guelph Library)

From the Diaries

January 1, 1931[1]
A clean page is thrilling, a brand new year and a fresh start in this old, old diary. I love writing in it. All the days since last I wrote seem so utterly lost. Some things stand out in them but you can't remember all the thoughts and feelings, and you can't be so sure of your development. I must keep writing, it makes me feel that I am living with more purpose. Each day must be recorded and there must be something to record, otherwise days are only days, each one gone forever when a new day comes. It's nice to forget some awful blundery days, but it's good to look back and learn not to blunder again. And some day it will be so much fun, maybe, for some darling sweet children of mine to read what a wonderful person their mother hoped to be. I sound didactic. Oh boy—it's going to be so much fun writing in here again. I love it.

January 2, 1931
I've been keeping house and cooking meals. It's fun, and it's so important. I used to think cooking so prosaic and ordinary but now I think it may be my nearest approach to being artistic, and it's so nice to think of actually building up people with the things you make, making them good so people want to eat them, and making them feel healthy and happy. I love it.

January 4, 1931
Church—our church—with Keith. Then sauerkraut for dinner—I'm fond of it. In the aft. we took down our Christmas tree—nice tree—I love a Christmas tree. After tea we read "Green Pastures," a beautiful play by Mark Conway [sic], giving a southern Negro's idea of heaven and God in a black alpaca coat and a 10ct cigar.[2] Not sacrilegious at all, but what you'd expect, it's so beautifully, musically written.

January 5, 1931
Advertised in the paper for a maid today and had about 50 phone calls. Poor women wanting jobs, most of them married, their husbands poor and out of work. Stupid, stolid German women. Austrians. Russians with red cheeks and big bones and Canadians too, all smiling and eager.

I had to turn them all away. It was so hard. I kept our Ethel.... Very tired tonight, but the snow is fresh and white and sparkly.

January 8, 1931
Ethel came. She's nice. Keith came too in the aft. to say goodbye to me. I don't like saying goodbye to him and yet this morning I was somehow anxious to get back to Toronto and work hard.[3] Keith's mother came before he left and it felt so awful and cut off. I shook hands at the door and he went away. When Mrs. Staebler left...I scurried like anything and tore to the train and here I am.

January 9, 1931
School—I don't like it very well. I despise shorthand. I met Wilfrid on the street. He's married now and he walked home with me and came right in as if I were his wife. I wouldn't like that, tho she really has nothing to fear as far as I'm concerned—but being married makes you very puritanical.

January 10, 1931
I loathe shorthand. It's so darn aggravating. Home tonite. Talked to the darlingest man on the train. He had the most infectious laugh and he sings over the radio and on the stage. Also he writes poetry. He was sweet. Old darling Keith met me at the station and took me to hear [tenor] Edward Karsame Ransome of the Metropolitan Opera Company. He used to be a butcher in Kitchener. He had a powerful huge voice but no sweet pure lyric lovely notes. Keith has been feeling very poorly about business being so bad. Dear old fellow.

January 11, 1931
I love cooking and using new recipes.

January 12, 1931
Worked hard as is possible on a Monday, writing and everything. I love getting up lessons, [illegible] it's so darn interesting. I love the old houses in Toronto. I wish I could paint them. Everyday I wish that and my hands feel groping and anxious to do something, just longing to touch something and make something.

January 14, 1931
History lesson—I'm so blooming fond of teaching that I just can't even

think of anything else. Got a marvellous idea today. The importance of teaching bookkeeping in high school. I never had much use for commercial subjects and I still can't stand shorthand, but bookkeeping, I think, is marvellous. I love drawing red lines for one thing and it's fun having things balance and I think there isn't a girl or a boy in the country who wouldn't be better off for having some knowledge of its principles. I should love to teach it—to teach it as a practical honest-to-goodness thing necessary to everyday life to make kids want to have it for their own personal good to keep track of their own money and especially if they are married. I'd like to work out a special scheme that would be practical for them.

January 15, 1931
My birthday, I believe. Mum, the old darling, sent me a check for $20, and Norma and Ruby sent me sweet hankies.... Keith gave me good wishes and I really don't mind cause I'd sort of like to forget about adding another year on Jan 15th.

January 16, 1931
I'm getting to be awful. I just haven't thought about Keith all week not even at night in bed. I've been working so hard and thinking about work and being fond of it. And today Helen [MacDonald] and I met downtown and bought lovely goods and started to make dresses for ourselves. I'm copying mine from a picture in the *Globe* and working the pattern myself.[4] It's darn hard work but fun when it turns out right.

January (undated) 1931
Last year when I was home I longed for Toronto and now I am here, I'd like to be some place else, never content, and the reason is that I let myself stagnate. I don't make the best of the thing I should be doing. I don't use my imagination enough to glorify my surroundings. I'm not alive enough. I stagnate. I forget that I'm alive and young and lovely. Keith tells me I'm lovely, and I feel myself get stale and dull and lose my sparkle and my goodness for all the interest and beauty and loveliness in life. I must never forget them.

February 5, 1931
On Tuesday I went to a dance with Fred Kergin and I had more fun—it was great. We danced and laughed and felt so nice and friendly and when we came home, there was a white full moon and a blue, blue sky

and stars and billowy little white clouds scurrying along between the apartment buildings and we looked at them and Fred said they were like that on summer nights when he was out on his boat alone and up all night, and right that minute I wanted more than anything else on earth to be able to live near the sea, or even a lake, and have such a glorious windy wild life. I've always longed for it...and if I must have the sea, I can write about it, like CGD Roberts said, "never write with your eye on the object—in autumn write for spring—put your personality into it—write about the thing you are longing for."[5] Sit by the phone and not think at all, but just feel the bigness of it, and all the greatness beyond across the water and all the rest of the world, way off somewhere. Ah dear, and Kitchener hasn't even a river, not even a tiny stream.

February 24, 1931

I went home on Friday in the usual manner and was met in the usual manner by my dear boyfriend and all weekend we had so much fun, tho I had beastly headaches occasionally. We read the preface to *The Apple Cart*, it's wonderfully clever.[6] I wish I knew more about things political. On Sunday night we had a business meeting and discussed our finances, present and future. They look quite bright, about 20 years from now.

Today I went into the Women's Union for tea and my dear friend Wilson MacDonald was there.[7] I enjoyed it so much. There were so many pretty girls all making the biggest pass over that man, telling him how thrilled they were about owning a book of his poems and how "delightful" they were etc. etc. on and on—poor man to be so gushed over. I'll bet he felt good and glad when he got out in the nice spring sunshine again. He looked at me several times like an old friend—understanding.

March 3, 1931

March 3rd—Keith's and my anniversary, tho he has forgotten, but exactly five years ago today he nearly kissed me and two years ago he decided finally to stop going with Marguerite [Shantz] and right today in this morning's *Globe* I read that Marguerite and Stuart Good were married on June 14, 1930. I'm glad.

March 7, 1931

Home again. Went to a little party at the Granite Club. Keith played most of the time. I don't know what to do anymore. Every time I come home there is a big quarrel about something—staying up too late or hurting Norma's feelings—or somebody's. I must be terrible and I always feel so darn awful about it and every time I try to be so much better and only manage to do another awful thing. . . . Mother thinks I'm a terrible, ungrateful thing and just because I like seeing Keith and stay up a bit latish—12:30 sometimes. I don't think I'm really any worse than any other people's kids—but I guess I must just be plain selfish.

November 3, 1931
And I am well established in Ingersoll. I love it. So much has happened since March 13—exams and getting this school-teaching job and passing and Lib [Ruddell] and Gerry [Eastman] married and living in a darling house all their own and going to call on them every Saturday night and having fun and going to summer school and taking PT and gaining eighteen pounds and coming to live with the Swallows who are the most charming English people and teaching itself and all the dear silly bad kids who simply won't learn and all the nice people in Ingersoll and the stories about them.[8]

November 10, 1931
I must read more and do more. My time is occupied, every minute, and still I can't do all I should and would like to. I want to read a lot of books about Russia and I'd like to write some more about Ontario. I must study more about all the countries in the world. I feel so intensely ignorant. (54–55)

September 17, 1932
Poor Daddie, for weeks now he's been coughing and coughing and hiccoughing and yet he lies so uncomplainingly, never a word, except maybe once a week, "This is . . . not very nice." Today he said his spoon seemed so heavy—he could hardly lift it to his mouth. He thinks of everything and he's so afraid he'll be a care to us, wants us not to bother getting him things or making them for him. He lies all day—half asleep, so weak he is—and he eats such a little bit. I don't know what he thinks about the future. He says he knows he'll never get better but we must accept it, it's only natural, and he may be a bit young, only fifty-seven, and there were still so many things he'd hoped to enjoy, but he had no regrets, he hadn't done many bad things in his life and if his time here is over, that's all, and he keeps on waiting, just waiting, so patient, hoping it will be not too long, for our sake.

June 4, 1934

I've just read over my last entry in this book.[9] I remember so often I wanted to write more about Daddie but I just couldn't at that time. He was so marvelous I only wish I could have been with him more.... But I must stop thinking of it [father's death] now. I hope I'll keep on writing here faithfully as I did when I was at school. It seemed a great help then, days didn't fly into nothingness and utter forgetfulness. They're too precious to let go forever without one word being said for them. So many things have happened this past year, and though I know I'll never forget all of them, I'd like to be able sometime to see how my ideas of things have changed. I was so busy last year looking after Daddie's factory... and planning the wedding. (62–63)

June 5, 1934

So hot, and still no rain. Three weeks now since the last and the temperatures around ninety all the time. This starting again is difficult. I'd like to put in all I've missed but I can't, so I might as well start now.

January 24, 1936

I hope I'll keep this up. I've reached the place now where it is an effort to write. My signature is about the extent of my penmanship. Last entry June 1934—a lot has happened since. We've built a house we planned every detail of. It feels so much like us. We're terribly broke now and in debt. My greatest wish is that I could earn some money by writing. Wishing doesn't seem to do any good tho! I sit for hours, almost, with a pad and pencil and write nothing. My mind seems absolutely blank. I have several good ideas for articles, but can't seem to get them developed. By writing here every day I hope to loosen things up in the old cranium. The snow is deep and it is cold. The wind is howling loud and long. Nuts. Anyway, nice trying to get a little theatre group going. Nice putting on *The Devil's Disciple* by Bernard Shaw.[10] I'm Judith Anderson and Keith's Gerard Burgoyne. It's fun. Last year we were in *The Ghost Train*.[11] I was Peggy and Keith Mr. Winthrop. It was most exciting. My debut.

Mother's birthday—fifty-five.

January 26, 1936

There's so much more beauty in ugly hands, hands that are red and roughened with toil, hands that have knitted and scrubbed and sewed, capable, large, and trustful.

January 27, 1936
Darn—I've been trying to write a story nearly all day. I have a very lovely magazine story plot but I write like a Sunday school teacher: pedantic, didactic, stilted, stupid—no use. Oh why can't I gain some fluency? I sit for hours and write three or four sentences that I'd be ashamed to reveal even to my husband.

January 28, 1936
Burial day of King George V.[12] A beautiful, sunshiny day with long blue shadows on the snow. We went to the memorial service at the church. It was very beautiful. The church was crowded with all kinds of people. The two theatres were filled, too, and four other churches. It was a most memorable occasion. Everyone looked so honestly sad. I can't write about it.

April 7, 1937[13]
Family's for tea. Social Council Exec[utive] Meeting—made convenor of Civic Committee. Damn. I'm getting tired of this kind of stuff.

August 11, 1938[14]
I feel horribly despondent today. Everybody is becoming so damned loose and awful. We used to have high ideals. I think I still have but everybody else seems to have lost theirs. What will happen to these people? My very best friends whom I've loved and trusted. Keith likes the drinking too. Am I going to be left alone—all alone?

August 22, 1939
This diary used to be a great satisfaction to me, a place to air my innermost thoughts and for so long now I've neglected it and kept my thoughts to myself or spilled them in places that I shouldn't have; so I'd like to try and keep this up again every day. I seem to pass through so many stages lately. I've been most introspective and disgruntled. I seem to be always on the outside of things other people are doing and saying. It's a very lonely feeling.

Notes

1 Box R3–1. Diary 1931–38.
2 Marcus Connelly, Pulitzer Prize-winning playwright, whose *The Green Pastures* (New York: Farrar and Rinehart, 1929) is an re-enactment of Old Testament stories featuring African-American characters speaking in black

southern dialect. Performed for the first time in 1930 at the Mansfield Theatre in New York City.

3 Staebler had enrolled in the Ontario College of Education in Toronto and
was living in Toronto during her studies.

4 The *Globe* was to merge with the *Mail and Empire* in 1936 to become Canada's
national newspaper the *Globe and Mail.*

5 Charles G.D. Roberts (1860–1943), one of a group of poets, including Bliss
Carman, Archibald Lampman, and Duncan Campbell Scott, prominent in
Canada between 1867 and World War I. Often referred to as the "Poets of the
Confederation," they were deeply engaged in the development of the new
nation's literature. Roberts was the first of the group to publish. His collec-
tion *Orion and Other Poems* appeared in 1880.

6 Play by Bernard Shaw (1856–1950), first performed in Warsaw 1929 and
published in Berlin in 1929. Born in Dublin, Shaw was a prolific playwright
and author of numerous works, including *Pygmalion* (1913), later made into
the popular musical *My Fair Lady.* He was awarded the Nobel Prize for literature in 1925.

7 Wilson MacDonald (1880–1967) popular Ontario-born poet, author of five collections of poetry, including *Out of the Wilderness* (1926), *A Flagon of Beauty*
(1931), and *Comber Cover* (1937).

8 PT refers to Physical Training, one of the subjects Staebler was to teach.

9 There are no entries between September 1932 and June 1934, a period during which Edna's father died (October 23, 1932) and she was married (October 14, 1933).

10 *The Devil's Disciple* was first performed in 1897 and published in 1901.

11 Nineteen twenty-seven play by Arnold Ridley (1896–1984), British playwright and actor.

12 George V (1865–1936), king of Great Britain and Ireland from 1910 to 1936.

13 Box R1. Travel Diary 1937.

14 Box R3-1. Diary 1931–38.

3

the
1940s
Must Write

FOR EDNA STAEBLER, as for an entire generation, the 1940s could be divided into two halves, the first dominated by World War II (1939–1945), the second half ushering in the postwar era. As diary entries on May 31, 1940, November 14, 1940, and May 18, 1942, indicate, Edna found that the war generated mixed emotions, troubling questions, and overall uncertainty. Many entries probe the possibilities and limits of philosophy and spirituality in the face of conflict and suffering.

As she struggled to understand the war and its impact on the world around her, Staebler also grappled with a "constant war" within herself (January 26, 1946). "I grasp at things that prevent me from writing and yet am depressed because I fail to write," she observed January 26, 1946. "But I have these other responsibilities—Mother, Cdn [Canadian] Club, Library Board. They take time, ideas. If I don't do my best for them, I feel guilty, ashamed. I fail." The constant conflict Staebler felt between her desire to write and the demands of her responsibilities drained her energy. "I must write," she wrote February 8, 1940. "This business of being married and doing nothing with a brain, which may or may not be any good, is too, too awful." Staebler resented "being just a housewife" (February 8, 1940). In her address to the Writers' Union in May 1997, she recalled early married life:

> I learned to knit and sew my own clothes. I designed and watched the building of our house. I made frilly curtains for all the windows, braided a large living-room rug, hooked a mat. I went to meetings and parties and dances, acted in little theatre plays, lobbied to get

women on public boards, did interviewing for the Gallup Poll.... I
read hundreds of books—novels, plays, biographies, and books about
writing: Virginia Woolf, Mary Webb, Arthur Koestler, T.S. Eliot.[1] Some
of them expressed thoughts I'd had and I wondered, "Why didn't I
write that?" And all the time I felt guilty as hell because I wasn't trying. ("My Writing Life")

Family offered little encouragement. According to her mother, trying
to write was a waste of Edna's time. Meanwhile, Keith Staebler had
grown very distant. The advent of World War II presented a deep challenge to the former pacifist who, though he did not enlist, supported
local contributions to the war effort through various work-related asso-
ciations.[2] War and the activities it brought to Kitchener, including an
army training centre, were not the only developments in the Staebler
lives at the outset of the 1940s. Within a period of six months spanning
the end of 1939 and the beginning of 1940, Keith Staebler withdrew permanently from intimate relations with Edna and suffered a nervous
breakdown. "When World War II started, my popular, talented, party-
loving husband had a nervous breakdown," Edna recalled. "When the
war ended he was manic depressive, alcoholic, and having three ses-
sions a week with a psychoanalyst—for fifteen years" ("My Writing
Life"). Edna suspected that Keith's decision not to enrol in the army created tremendous personal tension for him. Another cause for worry in
the Staebler relationship was "the baby problem" (October 12, 1944).
After a decade of marriage, the couple remained childless. They considered adoption, but Keith's drinking and difficult behaviour posed a
serious problem.[3] The Staebler marriage maintained outward appearances but it was far from what Edna had expected. "Last night K worked
at the office till three o'clock and I didn't sleep till after four," she recorded
October 12, 1944, "and that's how our life is now all the time." "He isn't
interested in all the things that I share with the other people," Edna
observed. "He wants me to be alone with them. But is it right? Is our
together relationship suffering because of it?" (January 7, 1945). Keith did
not discourage Edna's friendships with other men. During the war years,
soldiers from the Kitchener training camp were invited to Sunday dinner at the home of local residents. The Staeblers became frequent hosts.
Among their guests were Bill Reeves, Philip Knowling, and Fred Kruger,
all of whom figured in Edna's life during these years and make diary
appearances.[4]

Developments during the first half of the 1940s—the war, difficulties
in her marriage, tension between her social responsibilities and her

desire to write—left Edna deeply introspective, and her diaries served as the outlet for her thoughts. These were disturbing, often depressed, years for Edna. Then life took a major turn in 1945.

Two events in 1945 pointed Staebler in new and satisfying directions. The first was a sojourn in Neil's Harbour, a small fishing village in Cape Breton. The second was her encounter and subsequent lifelong friendship with John Robins, a professor of English at Victoria College, University of Toronto.[5]

Staebler's three-week stay in Neil's Harbour in the summer of 1945 became a definitive moment in her life, one that she has recounted in various public addresses and articles and, most importantly, in her book *Cape Breton Harbour*. Following a trip to Halifax in 1943, where she discovered the beauty of Canada's east coast, Edna decided to return in the summer of 1945 and travel the Cabot Trail with friends she had made in Lunenberg two years earlier—Earl Bailey, a painter, and his brother Don. Edna and Earl, who was confined to a wheelchair as a result of physical disabilities from childhood polio, had exchanged letters to one other on a range of topics about art and writing. Edna's expectations for a trip with like-minded friends around the Cabot Trail collided with Earl's more romantic intentions. Edna insisted the travellers part company and found herself alone in Neil's Harbour. She determined to stay the night while she figured out how to get back to Halifax. The small fishing village had no tourist accommodations and Edna welcomed the offer of a room in a house shared by two sisters and their mother in Neil's Harbour. One night became two weeks, and then three, and then Edna realized that she had at last found something to write about:

> The fascination of the sea breaking on rocks and the promise of swordfishing kept me from leaving. Each day that followed I said, "Tomorrow, tomorrow, tomorrow I'll leave." But one day I went out with the men in a snapper boat, on another I hitchhiked over the mountains to Cheticamp, every day I swam in the saltwater pond; I square danced one night on the platform in front of the Orange Lodge Hall. I listened to the friendly people who spoke to me in their Newfoundland dialect and became so engrossed that I no longer worried about my problems at home. I stopped being introspective. ("My Writing Life")

Staebler had discovered her subject. She also found new, lifelong friends in Neil's Harbour, whose names recur throughout the diaries: Clara May and Henry Ingraham, with whom Edna stayed on her next visit to the harbour; John Anderson, a writer living there; Ray Zwicker, a Halifax artist who came to sketch in Neil's Harbour; Tom Glover, a Sydney schoolteacher who vacationed there; and a host of other Neil's Harbourites. Staebler's story of Neil's Harbour would undergo numerous drafts and endure a long wait before finally appearing in print over a quarter-century later. Published as *Cape Breton Harbour* in 1972, the book received positive reviews. Its long genesis, however, was often cause for discouragement. Staebler continued to find the process of writing difficult (February 6, 1946), and family and friends remained dubious. "I wrote every day—sometimes taking hours to make a sentence come right," she told the graduating class of Wilfrid Laurier University in October 1984 ("Convocation Address"). "I learned to say no to people who wanted me to do other things. During the first two years of writing, my mother kept saying, 'Why waste your time?' And though I'd filled thousands of pages with typing my husband said, 'You're not a writer till you've had something published.' And a neighbour said, 'Put up or shut up.'" Before the decade was out, Staebler did have something published—and not just anything or anywhere. "Duellists of the Deep," an article based on her excursion with fishermen in Neil's Harbour, was accepted for publication by *Maclean's* magazine. It was the lead article in the July 15, 1948, issue, and it launched Staebler as a journalist who would go on to win the Canadian Women's Press Club Award for Outstanding Literary Journalism in 1950. Edna Staebler the journalist became friends with Canadian writers such as Pierre Berton, W.O. Mitchell, and Margaret Laurence, among many others. In the early days of writing about Neil's Harbour, however, it was her friend John Robins who provided her much-needed encouragement.

Dr. John D. Robins came to speak as an author and professor of English to the Kitchener-Waterloo Women's Canadian Club on November 15, 1945. Edna Staebler was president of the club. Meeting Robins led to a lifetime of correspondence, largely on the topic of writing. Robins's letters were vitally important to Edna as she endeavoured to master the craft of writing, and she carefully preserved them.[6] As she pointed out to members of the Writers' Union in her address, she "knew no writers, there were no local colleges or universities where writing was taught" ("My Writing Life"). Dr. Robins read what she had written, however, and encouraged her efforts. Edna's labours eventually paid off. The success of her article about swordfishing ("Duellists of the Deep"), excerpted from her work in progress on Neil's Harbour, resulted in an invitation for a second article. *Maclean's* article editor Pierre Berton suggested that she write about the Mennonites of Kitchener-Waterloo. "How to Live without Wars and Wedding Rings," published in the April 1, 1950, issue of *Maclean's*, sealed the journalism success that would constitute Staebler's writing during the next decade of her life. It also laid the foundation for the Mennonite food cookbooks that established Staebler's reputation in years to follow. Meanwhile, throughout the second half of the 1940s, Staebler continued to work on her book about Neil's Harbour. She made three return trips (in 1947, 1949, and 1951) and stayed in touch with friends there by phone and letter. Staebler's decision in the summer of 1945 to stay overnight in Neil's Harbour had a lasting impact on her life and writing.

Notes

1 Virginia Woolf (1882–1941), author of *A Room of One's Own* (1929), a feminist classic, and other works acclaimed for their innovative experimental techniques; Mary Webb (1881–1927), best known for her novel *Precious Bane* (1924); Arthur Koestler (1905–83), whose novels, such as *Darkness at Noon* (1940), explore the ethics of revolution and survival; T.S. Eliot (1888–1965), whose work *The Waste Land* (1922) captured the voice of the disillusioned of the interwar period. Among other books that Staebler read during this period, Brenda Ueland's *If You Want to Write* (1938) was particularly influential (February 8, 1940). Not only did Staebler read and reread the book many times, she typed out the full text twice. She also arranged to meet the author, in the spring of 1961, by travelling to a library convention in Minneapolis where Ueland lived. It was the book rather than the person, however, that Staebler continued to turn to for inspiration.

2 He was a member of the Sales and Advertising Club, for example, which raised money to buy a tank. See Ross, 74–75.

3 Recalling this in later life, Staebler wrote: "Children's Aid refused to allow it because both K[eith] and [Keith's brother] Nort were alcoholics, and Nort's daughter [by his first wife, Helen Waimel] was in the Home in Orillia for the mentally disabled—she [Linda] had the age of a two year old until she died at 35" (October 22, 2000).

4 For more about these guests, beyond Staebler's entries about them in her diaries, see Ross 80–83. Fred Kruger had special impact on Edna, who often thought there was a book in the story of the convicted criminal's life.

5 A specialist in Old and Middle English, Chaucer, and English philology; head of the department of English at Victoria College, University of Toronto; and the college's librarian, John Daniel Robins was also a Governor General's award-winning author for *The Incomplete Angler* (1943), a humorous story about two amateur fishermen in Canada's north.

6 Among various book projects that Staebler envisioned over the years was the publication of her correspondence with Robins. While the book did not mate-

rialize, *The New Quarterly* literary magazine published a selection of the letters, edited by Harry Froklage. See "Edna Staebler Finds Her Voice: Fragments from a Life in Writing," *The New Quarterly* 93 (Winter 2005): 13–78.

∾

top "That Golden Thanksgiving weekend at Dorset, 1943." Edna and Keith with Norma and friends (photo taken by Ralph Hodgson, Norma's husband); *bottom* 1942. Edna with Small, her first cat after marriage to Keith.

top left mid-1940s. Keith, Philip Knowling, and Edna; *top right* 1940s. Edna and one of the Staeblers' war-time Sunday dinner guests; *bottom left* Norma and husband Ralph Hodgson with daughter Barbie.

top left 1940s. Fred Kruger; *top right* 1940s. Keith, Edna, and Bill Reeves; *bottom left* 1942, Edna.

top 1940s. Edna and friends at Dorset, Ontario; *bottom* early 1940s. Edna and the Morris Minor.

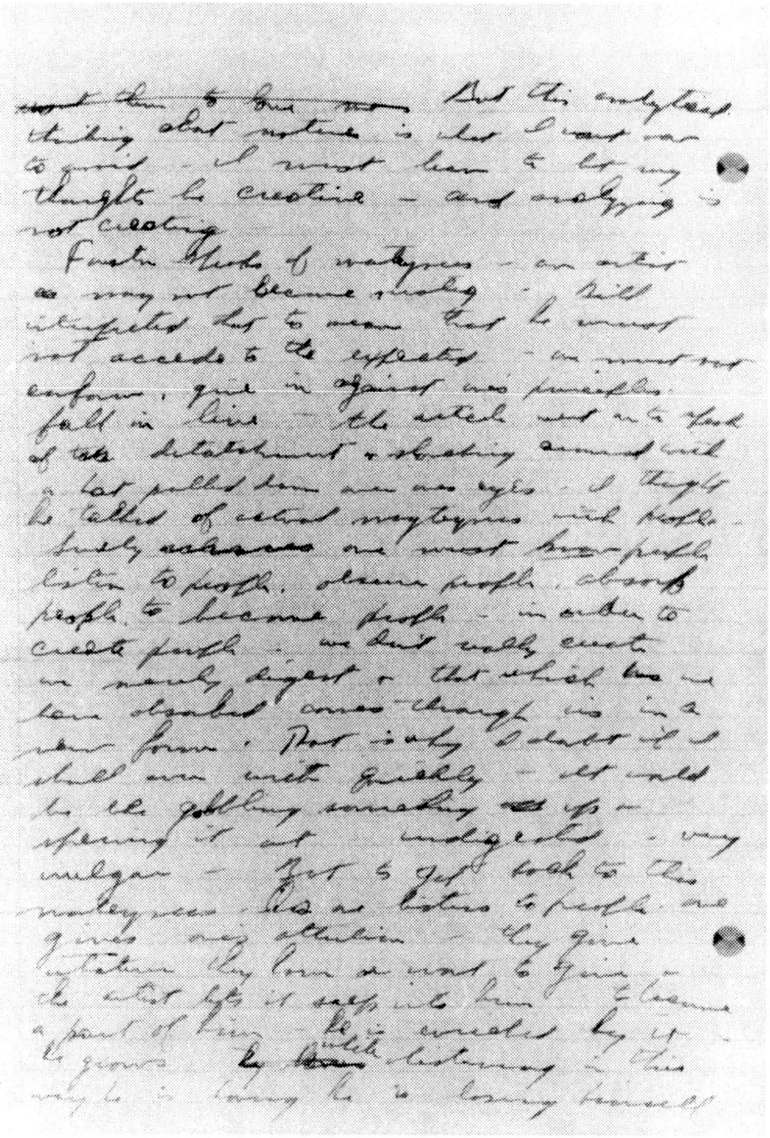

~~want them to love me~~ But this analytical
thinking about motives is what I want now
to avoid – I must learn to let my
thoughts be creative – and analyzing is
not creating
Foster speaks of wallpaper – an artist
may not become stodgy – if Bill
interpreted that to mean that he must
not accede to the expected – we must not
conform, give in, agree, [illegible]
fall in line – the artist must not think
of the detachment & standing around with
a hat pulled down over our eyes – I thought
he talked of actual wallpaper with people.
Surely ~~[illegible]~~ we must [illegible] people
listen to people, observe people, absorb
people to become people – in order to
create people – we don't really create
we merely digest & that which we
have absorbed comes through us in a
new form. That is why I doubt if I
shall ever write quickly – it would
be like gobbling something ~~[illegible]~~ up –
spewing it out undigested – very
vulgar – just to get back to this
wallpaper idea as we listen to people we
give no attention – they give
[illegible] they have [illegible] to give –
the artist lets it seep into him – it becomes
a part of him – he is enriched by it
he grows – by ~~[illegible]~~ [illegible] listening in this
way he is [illegible] he is losing himself

August 26, 1949. Edna Staebler Collection. (Archival and Special Collections, University of Guelph Library)

From the Diaries

February 8, 1940[1]
Hurrah, inspiration via a book by Brenda Ueland, *If You Want to Write*. It makes me feel like a potential genius. I must write. This business of being married and doing nothing with a brain, which may or may not be any good, is too, too awful. I must do something. I resent being just a housewife like all the dumb gals I went to school with and couldn't be bothered talking too much 'cause they had nothing to say, no vision, and now we're all married and they're all better housekeepers than I am, and I do nothing to prove to myself or anyone else that I have any brains at all.

April 11, 1940
Oh, why don't I write? I don't even try. I think about it and think about it, but I think of nothing to write about. My brain feels constipated, simply bursting with desire, but there are never any ideas. I have probably a one-track mind, and my thoughts are set in a little groove which sags. I want to write. I must write. I can't stand not writing, and that goes on and on and on. I either have no power or no imagination or no ability to get out of that single track. There must surely be something I can do in the world. At present I feel that I am a failure. I'm a fair cook, a bad housekeeper, I work hard most of the time, make my own clothes, mats, curtains, but any Mennonite farm woman could do those things better than I can.

May 31, 1940
The war is getting me down, I'm utterly at sea, I don't know what to think, really. In my heart I feel that anything that engenders hatred must be wrong and we should have no part in it. But in this case the cause seems to be right and it can't be right to be safely at home and let some other poor beggars fight it out for us. But how could Keith kill anyone? If only they could let people devote their brain power, but it still wouldn't be fair to use other people's bodies. Oh damn—how much of it is propaganda? How truly horrible and cruel are the German people? I can't believe them any worse than we are. But we are bad enough. We say terrible things should be done to the enemy and yet if they do them to us, or suggest them being done, we say they are barbarians.

November 14, 1940

Always at the back of my mind gnawing and persisting is the desire to write. Always the feeling that I should be writing, that perhaps I can write. But I never do it. I wish I knew why. Am I just lazy? Have I really nothing to say? Am I stupid? Dull? Uninteresting? Whenever I am unhappy, I almost do it. I lie in bed at night and think marvelous little things. Is the desire then just an outlet? Right now I am very busy and very happy. The war has made me happy. That sounds strange but it has made me so much more aware of things to love and to cherish.

February 6, 1941

Self-pity is the worst sin of all. I think it must be a denial of God. One's thoughts are turned so utterly on oneself that one fails to see and to love all the other things in the world.

Interest is the first thing, no, observation and awareness, *then* interest and a desire to understand. With understanding comes giving and loving and that means finding God. I think I must find out for sure. One doesn't have to be always, in fact one couldn't be always, ecstatically happy. That comes only rarely at times as a revelation.

February 7, 1941

Till now I think I've tried to make Keith's love be enough and have been terribly hurt and sorry for myself when it didn't always satisfy me. Sometimes I'd imagine myself in love with other men.... I'd know in my mind I wasn't really but I craved the excitement, though they never dreamed it existed. I'd pretend all sorts of fantastic things. All this because Love is not enough—romantic love is not enough.

We are always looking for something constructive, some magic formula that will suddenly direct us to the right path and make us happy forever. But there is no such thing unless we construct it somehow by really working hard to get it and then working twice as hard to keep it.

February 9, 1941

There is so much to write about, really. My mind is teeming with ideas, but they are all so vague, intangible, and indefinite. When I try to write there are great gaps. The reason for this, perhaps, is that I try to show things as they actually happened. I must learn that there is truth in things even though they are not reported word for word. It is the spirit of the thing that I must see, not the thing itself. And for that I must use my imagination, not just my memory.

I wonder what is behind this pathetic urge I have to write. I feel that I have always had it, and yet I have never written anything. Is it just an intense form of egotism which makes me want to force my puny personality on an otherwise unappreciative world? Am I too lazy to make the effort just for that? I don't know, but I don't think so. There are times when I feel things so ecstatically, so deeply, so desperately that I feel I shall burst if I can't make other people see them and feel them as I do. Some of the things are unimportant—a lovely child on a street car in Toronto, a silly dog, an old man, a house, so many things that bring an inner joy that is inexplicable. But how to tell about those things because, actually, they are nothing, just fleeting glimpses, yet full of meaning which has no meaning. But they cling to one's memory and will not be put out. Just now an old, matted collie dog passed the window, purposefully trudged by. A second later, a frisky wire-haired bounced after him. There's nothing in that, it would pass unnoticed, but somehow it is thrilling, it means something. I don't know what, it's silly of me to think it does, but it registers, perhaps because this is a sort of magic moment. Perhaps those magic moments come to us and whatever happens to pass just then is suspended and seems to have significance.

May 7, 1942
I'd like to get a job and be independent. If I didn't love Keith so desperately, I'd have cleared out long ago. But I can't be happy without him and I can't be happy with her [Keith's mother] interference, so what am I going to do? I can't go on as I have been or I'll end up with a complex. And in the meantime, the barrier between Keith and me grows higher and higher. And he's on the other side, with his mother and I'm fighting away alone. Not altogether. I have Mother and Lib and my family, but I want Keith. I don't want to possess his mind, but I don't want to be shut out of it.

May 18, 1942
I wonder what we really will do when the war is over. Will we remember the things that now mean so much to us? Will we again take an interest in the things that are now so small and unimportant? At the tea I had the other day, I heard one of the girls say, "Some day I hope I'll own a beautiful tea service like that." It sounded so strange when all that really matters now is life itself and keeping love and faith alive. A tea service is such a useless thing. It could never make anyone happy. It

isn't possible now to think much of anything that is not directly personal and vital to someone. There's so much to be done. I sometimes just ache with the insignificance and inability of myself to do something that would really help. Can we really help other people? Oh, I'm a fool, a weak, soft idiot. A reed in the wind inclining whichever way I'm blown. I resolve so many things and f f f f f f [*sic*] and over I go.

"Summer 1943"[2]
Seeing the [Halifax] harbour was the kind of thrill that makes your outside become too small for all the expanding that's going on inside, and you want to shout and do something to relieve the pressure of too much loveliness.

November 7, 1943
What is it that makes people happy? What magic suddenly lights a flame inside that burns brilliantly for about a minute and makes you feel that that minute is too big, too wonderful, too glorious to hold? It is so wild and ecstatic and it has nothing to do with people or things or time or space. It is pure magic and it is strictly personal, not to be shared, inexplicable. Or is it to be shared, at the height of physical, mutual passion? For a minute you can see into the infinite, you know everything, you've got the secret that means freedom and eternal joy. It is supreme truth. It's the heart of everything. It's purely spiritual. It's the doors of heaven opening and letting you see in. But it only lasts a moment. Then the sharp ecstasy of it is gone. The memory lasts awhile, sometimes you can recall it again and again, but it's always a sad thing to do.

Sometimes the magic comes fairly often, sometimes not for years. I think we must be receptive by living as completely as we can. I mean putting ourselves into everything we do, with all we have. All I've had, I think, has been concerned with things and people outside myself. Maybe that's the answer, a complete loss of one's self or a merging with something else, a perfect harmony, a complete understanding, for a moment. I don't know what it is. I can't express it, but I know it's the thing I'd like to do when I write. To feel that I've captured that magic, that absolute truth, that essence, and that perhaps I can give it to someone else. I've had it often from other people's works. Katherine Mansfield, Mary Webb, Thomas Wolfe.[3] But how to do it—I'll have to work like *Hell*.

September 7, 1944
I think my diary in the old days served a good purpose but it wasn't a

very honest one. I was always so self-conscious in the things I wrote in it, and so sentimental. Of course, then I believed that some day I'd be a famous writer and that my diary would be published, so I had to make it "nice." Now I know better. I just haven't got the stuff; however, I may keep on trying for a little.

September 10, 1944
What sort of things should one write in a diary anyway? Those very inside pestering thoughts that keep coming so damn often, the repressed, imagined conversations and actions with people that I know I'll never have and never be able to do, or have the courage to do. Or shall I write about the things I've done, the people I've seen, what I think about them? Or should I strive always for profound, meaningful thoughts that might show a development in thought, philosophical, rational, trivial? I don't know. The very sight of this book makes me feel serious, as if I must think only worthy things, soul-stirring, helpful things, showing growth, props to lean on.[4] Hell.

September 13, 1944
I wonder if it's just plain down curiosity that is at the root of all evil—or is it evil? This business of sex. Surely little boys seven and eight years old don't feel any sex urges. They must be merely curious—little girls too—so they try and find things out for themselves. And so it starts. Later on when the real urge comes, they wonder how it would feel to satisfy that, and away they go. But how did people like me escape so damn innocently? No one ever tried to take my pants down. I never wondered about things like that. I didn't know anything. I suppose I thought or was told it was "dirty" to ask or talk about things pertaining to the body. If anyone had told me anything I'd probably not have known what they meant. All those years I lived in a lovely little dream world of romance where kisses, nice, just-touching-the-lips sort of kisses, were the ultimate in human ecstasy. I read books all the time and preferred them to being with people I didn't understand and boys were beyond me, I guess. I wish I could remember better. I know I always was aware of boys and they liked me, except during the awkward, shy fourteen–fifteen stage, though even then there were a few, not in our own "set," but others. But now, I feel so ignorant and innocent and there's so much I'd like to know, to talk over with a man, to experience. K doesn't satisfy me, that's the dangerous part about all this. Someone told me last year that a woman loses her sweetness when she loses her innocence, and once she

has lost that she is never satisfied. She keeps on drifting and one other experience is not enough, she wants more and more. I don't doubt it. It can become an obsession. It haunts your thoughts, always wondering, wondering, wanting, till it can really be hell. I wish I'd never started. But is it right to live in a lonely world of illusion and refuse to admit that all these other things exist, to not want to know about them, to shut yourself away from them? Or do they exist only in the minds of people who are desiring—no, that's silly. I know they are real. People do things—Fred, Bill, [illegible]—all wanted me and if I'd let them, the desire wouldn't have stayed just in their minds. I suppose the reason men go from one woman to another, coupling them all and not taking them seriously at all, is because they first started when it was merely curiosity with them. Gosh, what a world, what a life. I feel like a very young, bewildered child who has just had a lot of things pointed out to him and doesn't know what to do about them or how to deal with them because there are so many and they are all so strange.

Tonight I wanted to do some writing but I just couldn't work. I got a permanent this aft and I'm tired, dead tired. I read a bit of *Light in August* by Wm. Faulkner.[5] It's morbid and dark. The part about the boy's first experience with a girl—it made me feel that awful yearning, burning inside of me and the longing to have someone to tell about it, to hold me close and want me. I thought of [name illegible]—always do in these black moods. I don't know why I should, except that I know he would understand and explain me. I can't tell K these things. They'd make him feel badly and he can't do anything to satisfy me. If only he could. If we'd only had a normal life together, instead of this constant striving busyness and always being alone.

Today, when we were having lunch, I could see K was worried. His eyes looked tired and he wasn't thinking at all of the trivia we were talking about. It wasn't any pretense of a conversation and I was thinking about other things too. We were miles away from each other in our secret minds and it was so frightening because it happens so often. We are together such a little bit of our time and when we do manage to be we don't know how to talk to each other. We both keep thinking our own thoughts and not telling them to each other. Of course, I'm so selfish and introspective and always trying to figure things out about myself and I can't talk always about me without being a perpetual bore. I must stop thinking about myself. I just go around in circles. I should study something serious and stop reading novels and applying them to myself. I'm at it again, damn it.

September 19, 1944
At last I have seen Bill [Reeves] and his family. And what a dramatic episode that was, and tragic and funny. I had just finished canning peaches and had gone upstairs to dress up. I looked like hell, I guess, in my oldest, dirty housedress and my old, grey sweater, terrible shoes with ankle socks, and no powder or lipstick, when I heard, "hello, Ed." I called, "who's there?" "It's Bill." I tumbled downstairs and into his arms so quickly—not one thought about myself. For so long I had wondered how our first meeting would be. I was sure we might be rather strange or appraising, but we were just wonderful. After a few minutes of complete joyousness, I came upstairs to dress and Bill got a screwdriver to fix the radio. Then the family came in and we got Bill some supper. K was out at Breslau on an army scheme and I did rather wonder about how Bill and I were going to spend the night—?—Just as Bill finished eating there was a knock at the front door and I opened on a plain, mousy woman and two little boys. I knew immediately that they were Bill's family. Surprise is hardly a strong enough word to describe my reaction. I welcomed them, though, and got them something to eat. God bless my family, too, for being there. They didn't stay long and we watched the children roam around. Poor Bill is very nervous. His scars are livid and horrible and he must have gone through hell to survive. What he needs more than anything now is lots of love and sympathetic understanding and quiet relaxation. Fortunately he is still being kept in hospital in London except for next week which he spends with [Kath] and the boys.

September 20, 1944
Ever since Bill was here I've felt so terribly in love with Keith and his last words before he left me tonight were about how very much he loves me, and he'd be home at midnight. Well, at one o'clock he phoned, I got out of bed and ran down. He said he was at the Walper House playing poker and had won eighteen dollars so he was taking the boys up to Waterloo for a hamburger and would be home in twenty minutes. That was two hours ago. He'd had quite a bit to drink, I could tell that, and just this morning I had decided to go to the Children's Aid office to ask about a baby. I don't want to adopt one, I want one of my own. But K has always been too busy to get me one. And since his nervous breakdown, he can't get me one. And now I'm so scared he'll break down again, and if he doesn't, I will, because I can't stand these late hours. I was dead tired and depressed today, and couldn't work all afternoon. And if I had a baby

to look after, I'd be crabby and sick because I'd have so much work to do and no sleep at all. So I guess I won't get one. Keith won't ever change. He's been like this ever since I've known him. But he wants a baby too. And I feel mean and as if I'm not being fair in not getting one. But how can I, he'd damn well have to sleep at a hotel so that I could get some rest. A fine family man—nix.

September 28, 1944
It is so wrong to judge other people by our own standards. To be critical of their actions because they don't do things as we would have them do. The things that are responsible for my development are not in other people at all, so I must not take them for granted and not try to force my ideals on them or be disappointed if they don't respond to me as I hoped they would.[6]

October 12, 1944
Felt very happy this morning. The baby problem has been so acute lately. In the spring, Angie Wilson [one of Edna's friends] said if I'd adopt one, she'd have one and now she's pregnant and is urging me to keep up my end of the deal. But last night K worked at the office till three o'clock and I didn't sleep till after 4:00, and that's how our life is now all the time and will be as long as [illegible name] is in the army and K in the Reserve and that's no sort of life to bring a baby into. I worried so all night about wanting Bill.[7] But this morning I felt free, and sure that all I must do is the very best I am able, and all the things that come and that it occurs to me to do will turn out all right. I feel so fruitful, and sure that I could have one myself if I had a chance and that someday I will.[8] And if I don't that will be all right too. I'm just not going to worry about it any more—or talk about it. I'll see what happens. Everything that has happened in my life so far has been wonderful and interesting. Sometimes it's been hell while it lasted, but after I've always been grateful that it did because of the experience. If I could only always remember to trust and believe that the best will happen. Sometimes I try to force things by my will—that isn't faith—and that is bound to bring disappointment to me if things don't turn out as I want them to. But to keep on loving and believing, that is the thing.

November 3, 1944[9]
Some compliments that people give have a tendency to make a person very self-conscious and spoil their charm. Conceit is a horrible thing

and might result from too much praise, unless a person has a very fair evaluation of himself. No matter how many things people tell me about myself I always know how far short I fall from being the kind of person I should be. Praise gives me self-confidence. The right kind makes me lose my fear; the wrong kind makes me self-conscious.

November 6, 1944
If I was my husband, I'd probably kick me out—or would I? But I'm such a fool. He knows I am and knows why I am and he loves me enough to accept me as I am. And so I think he's the most wonderful person in the world, and I wouldn't ever ever want to live with anyone else. No one else would ever put up with me.

November 15, 1944[10]
In my writing I try so hard to find words. I must not think so much of how to say a thing but think of the essential quality of the thing itself and the words will find themselves. I must be completely *aware* and I must write more. I must write every minute that I have.

January 7, 1945[11]
When a person falls in love, does that mean they must close all the doors to everyone else? That all conversations and thoughts are held from them or as if in the presence of a third person? Can there no longer be any intimacy with other people whom one has loved or does love? This morning I was thinking about a lot of people whom I love dearly and with whom I can talk intimately and freely. I wouldn't want anyone else to hear my conversations or read my letters to them. But should I feel that I must not say or write anything to them that K could not share? It is as if I were living in a house with a person in every room, each with a different interest for me. I would like to be able to go to each one. But is that right? Should I have such freedom? Because I am married to K, should I have to stay in the hall (as it were) with him and be intimate with the people in the rooms of my house only thro' the doors, in his presence, his mental presence? But I can't share everything with him that I have with all those others, i.e., Dottie and I frequently discuss religion; K and I seldom do, we don't share the same views, or is it because I satisfy myself with Dottie and don't need his ideas on the subject?[12] That can't be right. But he doesn't come to me; he isn't interested in all the things that I share with the other people. He wants me to be alone with them, but is it right? Is our together relationship suffering because of it? Or is

it better for people to be independent of each other? Not altogether, surely, but enough so that they can stand on their own feet and work out problems by themselves.

January 11, 1945[13]
This business of living is so darn interesting and exciting that at times I feel I shall burst with it. If only I knew what to do about it, instead of being up amongst the stars one minute and grovelling in the mud the next. It is the horrible feeling of *wasting* my life that gets me down, and it is the exultant feeling of interest and joy and power within me that sends me up. I feel so *vital* then. But surely there should be times in between when I am on an even keel and should be able to really do something, really create something or do something worthwhile. Always that damn desire for something permanently interesting, something I can do at any time, at any age. Reading? Not enough. Not expressive enough. Writing? Of course, but when I try to do it, it comes out all wrong and I become depressed. I haven't enough *will* to stick at it. I deserve to be depressed (5).

January 26, 1946
Letters came today. It is strange how much more powerful can be the effect of an idea expressed in a letter than the same idea read in a book or heard in some other impersonal way. No doubt this is because the receiver of the letter feels that the idea was meant for him and that the person who sent it had enough regard for him to take the trouble to think about him that makes the idea have more meaning for him than if he had read it or received it in a more impersonal way, and so it is more likely to influence his life. So God help me to send the right thoughts.

This constant war that goes on in me between volition and determinism must be decided before I can do my real work, and yet can it ever be decided? I find myself grimly determined to do a job, get some writing done. I'll sit for hours and no thoughts come. There is no inspiration. Then someone phones, ah—providential. I'll talk for an hour and so my life goes on. I grasp at the things that prevent me from writing and yet am depressed because I fail to write. It is time I made a decision and stuck to it, took the consequences of it. But I have these other responsibilities—Mother, Cdn Club, Library Board.[14] They take time, ideas. If I don't do my best for them I feel guilty, ashamed. I fail. I must give them my best, and if I do there is still plenty of time to give my best to my writing. It is the constant conflict, the revolt that saps my energy and results in nothing being done well in either field. So, I must believe that if I give my cheerful best always to whatever job I do, whatever contact I make, I shall get everything done that I want to do, if my life is predetermined. Okay, make the best of that, enjoy that. If I have a free choice, then again it is up to me to DO something. There is never any excuse or reason for depression. If I am low, everything I do is poor, selfish. I am my own enemy and I am also the enemy of the world.

Man cannot reproduce himself like the amoeba, so he cannot live alone. He is a gregarious creature and so the thing that is best for the herd is best for him and vice versa. To preserve his own life he must save the lives of his fellows. To receive he must give, they are the same thing. But what about the survival of the fittest? As long as man wanted to be the fittest animal, that was a fine idea, but man still instinctively wants to be the fittest man, and so he strives constantly for superiority over his fellows in so many subtle ways, unconscious ways. He wants attention, praise. If he fails to call attention to himself by his deeds, he builds himself up in his mind by daydreaming. The most difficult thing he can achieve is self-effacement, humility, and yet achievement would bring him the glory that he seeks, instead of being only himself, one very small, isolated, unhappy bit of humanity with the weight of the universe resting on his shoulders, pressing him down or spinning dizzily round his bewildered head, he would know that all the universe was part of him, that he was part of it, that in himself he is nothing but every person he meets, everything he sees, everything he hears, everything he reads, and so in himself he is everything. He must be aware of his allness and his nothingness. When he realizes that his allness depends on his nothingness then he will be free of conflict, able to work creatively because then he needs no longer think of himself but can use all his energies in being aware of all about him, constantly learning, digesting, and forming new patterns. There is nothing new, but there is infinitude of new combinations. Each person is a different combination, so everything that person produces must be original. (p. 11)

February 2, 1946
Today I read *Falling Thro' Space* and *The Last Enemy* by Richard Hillary, and Arthur Koestler's essay about him, and it.[15] It seems that in everything I read I find that same eager wondering—why—what purpose? In so many people I meet, there is the same question in me. I believe it is necessary to make a decision and then to work hard toward the goal decided on. So God help me to write and in my writing to show the

goodness in man—the beauty, the truth. Reality is not meanness and cruelty and ugliness. That is only half, I hope less than half. If I can find goodness and show it, maybe that will spread, make it grow. But I must WORK.

February 5, 1946
After feeling greatly moved, writing a long letter to Gladys Arnold, I felt that awful proud self-righteousness stir in me again.[16] Just after the moment of miracle, the opposite feeling comes to me. Why must this be? It makes me so utterly distrustful of myself and no doubt as long as this feeling comes, I am not free. I am not integrated. Or is Koestler right? And so it is the return from the *vie tragique* that causes the conflict.[17] But I must work to eliminate it. I shouldn't write to people or talk to them about the big ideas. I should just prove them in creative work. Then I would have the feeling that I was everything, not the evidence that I am nothing. But no matter what I write, I should still be nothing. I shall always be nothing.

I've thought more of this. It wouldn't be possible to live always on the *plane tragique*. We must come back to the trivial for balance, for contrast. The other plane is too lofty; we would lose contact with the world of reality. As for the elation I feel after I have written something that moves me, perhaps that is natural, but I must still feel the gratitude for having been directed to write it instead of giving myself a pat on the back.

February 9, 1946
In writing my book, I want to have humour, but I must direct the laughter to myself, not laugh at anyone else.[18] I want the whole thing to flow freely and to do that there must be a central idea and I want that idea to be the love and beauty that I found in all I saw, felt, heard, tasted.

God, where is it gone? Five minutes ago I had a sudden revelation of completeness and now I can't find any words for it at all. In it I know that volition and determinism were one; that negative and positive were One. How did I find it? What led to the realization? I believe I began with the thought I had of laughing at myself in my book. I thought how ridiculous it is to be disturbed because I can't learn everything, know everything that is to be known in the universe. Then I remembered someone saying Einstein was such an all-round sort of person. Oh damn, in these few minutes I seemed to have everything, to have it all in my mind, and now there is nothing in it but fuzz.

I suppose that revelation comes at times to let us know that it does exist and that we must work always thro' the fuzz to find it. That is the thing every artist wants to capture, to put into words, or on canvass or into music. And if he succeeded he'd not have to keep on trying.

In my book I must build up, show my growing interest in the people, their growing confidence in me. At first I was aware of the natural beauty of the place, the people's occupation. Then I knew I couldn't write about these things unless I knew about the people, why they did things and felt and acted as they did. I had to know them. So the experience kept growing till it reached a peak in the evening with Tom Glover.[19] The beautiful sunrise, the day's fishing—all come at once. Then, next day, the tiredness, the need to rest and think and digest.

February 15, 1946

Nothing is more boring than people who talk about their offspring to people who aren't interested in them or who haven't any of their own. So creative offspring must be just as boring. To discuss problems of method with someone else who is realizing the same problems is all right. But it isn't a good idea to talk about a work or to show it or read it to ANYONE. You know yourself if it does what you want it to do. If you're satisfied, let it go at that. And heaven help you if you're not satisfied, you'll know why better than anyone else. You can't please everyone, especially those closest to you. So, don't show it, don't send it. Let the work alone prove its own worth. If it's good enough it won't need any help from anyone else. No matter how pleased I am with what I'm doing I must restrain myself.

February 16, 1946

I must stop being so damn serious and theoretical about everything. If I can remember to LOVE every passing minute, I'll be OK.

Fear is confusion and chaos, so faith must be stillness and order. It comes in listening to music, as well as many other things where thinking and feeling are completely quieted.

March 3, 1946

There is no doubt in my mind at this moment that all my living is directed. That a Power is available to me which can not only make me joyous and creative but which will give me insight into the lives of other people, which will help them, too, to realize their potentiality. As I look back on my life I can have no doubt of these things. The constant psychic flashes, the contacts, the strange inexplicable things that have happened always with that feeling of "There is no REASON for this" and yet there was more reason than there was for many of the forced, confused actions which I thought I controlled myself. If from now on I do not WORRY, do not fear, but know always that every passing moment is mine in which to learn, receive, and give and produce, humility will come from the gratitude I feel in knowing that I am constantly being given something from everything I hear, all I see, all I feel, smell, taste, and can laugh at. It is, I suppose, inevitable, that I shall love some people more than others. Our lives run in parallel lines but never ever can any of us possess each other. Possession means a blotting out, a carving up, a destruction of the other person. But if I love I shall keep on finding in the other person these things which are loveable. I shall know that the other person has the power to create, that everyone, even the humblest, knows something, can do something that I can't and so has something that I can admire and praise. God—life is wonderful.

April 14, 1946

My mind has been racing madly in so many directions. I wish there were some way of recording thought without the mechanical process of writing it on paper. Now more than ever I am convinced of a Power which motivates, which drives us, which governs our lives. If we can submit to it eagerly and fully and fearlessly, we should become creative and powerful in our own way. Phil [Knowling] says he is a driven man.[20] There are times when he longs for a home and comfort but he knows first he must travel in every country in the world and write about the geography, the people, their politics, their way of life, his own suffering and ideas and joys. He says he feels a ruthless resentment against anyone and anything that interferes with his purpose. He will not be stopped except in the performance of his duty. He has no fear of death. He says he feels it could come to him at any time and if it does, he will have no regrets of a life well lived. He has a remarkable gift of telling things clearly, dramatically, and beautifully, in a way which stirs and stimulates the imagination and rouses the other person to heights he didn't know he possessed. He spoke of feeling like an iced river. He is one of those people whose vitality melts the ice and sets the stream of another's emotions flowing. His true humility is an inspiration. His interest is completely attentive and concentrated on the other people and things around him. He is a complete observer with little thought of himself or his effect on another. The significance of this meeting intrigues me. Again I found myself telling things in a way that I didn't know I was capable of and putting into words things that I didn't know I knew. He made me feel very wise and interesting and full of power because he is all those things. He brought them out in me. He says I must write, that I can do it. He's talked to wonderful people all over the world who have done creative things and he says my mind is as free and varied and interesting and strange as the very best he has encountered. That frightens me in a way, yet I know that there is power available to me and if I used it impersonally as it should be used, I could really write. The first step is attention, complete and undivided, disciplined. That becomes concentration and with that comes inspiration, the free flowing of the stream of consciousness entirely free of self. If only I could set down all the things that have come to me in the past forty-eight hours, I could write six books. First I must finish up Neil's Harbour in a lightly entertaining way. By that time, perhaps I shall have come far enough away from the details of what has been happening lately and get a perspective so that I can write a novel about the strange interplay of one's power on another in the lives of those people that have touched me in the past four years.[21] Meantime it is necessary to keep copious notes. To be writing all the time. Just a few words are necessary to bring up a picture, a feeling, a complete idea. I must let nothing stop me. I wish, like Phil, that I could go alone to a cabin by the sea where I could wander and read and write. Now I feel that as long as I am with other people, my life goes on, developing, piling up. I need time to catch up with it now. I've reached a definite stage where I need to concentrate and consolidate and rest and work. However, I can't have it so I'll have to try somehow to live and work at the same time.

April 15, 1946

It is strange that when I sit down to write, no thoughts will come tho' a few minutes earlier my mind was teeming with ideas. I seem to be in an agony much of the time because there are so many millions of things that I must write and that somehow I didn't get out. This morning in bed I was thinking about being driven, that in all probability all people are driven, tho' few have the courage to yield completely to the force that motivates them. Perhaps it is because that force is confused. Energy is, of course, the basic thing and it comes in various forms to all of us, as fear, rage, wonder, and sex, and in each person one of those is dominant and closely modified by one other. But if all four are allowed full sway, the person becomes sort of neutral and ineffective. I know how often I have worried about physical passion driving me to do things that I have been ashamed of, but I know now that, actually, most often it was wonder that moved me, this damned curiosity which eats away at me and must know the inner secret, the meaning behind everything. The search for perfection in art. It drives us unmercifully. The need to be creative is inherent and if it is thwarted, the spirit in us dies. Some people create physically, they crave sexual intercourse and if they aren't satisfied in one place they keep searching, promiscuously, driven to find the perfect lay. Lovemaking is an art and must be studied to be perfected.

Any imitation is cheap, unsatisfactory, as in all art forms. A woman who yields herself is likely to become possessive because she is afraid a man may leave her. She can be deeply hurt if he does. It is a blow to her vanity, her self-respect. But if a man can leave her believing he still wants her, she can still retain that cherished regard for herself. There is a tendency in everyone to project his own desires and ideals onto another person, to believe that in him is the perfection that she believes is in herself, and so a person falls in love and is terribly disillusioned if and when she finds out that the other person isn't all she believed. But if a woman is experienced, has known intimately many men, she knows that in each one she will find something that responds to something in her, but never to everything, and she will accept each person for the best that is in him and understand those things which are not good. By looking for the things that respond to her, she evokes them in the other person and gives him a sense of power, which he does possess, or rather which is available to him. I think every person should have that independence of spirit which would enable him to stand on his own feet no matter what happened to him. No person should become a burden on another, make another feel responsible for his happiness, because there are always so many other people, all possessed of the same qualities, who could be just as satisfactory, tho' that is not the reason. The reason is that to everyone is available the power which will drive him if he yields to it. We get so bound up in other people's ideas, advice, everyone thinks everyone else should be and live as he does, not because he's happy but because he thinks he's right. We must learn to respect each other's integrity and to leave each other alone to work out our own lives in our own way. An exchange of ideas, a sharing of experiences, that is helpful and from that we learn. But there must be no forcing. (31–32)

April 16, 1946

God, what a life this is. I nearly go mad sometimes with the fullness of it, and the desire to share it. Some day I must write it. At the present moment there is so much and I want to get it all down *at once.*[22] But I must be patient, taking one step at a time proving myself as I go along. This morning I was thinking of Phil Knowling, who is *perhaps* the personification of all I have ever dreamed of in a man. A world traveller, serious and a writer, emotionally mature, sensitive, with a love of beauty, a mystic—everything—the same desires and ambitions that I have. I was thinking that if he asked me to go with him, I would want to go. I do want to go but I know I couldn't go. I haven't yet earned the right. I couldn't be happy with him till I'd proved myself. I must first of all see Keith on his feet. He'll do it, I know. He'll become a creative and emotionally mature person too, a damn fine one whom I may never want to leave. And I must write and publish what I write, to prove that I *can do* it. As long as I talk about these things and don't do them, I am failing. So, I must work like HELL. Then, I'll do whatever comes for me to do and I'll know that whatever it is, it is right. (32)

April 25, 1946

Can one ever be unselfish? If a person is driven by a desire to do something, must he not be ruthless if it is to be done? If the thing in him is strong enough, it can't be stopped. No one can stop it. Jesus was selfish really. There is no record of the year when he must have lived experimentally to gain the wisdom which he later taught. And he must have hurt his family and friends greatly by preaching as he did, risking his life. And great musicians, living in poverty to compose, when they might have done some other work and supported their families more comfortably. But the important thing is that the thing that is being done will give more joy, more peace, more truth to more people than the few who are deprived that it may be given. That is the essential. So, as long as the drive is not a purely selfish one, as long as one's faith in it is strong and one knows *for sure* that it is good, then it is right to give it all one has. But still, how does one know that? One night we were discussing selfishness and K said the only pure form of unselfishness is that a man give up his life. There are different ways of doing that. I was wondering today, as I often do, just what love is. I say I love people, I love K, yet there are so many times when I know that it is not true, when there are things I want to do more than be with him. I say I love Lib, but there are times when I am jealous of her.[23] I say I love Tom Glover, but am I really dependent on him in any way? Or any of these people whom I love? If I love them, how do I prove it? By giving up my life for them? But have I that right? I'm pledged to K. Does that mean that my life belongs to him? That I should love no one else but do everything he wants me to? I want to travel, to write. K wants me to be an average, comfortable wife who will adopt a couple of children. If I really love him, I suppose I'd do that and give up the other things I've wanted all my life. But if I could write well, really well, put into my writing something good, would that justify my depriving him of what he wants? Or could I do both? I know I can't give up the idea of writing. All the things that have happened to me lately prove to me that I must do it, that I can do it. Then why in hell don't I get busy instead of wasting time like this talking about it? I've got to *prove* I can do it by doing it.

I know the right answers, I've learned them. Now why not *use* them? I keep putting it off, "but I must do the house cleaning," "I must write a letter," "I must phone someone, read something," and all the time I think of things to write about. But I don't write them. God, the novels I've planned this week. The articles I've written in my mind during the past two years, but none of them on paper. It's about time now. First I didn't know what to write about, then for a long time I lacked confidence, doubted my ability, now I've had the assurance of people whose opinion I respect and value and that should no longer be an obstacle. Now, there is only K, and he wants me to do it and if I organize my house work, I do have time. (49–50)

April 27, 1946

Will my life go on always as it is now, up and down, secure and happy often, for a short time, then disturbed and depressed and wondering? Is there no way, no simple, sure rule that can be applied to meet every situation and each new encounter, each situation? (50)

May 5, 1946

It would not be impossible to write several autobiographies, in each one tracing the life of a different self. They would be surprisingly varied, the results, the end, completely different.

Success comes in getting what you want, happiness, in wanting what you get, and utter misery in not knowing what you want and being unsatisfied with what you have. I wonder if there could be a way of combining the success and the happiness. Or is that having one's cake and eating it? I can be happy if I am constantly aware of the wonder and the beauty and the mystery in things and people around me, in finding and knowing them and me. But I want to show what I find. I can't be completely happy unless I express what I think and feel about these things. So I guess my path is clear. I'd better get to work. Dr. Robins thinks my book sounds all right. When I was with him, I talked about it as if it was an accomplished fact, and so it has become in my mind, and he says that's as it should be, or it soon will be. Some day, when I finish NH [Neil's Harbour] I must write a novel, tracing one of the lives of my life thru to some sort of end. There is no beginning and no end, of course. It is part of infinity. In tracing the various lives, they should converge, if I am ever really integrated, or in harmony. So, they would not become one life, but harmonious lives, running together parallel, not crossing each other. (58–59)

January 15, 1948[24]
Happy Birthday. Tried writing most of the day—no good. Piano concert at night—beautiful. How they must work to keep up the precision. I waste and lose too much time. I don't know where it goes. I seem to do so little. It should be so easy to write two or three pages a day, I can write a letter in an hour. Why can't I write my book?

January 19, 1948
Tried all day to write—no good. I seem to suffer from a form of paralysis. Nothing comes out. I just sit, sit and feel horrible. Yet I know that some day it will come out, freely and as I want it to. I must just be patient.

August 9, 1948
At the moment I seem to be pulling C.S. Lewis to pieces. I don't mean to be, not the man himself. His life is as it is and that's all right for him. It is his authority that I am denying. How can an Oxford don who meets only the "best people" intellectually, a man who sits and writes and thinks and theorizes, really know life as it is lived by all sorts of people? What hope of heaven could a poor ignorant fisherman, a farmer, a labourer have if C.S. Lewis's ideas are the *only* right ones, as he claims they are? No, it must be something simpler than that, something inherent, not dependent on words and ideas about original sin and grace and all those fancy things.

August 15, 1948
You can't tease a person who hasn't a sense of humour.

If you can't and don't laugh at yourself, you haven't a sense of humour.

A mature person can laugh good humouredly (to himself) at faults in others that would irritate an immature person.

In reading philosophical works one might agree with some ideas and disagree with others. Instead of saying, then, "I don't agree with him," or, "He is wrong," one can be glad for the agreeable parts and can ignore the others or be grateful for them because they make one put one's own ideas into more specific form. State positively one's own philosophy, not merely negate the other person's, i.e., the Conservative party is against communism, that is its main platform, but it has nothing specific that it is *for*.

I've been reading a book about C. S. Lewis and I cannot agree with his teachings: original sin, a wife must obey her husband, fundamentalist Christianity, etc.[25] Why do I read these books on philosophy, theology, and psychology? Why don't I just write here the things I learn from experience and use them as my guide? Why don't I strengthen my thinking habits by using the things I have learned instead of confusing myself with the conflicting opinions of other people? Why must I keep always searching instead of knowing? Actually, it is a form of justifying since in all the books I try to find approval of my way, of what I want. Each person who writes writes from his own experience, if he is honest, and so his philosophy is a sort of rationalization of his own being. I believe religion is so deeply and undoubtedly personal that no man can tell another what he must be. It is something that cannot always be expressed in words. Theology, like philosophy, can be an intellectual exercise. I don't like Lewis's thought that if his is right, everything else must be wrong. It is like saying if a rose is beautiful, a lily must be ugly. Nor do I believe in original sin. I like to think that the source of all things is God. So men are fundamentally good, but through ignorance at times do things that are evil. If one believes man is a sinner, an evil person, one must be always trying to change him and reform him and preach to him and make him feel guilty and helpless. The theologians and preachers would soon be out of a job if man were considered basically good, which is just the sort of defensive attitude that I must not have. I must not be against theologians. I must have a positive belief of my own and it must be simple.

September 19, 1948

I think in my book I have been trying to keep myself out of things, to be above all that happens to me, impersonal, cold, afraid to really give myself because of what people might say of me. Why should I be afraid? Why not be natural and honest instead of trying to hide and control my feelings?

[…]

It always gives me faith to remember Freddie [Kruger] when he came here from the Pen—the Power of Love was at that time very, very evident to me. I wish I could never forget it, would always have faith in it, and when I run into a snag, instead of dissecting it and analyzing, would look straight at the heart, at the thing I know is there. I have proved that so often, but I forget it so easily. I am very stupid.

It is breaking other people's rules, rules that have been imposed on us by custom and tradition, that makes us afraid. If those rules are wise and good we have no reason to be unhappy—if those rules are our own personal rules too. We must have our own rules and the simpler they can be the better. And only if we break them need we really be afraid, not afraid, but sorry and determined not to break them again, and not sorry either because we should always be glad for anything that helps us to learn and understand and love more.

October 23, 1948

Ade Sewell just called to find out if he could do anything to help Nort.[26] Ade says he has humility and true joy when he is contemplating the free, simple things of nature. As long as a man thinks he is a man apart from the rest of the world, a man with special privileges because he is an artist, he is no longer an artist, he is a dilettante. The true artist is just like any other man with a job to do and he does it. He doesn't dramatize himself and talk about himself as if he were different from everyone else. He is different in some things, but so is an engineer or a milkman. Instead of creating interesting life in my work, I keep wanting to live interestingly. I can't stand monotony and yet I suppose I must lead a monotonous life if I am to get my work done. I need the contrast: exciting work, monotonous background; exciting life, no work. And yet at mealtime I see my cat sitting on the floor beside my chair as I have seen him sit meal after meal for seven years and I have a sudden revulsion. I think how many more times must I see that cat sitting beside me like that? But then I quickly forget the monotony as I become aware of his large-eyed stare.

[…]

I think I'm playing sick. I'm not unwell. I'm merely lazy, pampering myself. I tell myself I want to write, want to finish my book, want to write many other things. I read books on writing. I have just finished an especially inspiring one. I know exactly what I must write yet I seem to be deliberately keeping myself from it. I must let myself sit down at my typewriter and go ahead. I lie instead on my bed and read a little or write here, or write a letter, or go for a walk, or talk to the children and feel wonderful. But underneath it all, in all the between moments, there is the empty feeling of not working.

November 17, 1948
I'm a terrible liar, really. When I tell people things that have been told to me, I often find them coming out as quite good stories and not at all the way they were told. I wish I could remember them that way afterward and write them down.

November 22, 1948
Learning to become a writer is harder than learning to write. The discipline, the keeping of my mind on my work and not letting it stray to my worry or to my dreaming, is the hardest thing of all. If I ever master that, I'll be able to write.

November 23, 1948
Feeling is universal; the expression of it is individual.

(no date)[27]
What you want to do more than anything else in the world is to write, to express the feelings that almost make you burst at times.[28] You don't want to be famous or to make a lot of money. You just want to give other people the benefit of your experiences. You want to show your joys and sorrows. People love sharing sorrows. You tell all your friends how you feel, what you want to do, and after a few years you convince them and they begin to say, "You must write—I'm sure you could." And when a visiting relative comes to town, they say, "I want you to meet my friend, she writes." You look a bit confused and deny it because you're afraid someone may ask you where your things are published.

Your friends' encouragement makes you more determined. You think, "I really must have something or they wouldn't say that," so you go to the library and get books by famous authors telling how they did it.

And you're sure you are exactly like them, become starry-eyed and sure that you're writing. You really must spend so many hours a day at it.

But first of all you must make a new dress, clean up the house, and finish the preserving. Next week should be clear and you'll start then.

So on Monday morning at ten you get out a pad and a pencil and you sit and you wait. The flow of inspiration will come—several authors spoke of that. Well, what's the holdup? How long should it take for one's imagination to get going? Keep your mind a blank then the ideas will begin to flow freely. A cigarette might help (?). You wonder what to make for dessert at noon. You mustn't wonder. Keep your mind free. Was that a knock? No. Hell, where were we? Twenty after ten. Let's see, something should surely come soon, gently: "ideas flow gently, figures move before your eyes as in a dream," but you don't want to write a story, do you? You want to write. You don't see any figures, nobody doing anything in your mind. It's a blank, or is it? It's beginning to ache. Is an ache a blank? Maybe that's a labour pain; maybe creative effort must be accompanied by physical pain. Should you take an aspirin? No, you'd better just let things come as they will, don't disturb the workings of inspiration. 10:30. Hmm, well, funny, nothing has come yet. You can't understand it. You close your eyes; the world looks red through your eye lids. What about a fire? Or blood, a story about a fire, or blood. There's an idea, but, oh, that's no good. You have to love something to write about it, before you start sitting down like this and writing is no good. That idea for an article you had last month would be better than this sterility. Let's see, you put down the headings: 1, 2, 3, 4. Now then, you'll begin. But you don't, you wait, and nothing comes. Eleven o'clock, the phone rings; you've decided not to answer the phone. It rings and rings and rings. You answer it; you talk and talk without any difficulty. It's time to get lunch. To hell with writing.

March 22, 1949[29]
If only there was some way of recording every precious passing moment.

July 11, 1949[30]
Every book on writing advises the faithful keeping of a journal. I hope in this to set down any thought that comes to me every morning and at the same time to make my writing legible. For far too long I have been trying too hard to be too good. It has made me very introspective and given me a very precious feeling about myself, made me afraid to

mingle with the world, to enjoy or give myself to anything that comes along lest somehow I be tainted by it. I have become a horrible prig and very, very dull, giving and receiving nothing when those precious moods were on me. I have privately let myself be immersed in my problems, arguing continuously with myself or whoever has upset me: K, Mrs. S[taebler], or anyone else who has disagreed with me. From now on, I must control my thinking, develop habits of thought that are constructive, productive, and delightful. (I sound so naïve). I must remember:

1) To seek first of all the kingdom of heaven (the inner meaning).
2) What profiteth a man if he has given the world and loses his own soul (public opinion).
3) Be *still* and know (my dreams).
4) Observe, be sensitive, seek always truth, beauty, and kindness and *write* about it. You become what you look for.
5) Don't try to become, simply search. Open your eyes and your heart and your mind. Writing is feeling and observation. I am nothing but the sum of all those things that have been granted me. Remember— I am nothing if I think I am everything or anything. I become something only when I am aware of something to become.

On Saturday morning at the market I saw many dull or unhappy faces while I fairly skimmed along in joy at the sight of the movement and colour. I felt so sorry for them. Why? Because they didn't look as joyous as I felt. They didn't know the things I knew.

Superior being, no, I must not feel better than they. I must simply be grateful for having had my eyes opened and must show what has been given me. In other words, I must observe and feel and *write* every day and every spare moment. No more of this mooning and dreaming and rationalizing and justifying. I must get the thoughts down, even if they're dull as washing dishes.

August 26, 1949 [31]

My article on the Mennonites was delivered to *Maclean's* yesterday. God save it from their cutting pencil. It is much too long. I hope they won't destroy its life and leave only the externals. Spent the evening with the W.O. Mitchells.[32] They are so earnest, so eager, so completely natural. Bill is like a lion, he roars and immediately after he purrs and yet to say he is like a lion is rather ridiculous since essentially he is a gentle soul, but fiery. He read, and we discussed, E.M. Forster's article in *Harper's*, "Art for Art's Sake."[33] Bill loves Forster. I must read him. I don't know why but something in me turns away from him as a man who stands on the brink of life and will not let himself be drawn into it. I may be wrong. I know nothing about his life. "There is nothing new under the sun, but there are always new filters etc." Bill said he thinks I should rewrite my Neil's Harbour book as a novel. He thinks it could have terrific power, whereas now it is just a sort of snapshot album. He is right, but can I wait long enough to change it? I need *now* the freedom that having a book published will give me. Or will it? No, one must always struggle for freedom, struggle with oneself, that is. I could have much more freedom here every day if I would not let myself be interrupted by all the people who come to me here. But I don't want to hurt them. I want them to love me. But this analytical thinking about motives is what I want to avoid. I must learn to let my thoughts be creative, and analyzing is not creating.

Forster speaks of mateyness.[34] An artist may not become matey. Bill interpreted that to mean that he must not accede to the expected. One must not conform, give in against one's principles, fall in love. The article went on to speak of detachment and slouching around with a hat pulled down over one's eyes. I thought he talked of actual mateyness with people. Surely one must *know* people, listen to people, observe people, absorb people to become people, in order to create people. We don't really create. We merely digest and that which we have absorbed comes through us in a new form. That is why I doubt if I shall ever write quickly. It would be like gobbling something up and spewing it out, undigested—very vulgar. But to get back to this mateyness. As one listens to people, one gives one's attention. They give whatever they have or want to give and the artist lets it seep into him to become a part of him. He is enriched by it, he grows while listening in this way. He is loving, he is losing himself and becoming the other person. There is feeling between them. There is a flowing together of their essential elements—a fusion. No, not a fusion, that is too static, but rather a harmonious blending of entities, and the artist may not have said a word. He has simply listened and looked into the other person's eyes and he has received a man's soul, he has got understanding. And he has given *attention*—undivided, absorbing, loving. And the person to whom he has given it is somehow secured, feels a bond between them. He does not know what has happened. He has just met a man to whom he could tell everything, a man with whom he is at ease, a man who makes him feel important and happy. He wants the feeling to last, the friendship between them to continue. He wants the artist to be his friend. The experience he has had has been unique. But to the artist it is only one of many, and because it is one of many, because he understands it for the fleeting glimpse that it is—a fragment of eternity—he withdraws. He cannot become the person's mate. Always a feeling of something shared will be between them but the artist won't have time to continuously be with the other person and that detachment is difficult. The other will no doubt be hurt and want the artist to keep on seeing him and listening to him, to be friends. He doesn't know that the artist has become him, that he is forever a part of the artist through whom he will filter and take form and so often he interrupts the artist, and he keeps away from him, and feels that the artist has slighted him. And the artist then too is hurt. But how can he do his work if he spends all his time being friends with all the interesting, lovely people he meets?

Notes

1 Box R3-1. Diary 1939–44.

2 Staebler wrote "Wednesday, no Thursday" on this entry, which is from Box R1, Travel Diary, Halifax 1943.

3 Katherine Mansfield (Kathleen Mansfield Beauchamp 1880–1923), New Zealand short-story writer whose experimental style provoked her British contemporary Virginia Woolf. Mary Webb (1881–1927), born in Shropshire, novelist best known for *Precious Bane* (1924). Thomas Wolfe (1900–38), American novelist who established his reputation with the autobiographical *Look Homeward Angel* (1929).

4 Some of Staebler's diaries, like the one referred to here, were book-like in form.

5 William Faulkner, *Light in August* (1932).

6 The word "not" in "I must not take them for granted" is crossed out here, though the context suggests it should not have been.

7 This appears to be a reference to Bill Reeves, one of the soldier dinner guests welcomed by the Staeblers.

8 "One" seems likely to mean a baby here.

9 Box R3-1. Diary 1939–44.

10 Box R3-6. Edna's Journal–December 1945–April 28, 1946.

11 Box R3-6. Edna's Journal—January 7, 1946–September 5, 1954 [p. 4]. This journal is typewritten. While the title suggests a start date of 1946, there are entries dating from January 1945.

12 Dorothy "Dottie" Shoemaker, a close friend of Edna's, and librarian at the Kitchener Public Library.

13 Box R3-6. Edna's Journal–January 7, 1946–September 5, 1954. Entries between January 11, 1945 and May 5, 1946 are all from this journal. As noted in the

introduction, where Staebler has paginated, an entry's page location is included at the end of the entry in parentheses, as in the case of this entry (5).

14 Staebler was president of The Canadian Club and a member of the Kitchener Library Board.

15 Richard Hillary (1919–43), author of World War II bestseller *The Last Enemy* (1942), first published in the USA under the title *Falling Through Space*, drawn from his experiences as a wartime pilot. Arthur Koestler's article on Hillary, "The Birth of a Myth," was first published in *Horizon* (no. 40, April 1943) and republished under the title "In Memory of Richard Hillary," in *The Yogi and the Commissar and Other Essays* (New York: Macmillan, 1945), 46–67.

16 Gladys Arnold (1905–2002), Canadian foreign correspondent who covered World War II for the Canadian Press. Arnold was a guest speaker at the Canadian Club in the autumn of 1945. Edna enjoyed discussing literature with her. Arnold's memoir, *One Woman's War*, was published in 1987.

17 French for "tragic life."

18 Edna had begun to work on what would become *Cape Breton Harbour* (1972), based on her sojourn in Neil's Harbour in the summer of 1945.

19 Staebler met Glover in Neil's Harbour.

20 Phil Knowling, another guest speaker at the Canadian Club and a frequent houseguest at the Staeblers. Born in Newfoundland, he had traveled extensively in service during the war and Edna enjoyed his stories.

21 A reference to difficulties in Keith's life and in the Staebler marriage.

22 This section of Staebler's diary is typewritten.

23 Lib Ruddell, childhood friend, married to Gerry Eastman. Referred to as Fay Roberts (later Adams) in Ross's biography, Lib had an affair with Keith Staebler while Eastman was overseas during the war. Edna confided in her friend about the troubles in her marriage. She would not learn of the affair until the fall of 1946, after this entry.

24 Box R3-1. Diary 1948.

25 C.S. Lewis (1898–1963), British literary scholar, critic, and author of stories for children, including the widely read *The Lion, The Witch, and The Wardrobe* (1950).

26 Norton Staebler, like his brother Keith, was a talented musician who also worked in insurance and also struggled with a drinking problem and mental health. He died tragically at the age of 42 in 1955 when he was struck by a car. He had a daughter by his first wife, Helen Waimel, a sculptor born in Estonia whose works were purchased and displayed in parks by the city of Kitchener, and a son by his second wife, Helen McLean.

27 Box R3-1. Diary 1941–49. This excerpt comes from a journal entitled "Notes & Journal writing about various subjects—including Fred." Entries in this journal are undated and unpaginated.

28 In this entry, Staebler uses the second person "you" in a style that recalls Brenda Ueland's *If You Want to Write*, a book that was very important to Staebler.

29 Box R3–1. Diary 1948.

30 Box R3–1. Diary 1941–49.

31 Box R3–1. Diary 1948.

32 W.O. Mitchell (1914–98), Saskatchewan-born novelist and short-story writer, best known for *Who Has Seen the Wind* (1947) and *Jake and the Kid* (1961). Mitchell was fiction editor at *Maclean's* at the time.

33 E.M. Forster, "Art for Art's Sake," *Harper's* no. 199, 1191 (August 1949): 31–34.

34 From "matey" meaning like a mate or mates; friendly and familiar (*with*); sociable, companionable (OED). Forster writes, "Estimable is mateyness, and the man who achieves it gives many a pleasant little drink to himself and to others. But it has no traceable connection with the creative impulse, and probably acts as an inhibition on it. The artist who is seduced by mateyness may stop himself from doing the one thing which he, and he alone, can do— the making of something out of words or sounds or paint or clay or marble or steel or film which has internal harmony and presents order to a permanently disarranged planet. This seems worth doing, even at the risk of being called uppish by journalists" ("Art for Art's Sake," 33).

4

"Duellists of the Deep"
1948

Edna Staebler's first publication, "Duellists of the Deep," appeared in Maclean's *magazine on July 15, 1948. It was reprinted in* Whatever Happened to Maggie, and Other People I've Known, *published by McClelland and Stewart in 1983. The version presented here is from the latter publication, which Staebler preferred because it was free of some of the* Maclean's *edits.*

DURING THE FIRST two years that I was working on *Cape Breton Harbour*—my book about a stark little fishing village on the Cabot Trail—my mother kept saying, "Why waste your time? You're not a real writer, you have to have talent." My husband said, "Stop thinking about yourself as a writer; you're not a writer until you've had something published."

I kept on writing. I wrote every day; I enjoyed what I was doing: reliving my adventures in Neil's Harbour. I sent out a couple of paragraphs to *Saturday Night* and *Canadian Poetry Magazine*. They were accepted as poems! My family was surprised but not convinced.

I wondered: could I make a story of the day I went swordfishing in a snapper boat with three Neil's Harbour fishermen? I worked on the piece for six weeks; it was twenty-four pages long.

When I was sure I couldn't rewrite it again I put on my "newlook" suit and flower-trimmed hat, drove to Toronto, and asked the man in the kiosk at the *Maclean's* magazine office if I could see the articles editor.

"Sure, sixth floor, Scott Young." If he'd told me I could go up and see God I wouldn't have been more surprised—or excited.

Scott Young received me politely, asked why I hadn't mailed the piece in, and said he'd give me his decision within two weeks.

My swordfishing story, cut in half by the editors, was published in July 1948. (I heard later that when he saw me Scott said to himself, "Damn, another little cutie from the Pen Guild." But after he'd read the piece he said, "My God, she can write!")

∼

WHILE DRIVING ROUND THE CABOT TRAIL in Cape Breton I stopped where the waves of the North Atlantic were breaking on great rocks beside the road. Not far off-shore I noticed a little boat with a figure swaying at the top of her sailless mast. Suddenly a man ran out to the end of her bowsprit; for a moment he was suspended; he lunged with an arm extended, poised, recovered, darted back to obscurity in the hull. The figure on the mast dropped to the deck. A dory was lowered from the stem; a man jumped into it and was quickly separated from the larger boat.

I was excited. I knew the men had speared a swordfish.

Hoping to watch them bring it in I drove back to the nearest village where a scattering of bare-faced wooden houses staggered up a hill that hadn't a tree, and a mass of fishing shacks clustered round a couple of jetties sheltered by a rocky point with a red-capped lighthouse.

I walked down a winding lane to a wharf where perhaps twenty children, three shaggy black dogs, and ten men were chattering excitedly in the salty dialect of the Newfoundlanders who had crossed the Cabot Strait and cleared the shallow earth around Neil's Harbour eighty years ago.

The children, tanned scalps showing through sun-bleached hair, wore well-washed jeans or calico dresses; the ruddy-faced men, in khaki caps with visors six inches long, wore rubber boots, thick trousers, and flannel shirts over grey woollen underwear on a day that was warm enough for me to wear shorts and for the children to be barefooted. Shyly conscious of the presence of a stranger, they turned away with a half smile when their curious glances met mine.

"Here comes the *Robin B*," someone shouted. "Gotta fish!"

Passing the breakwater that was nearest the open sea came a vessel like the one I'd seen from the Trail. As it scraped gently against the wharf, a rope through a pulley at the top of a pole was tossed to the men aboard. They did something with it that I couldn't see, then three men on the wharf heaved ho. A leviathan was stretched from the deck to the top of the fifteen-foot pole! I was seeing my first swordfish. It was stupendous! The body was round; the skin a dark purple-grey, rough one way, smooth the other like a cat's tongue; the horny black fins stood out like scimitars, the tail like the handlebars of a giant bicycle; but the strangest thing was the broad, pointed, sharp-sided sword, an extension of the head, an upper bill three feet long! As the rope was slowly released, the men guided the creature down to the dock where it lay like a rolled up rug.

A little boy knelt near the head; with a hook he ripped open the glazed membrane of the huge round eye that was uppermost. Out of the cavity ran clear, slurpy liquid. The child put his hand into the socket, pulled something out of it then looked up at me. "Want te heyeball?" he asked, thrusting his fist towards me.

Ugh! I couldn't touch the fishy thing. But everybody was watching to see what I would do. "Let me look at it," I hedged. He opened his hand and I saw a perfect sphere, clear as glass, about an inch and a quarter in diameter, reflecting colours like a bubble.

"Take it," he said.

I still hesitated. "I haven't any money with me."

The child shook his head. "Don't need none."

"You mean it's a present?"

He grinned and nodded. I couldn't spurn a gift. I held out my hand; the boy placed the crystal gently on my palm. It felt cool and tender as a piece of jelly or a gumdrop that's had the sugar licked off it.

"What should I do with it?"

"Take home and put in sun and it'll turn roight hard," someone answered. "Be careful not to break en." I held my treasure reverently; it didn't even smell like fish!

"How much would the fish weigh?" I asked anyone who could hear me.

"Over six hundred pound, I reckon," a blue-eyed fisherman answered. "He's some beeg."

"What does it taste like?"

"Don't know, never et 'em, we just ketches 'em and sells 'em for folks down in States," he said. "Don't fancy to try none of the big ugly things meself but some round 'ere cut off a bit near the haid and taked it home and cooked it; they say hit's got a roight noice flavour to it, loike pork, not strong atall. Americans must loike 'em or they wouldn't pay so much for 'em. We's gettin' thirty-two cents a pound today." I did some mental arithmetic. "No wonder you're so happy to catch one."

He grinned. "We be, but they's awful scarce." With a saw in his hand he knelt beside the fish. "Want sword?" he asked me.

"Oh yes, don't you need it?"

He laughed. "We just throws 'em overboard."

The fibrous grey sword was heavy and felt like bone. The cut end showed soft bloody marrow that was the essence of fishiness. A man saw me sniffing. "Stick in ant heap and ants'll clean en out for you," he offered.

"How long will it take?"

"About six weeks."

The man next sawed off the head, then the fins, the broad black tail and the fan-shaped crimson gill plates; as each piece came off the youngsters threw it into the water where flashing white birds darted at it before it sank to the shadowy creatures hovering in beds of waving kelp. With a knife the underbody of the fish was ripped open. I wanted to leave but the faces all round me were bland as blancmange; I couldn't insult them by running away. As though mesmerized I watched all the stuffing being pulled out of that huge cavity; like a gourmet in a nightmare I saw long white links of sausage, steamed puddings, buckshot, sets of false teeth, lumps of pink lard, clots of black jelly, and bright red claret splashing over everything including my legs.

The carcass, washed with salt water, was hoisted on a carrier and taken by four men to the scales. Everyone gathered around to learn the score—634 pounds—marked with indelible pencil near the tail.

The *Robin B* having moved to her mooring, another boat landed a fish. One by one the lucky boats of Neil's Harbour came to the end of the dock; those that had caught no fish went straight to the anchorage, the men coming ashore in dories that had been fastened to buoys in the water. Twenty boats had gone fishing; five swordfish had been caught and exuberantly acclaimed.

I decided I wanted to go swordfishing.

"Do you ever take people out with you?" I asked one of the fishermen. He answered warily, "We doos, now and again."

"Would you take me? Tomorrow morning?"

He rubbed the back of his neck and contemplated the water. "Well now, I'll tell you, miss, I ain't aimin' to fish tomorrow but if you gits down on shore by seven in morning they won't all git off without you."

Next morning I was on the shore at six-thirty. All the men gathered in little groups around the stages stopped talking to stare at me as I came along.

"Is it going to be a good day?" I heard myself asking timidly.

After a silence somebody said, "Yis, moight be." The rest just stared— at me, through me, past me. I wanted to run but the thought of my retreating posterior made me stay to try again. "Would anyone please take me swordfishing?"

The men exchanged glances; one of them said, "Well, I'll tell you, miss, ye'd be better off in boat with fo'c'sle. Ye see, we don't have much room in them small ones. You wait round till skipper o' one o' them snapper boats comes down."

Four larger vessels were tied up between the two wharves. I sat on the fish dock and waited half an hour till three men sauntered along.

"Woman aboard's bad luck," one said when I asked if they'd take me.

"I'm good luck, you'll see, I'll bring you good luck."

They looked at each other. "We been fishin' fer two months and ain't got but three...."

"Ever been seasick?"

"No," I answered firmly. (I didn't tell them I'd never been out on the sea).

"Come on then."

I was going! They helped me into the dory and rowed over to a blue and grey snapper boat. It was called the *Devil Diver*. The name gave me a tremor. I scrambled awkwardly aboard.

The snapper boat was forty feet long and ten feet wide with a Buick engine in the middle. It had a dory in the stern, a high, sailless mast from which the vessel was controlled, a fo'c'sle, foredeck, and removable swordfish rig, consisting of a plank projecting twelve feet over the water from the prow and a pulpit, a metal three-quarter hoop less than waist high, to which the long rod of the harpoon was fastened. A detachable double-barbed dart of bronze was socketed in the end of the rod; taut along the rod a thin, strong line ran from the dart to a great coil in a box amidships with a red keg tied at the end of the hundreds of feet of line. The keg could be thrown into the water to mark and retard a wounded fish.

We started at once. That they might spy a fish even below the surface of the water, two of the men, Diddle and Jack, had climbed the mast where they sat on rope-swung boards like performers on a trapeze, their feet resting on a bar. The other man, Jossie, sat on the wooden door that covered the roaring motor; he was the "sticker" who, when a fish was sighted, would run out to the pulpit, untie the harpoon, and make the fatal lunge. I sat on the only seat in the boat, a narrow bench near the motor.

Soon we had gone round the breakwater, round the lighthouse point, out to the open sea, climbing the hill of water that rose to the horizon. I sat very still, very straight, very stiff. Though the water didn't look wild, the boat seemed to heave. The fumes of the engine were very strong; I remembered that someone had told me the smell of gasoline always made people seasick. I thought I'd better move away but there seemed to be no place for me to go. I clung to the bench and looked at Neil's Harbour, now just a tiny clearing against the great dark hills. Jossie, relaxed in front of me, kept his eyes on the water.

"What do you look for?" I shouted.

"Just loike two black sticks, 'bout so high"—he held up his hands eight inches apart—"and so"—he stretched his arms as wide as they would go.

I tried watching the water for two black sticks—two black sticks—gasoline fumes—no, no—two black sticks—two black—gasoline.... I stood up. But there was nothing to hang on to so I sat down again, clinging to the bench.

"You might be more easy atop the fo'c'sle," Jossie said, swinging himself nimbly onto the roof of the tiny cabin and sitting on its front edge, his back towards me.

I shuffled to the rail of the boat. To get on top of the fo'c'sle, which was higher than my head, I had to climb up the side from the boat's narrow rail, avoiding the ropes that ran from the mast to the engine. The water was whizzing by and very close. I was scared skinny. I don't know how many times I missed but one time I didn't. I leaned against the mast and breathed the fresh salt air.

Then I felt dizzy. I thought, *This is it!* But nothing happened. I waited; I felt no nausea. I realized I never had felt any.

What the hell—I wasn't seasick, I was just unbalanced. It was time I started looking for swordfish.

How could I know when I really saw two black sticks among the billion sharp points of water that raised themselves capriciously round us? Dozens of those impish little wavelets deliberately deceived me as they danced up from the surface, imitated the curving fins, posed long enough to give me a thrill, then mercifully disappeared before I could shout what I believed I had discovered.

We were perhaps five miles from land and by simply turning my head I could see forty miles from the misty purple form of Cape Smokey in the south to fainter, farther Money Point at the northern tip of Cape Breton Island. Closest to us was a wall of red rock with the dark mass of mountains behind it. The village we had left was merely a break in the surrounding greenery.

The smaller fishing boats, weaving back and forth inshore, shone white, red, green, and grey with the sun against them in the deep-blue water; the snapper boats and sailing vessels from Newfoundland were silhouetted in the gleam between us and the horizon. There were schooners and jacks, ketches and smacks, snapper boats and skiffs from Port au Basque, St. John's, Glace Bay, Louisburg, and Yarmouth, from all the coast of Newfoundland and all of Nova Scotia; they had come to find, and kill, the wary, wondrous swordfish that from July to September mystifies and provokes the rugged men of the rocky northern seaboard.

Loving the sport, the gamble, the hope of fabulous luck, like men obsessed, they had piled up their lobster traps, hauled in their herring nets, coiled their codfish trawls, and become rivals in pursuit of the monstrous creatures that bask in the summer sunshine off the shores of Cape Breton.

In July the search for the precious prey is made near Glace Bay and Louisburg. When the middle of August comes, the men on the masts follow the broadbilled fish to the fertile grounds between Ingonish and Dingwall where the long swords slash and the toothless mouths gobble the defenceless mackerel and herring. By the end of September the roving gladiators have disappeared from the North Atlantic to go no one knows where.

The capture of the swordfish is as uncertain as the weather that controls it. The smaller vessels, with only two men aboard, are lucky to catch even three in a season; the larger craft, with as many as five watchers on a mast, searching many miles from land, may bring in a dozen fish in a day—or none. Almost the entire annual catch, averaging a million and a half pounds, is packed in ice and shipped to Boston.

When a boat came near us, I held my breath as I saw the men aloft sway four feet to the right, four feet to the left, to and fro, to and fro, like inverted pendulums. They shouted something that sounded like, "Got arn?"

Jossie shook his head, yelling unmistakably, "Narn."

I asked what it meant.

"Ave we got some and we ain't," he said.

There were no clouds in the sky. The sun was warm but the breeze was becoming a wind. Our boat leapt and fell in the swells, a wonderful, proud thing to feel. And all the time we kept watching for the precious sticklike fins. We saw several sharks; we saw dolphins; we saw a black-fish blow.

Then Diddle on the mast yelled, "*Fish!*"

"I see 'im," Jossie cried, running nimbly to the end of the bowsprit.

I couldn't see anything but those points of water. Risking my life, I stood up. I saw the fins, those two black sticks, eight inches high.

Jossie unfastened the harpoon, leaned against the iron hoop. The engine was switched off. We were close. Jossie was poised to strike.

"Aw—a trick!" he called and we all saw that the two black fins were fastened to a piece of board. The men laughed about it but I didn't think it was funny.

"Anyway, now you know what the fins looks loike when they's out of the water."

We settled down again after that and even I didn't stop watching the waves forming and disappearing. Sometimes the boat went towards the south, then straight towards the horizon, northeast, due north, south again, always moving, her men and I watching, waiting, hoping. The same anxiety was in a hundred vessels that searched the sea as we did. After a box lunch we saw a boat that had stopped some distance from us; almost alongside was its dory with two men. One, standing, was pulling in a line; the other, crouched over, was bailing.

"Must ha' been struck," Jossie shouted, pointing. "Swordfish be quiet, restin' fish," he told me; "wouldn't hurt nobody if they's left alone. Swords be made fer slashing, not stabbing, but when a fish is hit near the head 'e sometimes goes crazy loike and turns on a boat or dory, can ram 'is whole sword clear through a three-inch plank—and a man too if 'e's settin' in the way. Sword breaks off and fish dies quick after that, but a man dies quick too if sword goes through 'im or if 'e gits hisself tangled in a line and dragged down."

The wind was growing stronger, the water rougher; the waves were splashing over the fo'c'sle; I buttoned my jacket and tucked my green cotton legs under me. Around three o'clock I realized why I had been advised to go out in a boat with a fo'c'sle. I thought up genteel ways in which I could break the news to Jossie. I thought how unapproachable he looked as he sat staring at the water. I thought how ridiculous it was to be so prudish. For about an hour I tried to forget. When I knew I couldn't sit still another minute, Jack, the curly-headed blond lad, came down from the mast and sat beside me. "How do you like swordfishing?" he asked.

"Fine."

"Ever been out before?"

"No."

"Want to go out again?" He gave me a sideways glance.

"Sure."

"What's your name? Where do you belong? How long are you staying round here? Where are you staying at?"

I answered his questions briefly, hoping he'd go aloft. He asked me if I'd like a cigarette.

"Don't you smoke?" He looked surprised. "Not many city girls don't smoke." He painstakingly rolled a cigarette, lighted it carefully behind his hands, blew the smoke out slowly, and settled himself to enjoy it. "Nice day out on the water," he said, "though it's gettin' loppy."

I couldn't stand it any longer; I said, "I'm sorry, but I think I'm going to have to embarrass you...."

"What did you say?"

"I'm sorry, but I think I'm going to have to..." I stopped. I swallowed. I felt hot; I knew I was blushing. He looked at me sharply. I glared back and cried, "Have you got an old can I could take into the fo'c'sle?"

He didn't say a word; he went right to the stern, came back; without looking at me he thrust a battered tin pail into my hand then swung himself aloft. I slipped into the boat's little bit of seclusion and closed the sliding door.

Then, of all times, I heard, "*Fish!*"

The motor was stopped. Now, now, they would catch a swordfish. I zipped out of the cabin. Jossie was in the pulpit, the harpoon in his hand. I looked frantically where I thought he was looking but I couldn't see the fish. I couldn't climb quickly enough to the roof of the fo'c'sle. I thought I'd miss the whole thing. I leaned so far across the rail I almost tipped over.

Jossie dropped his arm. "Goddamn shark," he said. I saw it just as it disappeared: two broad fins above the water. Jossie's shoulders drooped. He fastened the harpoon to the pulpit.

The boat pitched up and down, rocked to and fro, rolled back and forth. I was sure we couldn't possibly see fins in the turbulent sea. The men thought the same, and at half past four the boat was turned towards the harbour. Tired and feeling as people do who have fished all day and caught no fish I slumped against the mast.

Suddenly I was pointing and shrieking, "Look, look, a fish, a fish, a fish!"

"By God, it is, a fish, a fish," Jossie yelled and ran out to the pulpit. Jack, on the mast, steered straight towards the prize. The motor stopped. We were quiet. Tense. We were close. Jossie held the harpoon in his hand. The fish was almost alongside. "Oh God, get 'im, get 'im," I prayed.

Jossie lunged.

The fish was gone. The rod fell slack in the water. Jossie jerked it back to the pulpit.

Diddle came down from the mast with Jack tumbling after. "Struck 'im right behind front fin," Diddle called as he grabbed the line uncoiling from the box amidships.

Jossie ran to the stern. The dory was lowered, and Diddle jumped into it with the keg and box of rope. Quickly he tautened the line with the dart on the end in the fish.

"'E's on," Diddle shouted, "'e's on," and at once was jerked away by the plunging, wounded swordfish.

We watched him go. Without the steadying drive of the motor, the *Devil Diver* was seesawing madly. I clung to the mast. Jossie grinned at me as he passed on his way to the pulpit to put a new dart in the pole. Jack started the motor and we were moving again. Jossie's place on the front of the fo'c'sle was constantly splashed as we plunged into deepening waves.

"Worst swell I ever were out in," he said as he moved back and sat beside me.

"What are we going to do now?" I asked him.

"Look for another fish till Diddle gits that one played out." We didn't go far from Diddle; except when he was hidden by waves we always kept him in sight. He stood in the little dory, pulling in line and letting it out as the swordfish tried to escape him by riding him round in the sea.

"Looks like 'e might be a big one," Jossie said when we'd circled for almost an hour. He seldom watched the water for another fish: he kept turning anxious glances towards the yellow dory. "Sometimes we loses a fish," he said. "Sometimes it takes three–four hours to tire out a big one. Sometimes a fish will turn on a dory before 'e dies." As we kept moving east, south, west, and north, all the other fishing boats were going in one direction, all going towards a harbour. Soon we were alone on the ocean with the little yellow dory. The hill of water towards the horizon seemed steeper than it had in the morning. The land seemed farther away.

"Wind's right nardly now," Jossie said.

It was useless to pretend we were looking for another fish: we kept our eyes on Diddle. He was pulling in the line, letting it out, pulling it in, letting it out as he stood in the little boat.

For another lonely hour we circled.

Then Diddle raised his arm. We rushed to the dory heaving up and down in the waves. Diddle was smiling broadly. The water around him was red, the great curved tail of the swordfish securely tied to the thwart. Diddle clambered into the *Diver*. With the help of a tackle the fish was hauled aboard. It stretched across the full width of the boat with its head running up the side, its sword above the gunwale. "Not the biggest one I ever seen in my life," was the first comment Jossie made, "but 'e'll go seven hundred pound." He thumped Diddle's shoulder with joy.

"'E was a dirty little bastard," Diddle said, "wouldn't go up or down, kep' hittin' the rope with 'is tail." He was grinning. Jossie was grinning too and so were Jack and I.

"You's lucky," Diddle said to me. "You can git a ship any time now. Jesus Christ, they'll all be beggin' ye to go with them!"

They hauled in the dory, the men climbed the mast, Jossie sat on the engine door, I sat on the bench. The *Devil Diver* leaped towards the harbour.

We rode straight up to the fish dock. A crowd was there to see. Jossie fastened a rope round the swordfish tail and the men on the wharf pulled it up.

"Oooooo, a good one, a good one," everyone said in a way that was almost a cheer. For a blessed moment the great fish hung high, then they let it down with a plop.

As we followed it over the rail, Diddle announced in his booming voice, "This girl's good luck, we want her to ship with we. Everybody else can't have her."

~

THOUGH I OFTEN WENT BACK to Neil's Harbour I never went swordfishing again with Diddle, Jossie, and Jack. In 1968 the swordfish was declared to be contaminated with mercury. The fishermen's favourite sport was over; they sold their snapper boats and tamely went out after cod, mackerel, haddock, and lobster, complaining bitterly that fishing was poor because the big trawlers and seiners of other countries were cruising close to their shore, getting all the big fish and destroying the little ones.

Then someone discovered that South Harbour was alive with oysters! The fishermen staked their claims and oyster fishing was profitable—until the oyster beds were fished out.

Then queen crab was discovered and the fishermen went after that—until there didn't seem to be any more.

In 1976, with the proclamation of a two-hundred-mile limit for foreign vessels, inshore fishing provided a living again.

And swordfish—still basking off Cape Breton's shores—though not saleable in Canada are welcomed in the USA. The fishermen of Neil's Harbour will tell you, "We don't roightly go after 'em but if we sees one out there we'll catch 'en, if we's lucky."

"How to Live without Wars and Wedding Rings" 1950

Edna Staebler's article about Old Order Mennonites, "How to Live without Wars and Wedding Rings," was Maclean's *feature article in its July 1, 1950, issue. It earned her the Canadian Women's Press Club Award in September 1950. Staebler was very proud of the award and of the fact that contenders that year included such notables as June Callwood, Mavis Gallant, and Marjorie Wilkins Campbell (Ross 141). Like "Duellists of the Deep," "How to Live without Wars and Wedding Rings" was reprinted in* Whatever Happened to Maggie, and Other People I've Known *(McClelland and Stewart, 1983) and in* Places I've Been and People I've Known: Stories from across Canada *(McGraw-Hill Ryerson, 1990) in the version that Edna preferred, which is included here.*

ONE DAY IN 1949 when I was calling on Bill (W.O.) Mitchell—then fiction editor of *Maclean's* magazine—he introduced me to Pierre Berton, the new articles editor. Bill said, "Edna's swordfishing piece was number one in the readership test; why don't we get her to write a piece for us about the horse-and-buggy Mennonites? She lives in the area."

They discussed the idea and agreed that I should try it.

But what did I really know about the Old Order Mennonites? I saw them in their black bonnets and shawls every Saturday morning at the Kitchener market, selling *kochkase* [a spreadable cheese of German origin] and vegetables. I heard stories about their strange ways and expressions. How could I find out anything more? "They won't tell you anything," I was told whenever I enquired about them. "They keep to themselves."

I decided the only way was to try to find a family that would let me live with them for a while. At the general store in St. Jacobs I was given the name of a family that was friendly and less withdrawn than most of the Old Order. I approached their farmhouse with some trepidation. A neat little woman wearing a prayer cap invited me into her kitchen. She and her daughter listened to me and shyly agreed that it might not be bad to have their way of life explained so people could understand why they live without cars and radios, telephones, pianos, and pensions.

The woman went out to the barn to discuss my proposal with her husband. She came back smiling, and it was arranged that I'd come to stay with them the following Monday.

⁓

NOT LONG AGO I STAYED FOR A WEEK with the family of Grossdoddy Martin, in the fieldstone house his great-grandfather built in the days when the Mennonites came up from Pennsylvania to break new ground in Upper Canada. The house and the family are among the oldest in Ontario—almost two hundred years have passed fruitfully and peacefully over the farm their pioneer forefathers cleared from the wilderness in Waterloo County.

The Martins belong to a splinter sect, the Old Order Mennonites, whose ways often seem strange to outsiders. They shun everything worldly, everything fashionable, but they don't mind a swig of cider. They use electricity and tractors, but will not buy cars or radios. They won't face a camera. They don't have telephones in their homes, or musical instruments. They refuse old-age pensions, medicare, and family allowances. They won't buy insurance or stocks. They won't go to court or to war and Canadian law has been amended to exempt them permanently from both. They speak Pennsylvania Dutch and have a look of contentment.

The style of their plain, sombre clothes has changed little since 1525. The men wear broad-brimmed black hats with round crowns; their coats, with old-fashioned cut-away backs, are buttoned straight up the front to a neckband, having no collars or lapels. Their faces are clean-shaven—moustaches, being ornamental, are not allowed. The hair of some men and boys is conventionally cut; others look as if a bowl had been placed over the head and the rim used as a cutting guide.

The women's dark print dresses, made from a traditional pattern, have fitted waists under a pointed plastron, and long, gathered skirts that almost hide their black stockings. Their uncut, uncurled hair is always covered by a white organdie cap tied under the chin, or a helmet-like black satin bonnet. In cold weather they are bundled in shawls. They wear no cosmetics or jewellery—not even wedding rings.

The Old Order Mennonites try to preserve the ways of their fore-fathers who crossed the Atlantic nearly three hundred years ago to escape religious persecution in Switzerland and settled first in Pennsylvania, then, in 1786, started coming to Canada. Although there are more than 160,000 Mennonites of various sects all the way from Ontario to British Columbia, there are only about 2,500 members of the Old Order. They cling to their homesteads near Waterloo and Kitchener, and their eight similar white-clapboard churches are on their own farmlands, all within a twenty-mile radius.

Like most Old Mennonite farm homes, Grossdoddy Martin's house sprawls. The main house, Georgian Colonial in style, is broad with a gabled roof; the plastered wall under the porch is painted sky blue. Adjoining is the *doddy* (grandfather) house, a small addition to which the generations of old folks have retired when their youngest sons took over the farm. Behind the kitchen is the frame summer kitchen; beyond it the wash-house, the woodshed, and the privy.

Prosperity smiles on the Martin house from its great painted barn. Beauty surrounds it: gentle hills form its horizons, its fields slope to the maple woods along the curving Conestoga River. On the day I arrived, fruit trees beside the house were snowy with blossom and daffodils bordered the neatly fenced lawn.

"You don't want to make fun of us?" The Martins were anxious when I asked if I might live with them for a few days to learn and write about them—though trustful, they were alert. From the beginning they used my Christian name; they were friendly, natural, and disarmingly candid. They answered my questions thoughtfully, generously, and asked me as many in return—only Grossdoddy, listening with a quiet smile, took no part.

I wanted them to speak in their dialect, an unwritten mixture of Swiss-German and English, but they didn't think it would be polite since I couldn't understand all the words. They asked me to correct their English. "We're shy to talk English in front of strangers because we don't say our letters always right: like for Jesus we say 'Cheesus.' We know it's wrong but we forget. Amongst ourselfs we always talk our own kind of German—it's easier; and if we don't, our own people think we're putting on style."

In their house there was little that was not useful except, in the spare room, two bouquets of paper roses that the parents had given the daughters for Christmas, and scenic calendars that had long outlived their dates. All the walls were whitewashed; the woodwork was painted bright blue. The windows had no curtains, but tins of geraniums bloomed on the sills. There were five bedrooms with pumpkin-yellow floors. The tiny parlour had a huge corner cupboard and wooden chairs set side by side against the pictureless walls. The kitchen was also the living-dining-room; the big black stove was always warm, and there was comfort in the couch and the rocker in the corner.

"Make the light on once," Bevvy, the mother, directed after supper on the day I arrived, and the family gathered round the long, oilcloth-covered table. David, the father, worked on his income-tax papers; Salome, sixteen, was absorbed by a romantic novel written fifty years ago; Amsey, seven, and Lyddy Ann, twelve, smiled at me over their schoolbooks; Bevvy placidly turned the pages of the *Family Herald*; Grossdoddy sat in the shadows near the passage to the *doddy* house.

"I was glad to quit school and earn money when I was eleven but often now I wish I went longer yet." David frowned at his papers. "If a person went to college his mind would mature in more of a hurry, I guess."

"The teacher wanted Salome to go longer," Bevvy told me. "She finished school already when she was thirteen, but Mannassah Brubacher's wife needed help chust then, so she went there to work. People hate us for our different ways and if she was in town she would have to act like a turtle for shame or change her Old Mennonite clothes; then she couldn't belong to us no more."

Salome looked up. "I'd like to learn but I wouldn't want to stay from home," she said. "In the city it seems each day is chust like any other day but in the country every day gives something different."

"You can always learn from things you read and people you meet." David's eyes were teasing as they glanced my way. "You think you're going to find out all about us while you're here, but we'll get chust as much from you."

At nine-thirty Bevvy led me up an enclosed stair and through a bare corridor to the spare room where I slept surprisingly well on an ancient rope bed with a straw tick and bolster.

Always the first up in the morning, Grossdoddy put on his stay-at-home suit over the long underwear in which he slept—I was told—and went into the parlour of the *doddy* house where Grossmommy, a black kerchief on her head, lay sleeping on a hospital bed. A young man rose stiffly from a couch.

"She made nothing out all night," he said, putting on his hat. "I see you next week again." He shook the old man's hand, then went out to harness his horse.

He was one of the relatives or neighbours who, in the kindly custom of the Old Order, took turns to come every night from nine o'clock till dawn to relieve the Martin family of some of the care of Grossmommy's lingering illness.

"We always look after our own," Bevvy told me. "And if we don't have enough money for doctors it's paid from the church."

"Why don't you take government benefits?"

"If we did we wouldn't feel independent," she said. "You know we got promised religious freedom a long time ago and that our men don't have to fight in a war."

"Would they if our own country was attacked?" I asked.

Bevvy thoughtfully shook her head. "Jesus said we must turn the other cheek; if everyone did that there would be no wars."

"But everyone in the world doesn't practise Jesus's teaching."

"Then we must be an example." Bevvy smiled. "In the last war our boys helped with the wounded and went in work camps and we bought war bonds." She added hastily, "But we didn't take the interest off them; that would be profiting from war."

When the morning milking was finished, Salome, singing "Throw out the Lifeline" in her clear, young voice, drew the full cans to the cooler in a little cart. Topsy, the collie, followed her.

The hens and beeplings fed, Lyddy Ann pointed out a red patch by the river. "Amsey went fishing at five already. Can you see him down there near the willow?"

At the kitchen sink David pumped rainwater into the basin to wash his face and arms. Bevvy, by the range, ran plump fingers through the curds that would be made into *kochkase* (cook cheese).

"Make the door shut, Salome. We won't wait for Amsey."

David was hungry: he had been doing barn chores for almost two hours.

Bevvy tucked a wisp of hair under the grey kerchief that had covered her head during the night. "I'll comb myself after breakfast," she said.

Chairs were drawn up to the table, heads bowed silently over ironstone plates—Grossdoddy reached for coffee cake with his fork. Everyone stabbed a piece and dunked it. Amsey came in, pleased with ten pink-headed chub. Porridge was eaten, the remains sopped up with bread so the plates could be filled with fried potatoes, summer sausage, and pickled beans. A bowl of *Schnitz und gwetcha* (boiled dried apple segments and prunes) was passed.

There was talk of the day's work to be done, of things growing; there were questions and answers, and there was laughter.

"Dat, you said slang," little Amsey chided his big Mennonite father with the warm brown eyes.

"Did I? Now what bad word did I say?" David pretended alarm.

"You said 'swell.'" The child was very serious.

"Och, ain't that awful? I must be more careful or my children won't be brought up decent," David declared. "But ain't 'swell' a bad word that could be used good?"

When we rose the plates looked as clean as when we sat down. Though it was only seven-thirty, Amsey and Lyddy Ann, eager to play with other children, ran across the fields to school. David went to plough with the tractor. Grossdoddy sat with Grossmommy; Salome sang as she washed the breakfast dishes.

At the little mirror above the kitchen sink Bevvy combed her hair, which fell below her waist. "We never cut them," she told me, "and we all do them chust about the same."

Parting her hair in the centre, she wet it to straighten its curl, folded it flat at the sides like the wings of a bird and then wound it into a spiral pinned firmly on the back of her head. As she tied a dainty white organdie bonnet with black ribbons under her chin, she said, "It's in the Bible that women should keep their heads covered when they pray and we might pray any time of the day or night." Bevvy never sounds pious: she accepts her rules as she does the planting of seed and the harvest.

Salome, looking through the window above the sink, exclaimed, "Isn't that pear tree beautiful? I often thought already I'd like to be able to draw it."

"May you draw pictures?" I asked.

"I may but I couldn't," she said.

"We chust mayn't have pictures on our walls or make pictures of ourselfs," Bevvy explained. "It is in the Ten Commandments, you know, about not making a likeness. Our retired bishop is real old and his children in Pennsylvania want him in the worst way to spend the rest of his days with them but he can't because he would have to have his picture taken for a passport and that would set a bad example."

Among the Old Mennonites example is a powerful force, I learned from the Martins. Young people emulate those who are older; the preachers urge adherence to the ways of their ancestors. If these humble people are permitted any pride, it is in their traditions. Their forefathers braved perils and hardships for their faith, clung to their beliefs, and died for them.

The Mennonite creed arose when the establishment of a state church in Switzerland was opposed, in 1525, by a group of former monks and scholars who wanted a religious order that was free of compulsion. The new sect spread rapidly over north Switzerland; it taught only love, faith, forbearance, and adult baptism, but its followers were exiled, tortured, or burned at the stake. Believing that evil would be overcome by goodness, they would not defend themselves against attack, and thousands of martyrs died without offering resistance.

In 1538 Menno Simons, a former Roman Catholic priest who had become a convert, reorganized and consolidated their congregations, which became known by his name. Services were held secretly in houses and barns; when educated leaders were imprisoned or murdered, simple farmers chosen by lot became preachers and bishops. The humble Mennonites, evicted from one place, would patiently begin again in another until they ranged throughout central Europe. Wherever they settled the land blossomed under their care.

Persecution continued for more than two hundred years. From 1683 on, thousands of Mennonites accepted the invitation of William Penn, whose Quaker faith was similar to theirs, to come to America where Britain promised them freedom from military service and the right to worship as they pleased.

Because they wanted to keep the security of British citizenship after the American Revolution, and because land was less expensive in Upper Canada than in Pennsylvania, hundreds of Mennonites brought their families in Conestoga wagons on the seven-week journey across swamps, mountains, and the terrifying Niagara. Some stayed near the Canadian frontier but most pushed on to Waterloo County, where they became the first white settlers in the interior of the province.

"And from them came all the different kinds of Mennonites around here," David told me.

"Except the Mennonites that came over from Russia," Bevvy corrected.

"Yah, that's right. We don't know much about any but our own. The others mostly all have churches in the towns and they don't dress or act like us Old Mennonites." In this way David dismissed the majority of Mennonite sects.

The first break from the pioneer church in Waterloo County was made in 1869 when a group was ceremoniously evicted because it wanted evangelism. The desire for English services, camp meetings, Sunday schools, young people's societies, higher education, and the free use of invention and of modern but modest dress resulted in further divisions. Quite separate from but similar to the pioneers were the 15,000 Mennonites who came from Russia in 1874 and settled in Manitoba and Saskatchewan, and the thousands who were forced from their homes by the Bolsheviks in the 1920s and found refuge in Ontario and western Canada.

"In Kitchener there is a Mennonite high school and in Waterloo and Preston an old people's home; there's Conrad Grebel College at Waterloo University," Bevvy told me. "And they have a Mennonite central committee where all the kinds of Mennonites go together and sew and send food and clothes and implements to Mennonites in other parts of the world to give to people in need, no matter who they are. I think that's real nice but our old folks don't want us to work in town so we have sewing bees in our own homes and send the committee what we make." Because it might seem boastful, Bevvy went on reluctantly, "We give them food and money too, but we mostly just care for our neighbours and our own; like if a man's barn burns down we build him a new one, if his cows die we give him some, or we help with his work if he's sick. That's the Golden Rule," she said simply.

"Why aren't there more Old Order Mennonites?" I asked. Bevvy blushed. "In Canada there's only us around here."

"There's some in Pennsylvania and Ohio," David said, "only they're a little different from us yet, but we visit back and forth and are related with each other."

"We can marry back and forth too," Bevvy added, "but it's chenerally only the leftovers that do; most Old Mennonites get partners at home where their parents can buy them a farm."

"We like to stay all together like," David explained. "It makes it easier for us to keep our rules if we aren't mixed up with other people."

"Do you think the rest of us are so bad?" I asked.

"Ach no." Bevvy was embarrassed. "We think there's good and bad the same as with us, we chust have different ways."

"Like the Newborns," David said, "they broke off from us because they thought we were going too fast by having the electric and tractors;

they wanted to be more backward yet. And the Markham Mennonites wanted cars and telephones so they got out, but they still use our churches every other Sunday and they paint their cars black with no chrome and dress about the same as we do."

One day the roadside post box had a packet in it for Salome. "It's the books we sent for with the boxtops." She opened it excitedly. One book was a novel, the other a collection of old songs from which she started singing "My Darling Nellie Gray." If I had told her that her voice is beautiful she would have blushed. She had no ambition or vain thought of performing on radio, television, or in Hollywood, though she has eagerness, imagination, wit, a gay red mouth, merry eyes, and the roundest of elbows. When a strand of her soft brown hair escapes its severity her mother reproves her, but Salome laughingly says, "It looks nicest when it's *shtmvelich* (tousled)."

"Here comes Uncle Isaiah." Lyddy Ann had started reading Salome's novel the moment she came home but she reported every movement on the road. An old man with a strong, stern face came into the kitchen and shook hands all around.

"How is Auntie Katie?" Bevvy asked him.

"She ain't goot. She's got the high blood pressure yet and the doctor says she must lose some fat but she can't—it's natural. Her mother and father together weighed near five hundred pounds." The old man shook his head despairingly, then settled in a corner to chat with Grossdoddy.

While we peeled potatoes for supper Bevvy said to me, "You haf such a nice apron."

"I'll let you have the pattern for it."

She grinned. "No thanks, we couldn't have one so fancy. Our clothes are supposed to be all alike and plain so we won't think about how we look. They protect us from temptation too; we couldn't go to picture shows or places of entertainment without being noticed."

"Leave me show her how we dress in winter." Salome ran upstairs; in a few minutes she was back, shaped like an enormous black beehive. Only her delicate nose and sparkling eyes revealed the lovely girl.

"Salome, I wouldn't know you if we met on the street," I exclaimed.

"You would." She laughed. "I'd yell at you."

A wool crêpe veil was folded over her forehead and pinned around the satin bonnet; a thick, fringed shawl fastened with a blanket pin covered a loose black coat, and a smaller shawl muffled her chin.

"It's cold in an open cutter," she explained as she took off the layers of clothes. "See, I fold my shawl straight—if I was married I'd have a point down the back." She handed me her black satin bonnet: it was stiff and heavy as a steel helmet and a little bit faded. "That I had since I finished school already."

"She'll have to take good care of it till she's twenty-one, then we'll buy her a whole new outfit and have her bonnet made over," Bevvy told me while Salome returned her things to the closet.

"Is that when she'll be married?"

"Not necessary, but she might be if she's found a partner she likes. Every Sunday evening the young folks go together to someone's house for a 'singing'; they learn our hymns that way and play games and Salome says some of them dance—but they're not supposed to. If a boy and girl like each other he might drive her home in his buggy."

I faltered over my next question: "Do they bundle?" [Sleep clothed with another person, fiancé.]

"Bundle? What's that?" Bevvy's innocence was honest; I couldn't pursue the subject.

"Does she go out with different boys?" I asked.

"Och, no, she sticks to the one she chooses at the beginning, usually. She could fire him at the end of a year or two and go with another but never more than two or she'd have a bad name and for the boys it's the same—no girl would want to go with a boy that would run from one to another. It's not like in the city where young people go out with strangers; we know the parents and grandparents of everybody from way back and we can pretty well tell if a marriage will be all right. We mayn't have divorces. Only one Old Mennonite married man we know ever went with another woman, and of course now he's out of the church."

After supper the children were in a gay mood. They cleaned the fish Amsey had caught after school; they patted the cats. Lyddy Ann picked violets; Salome played her mouth organ (the only musical instrument allowed). They pranced around the pansy bed; Lyddy Ann held sticks for Topsy to jump at; Salome sang a song. We smelled the honeysuckle and the daffodils; when darkness came we looked at the stars.

"I often wondered already how the streetlights look when they're on in Kitchener and Waterloo," Salome said wistfully.

"Do you never go to town?" I asked. The cities were only eight miles away.

"Oh yes, to the dentist."

"But we have always to be home in time for the milking," Lyddy Ann lamented.

Amsey was looking at the north star. "I would like once to see a ship," he declared.

"I too," said Lyddy Ann. "I would like to travel round the world."

"I would go with you," the little boy said, "and if we came to some cannibals they would eat me last because I am the skinniest."

At nine o'clock Bevvy called, "Come in now, children, and wash your feet before you go in bed."

On Sunday morning Grossdoddy drove Salome and me to church; he sat on one of each of our knees while we sat on the narrow seat of his buggy.

Martin's Meeting House, on the highway north of Waterloo, is more than a hundred years old; its painted clapboards gleam white. A wire fence surrounds its yard, kept neat by a munching cow, and the cemetery beside it where rows and rows of plain white slabs mark the grassy, flowerless graves. There are no family plots: here Nathanial Lichty, Josiah Ernst, Susannah Eby, Israel Weber, Veronica Erb, Rebecca Shantz—and the stillborn infants of David and Bevvy Martin—lie side by side.

Open buggies, two-seaters and boxlike *dachwaegles* (top buggies) came in a steady stream as the black-clad people gathered to worship. Horses pranced up to the cement stoop along one side of the building. Women and little girls in shawls and bonnets alighted; grandmothers went through a door near the front, mothers and children near the centre, young girls hurried to the back. Men and boys drove to the hitching chains, then entered the church on the farther end. In a crowded cloakroom on the women's side, shawls hung on wooden pegs and black bonnets lay on shelves; on the heads of the rosy-cheeked, chattering girls wore caps of white organdie with pale coloured ribbons tied under their chins. The style of their hair and their print cotton dresses had no variation.

Light flooded the church from small-paned windows, walls were whitewashed, scrubbed pine floors and benches were worn smooth and shiny. Women sat on one side, men on the other, on benches that were half the length of the church, each bench a step higher than the one in front of it. In the aisle between them were two stoves with long smokestacks. Suspended from the ceiling above each bench on the men's side were wooden bars with wooden pegs for the men's broadbrimmed hats.

A long, desk-like lectern in the centre front of the church had an open space before it to be used for baptism and feet-washing ceremonies. Behind the lectern five men sat side by side; a sixth man approached, kissed and shook hands with the others, then took his place among them. "That's our preacher," Salome whispered to me. "The others are preachers too and our bishop."

Chosen for life by lot from slips of paper drawn from a Bible, the Old Order Mennonite preacher, Salome told me, is also a farmer. He receives no pay, prepares no written sermons: his spontaneous word is believed to be inspired. And he has authority. If a church member buys what he is not supposed to, marries outside the Old Order, gets drunk too often, or does worldly things, the preacher will speak to him privately. If the vanity or sin is not repented, if it is irremissible, the erring one is denounced before the congregation. Though cast out of the church, he is not treated unkindly and, if contrite, may return.

Salome opened a hymn book printed in German script. Led by a man's voice, the congregation sat while it droned each syllable; the bishop preached for half an hour. The members of the congregation, turning to face their seats, knelt for silent prayer, their backs to the front of the church. "To live honestly and at peace with all men" was the text of the preacher's hour-long sermon in Pennsylvania Dutch.

Throughout the service the older men and women sat very still but in the long benches in front there was constant movement of babies and tiny children being hushed or taken to the cloakroom by mothers with bulging satchels. Two rows of lively little girls, their braids tied with string or a bit of shoelace, couldn't restrain a few giggles. The young girls who sat high at the back of the church turned solemn eyes towards the preacher or stole glances at the young men on the high benches at the other side of the room.

During the last hymn the little ones filed into the cloakroom. Babies in bright print or lustre dresses, black stockings and colorful booties were bundled up in black or purple shawls. The service over, women and children clustered on the cement stoop to chat till their men drove up smartly to pick them up in their buggies or two-seated wagons. Salome blushingly told me she was invited out for the day.

"Sunday is our visiting day," Bevvy explained. "Sometimes we have twenty people drop in for a meal."

"And don't you know they're coming?" I asked.

"Not always, they chust come after church. When Menno Horsts moved to the farm over there behind those maples they had fifty-six the first Sunday." She smiled. "Everyone was inquisitive to see their new house."

"How do you feed them?"

"Ach, that don't bother us, everybody helps. There's always lots in the cellar or the garden, and every Friday we bake cakes and buns and nine or ten pies. If somebody comes they're all eaten at one time and if not we haf them the rest of the week."

During the next three days the Martins answered many more of my questions.

"The preachers tell us to vote if we need a new bridge or something like that, but we don't know enough about politics to vote for the country. Artificial insemination of our cattle gives us better stock. With electricity we can do more work. Salome can run the tractor. Telephones we may have in the barn for business—if we sell fresh meat or the like of that—but not in our houses for pleasure."

"We wouldn't want our children to hear some of the things on the radio or television. If we had musical instruments we mightn't sing so much ourselfs. We never heard yet of any of our people stealing or getting in any trouble with the law."

I told them a story I'd heard about a man who tried to sell a car to an Old Mennonite. The farmer said he couldn't buy it because the devil was in it.

"But what about the gasoline motor you use?" the salesman asked. "It's the same thing—isn't the devil in that too?"

"Maybe, but he's fastened down and I can make him do whatever I want, in a car he's running around and might get out of control."

The family laughed heartily. "That sounds chust like something old Levi Gingerich would say," David said. "He'd have an answer for anybody that tried to get smart with him."

"We take a ride in a car sometimes but it would be a danger and a temptation for our young people to own one," Bevvy explained. "Anyways we love to ride behind our horses—they go fast enough for us."

"Some things we do to stay different and separate: it makes it easier to keep our rules. We don't know why we have some of them. They were handed to us from generation to generation; they're not written down. The bishop and the preachers have to change them sometimes or make new ones, but if we don't like what they tell us we can put them out of the church and do what we think is right."

"We don't believe in converting people to our ways; we leave them alone and want to be left alone—religion should be quiet and deep in the heart, not on the tongue. We're supposed to live simple so we can have more time to think about the Lord; if we got stylish we might get proud. We could never be clever like other people anyway—we're chust farmers, we love best to watch things grow, and work makes us happy."

"We like being boss on our own land," David said with an air of unallowed pride. "I would hate to have to work for somebody else that would tell me what I should or shouldn't do." On the last night of my stay in the fieldstone house, the family sat with me on the porch waiting for the car that would come to take me away. I said, "I haven't heard a cross or grumbling word since I came here. Don't you ever get mad? Don't your children ever quarrel or disobey? Are you never tired of working? Do you never break your rules?"

They looked at one another and laughed. "We've all been extra good this week because you were here," Lyddy Ann said.

"We were telling you what all we're supposed to do but we don't always do it." Bevvy grinned.

Salome brought me a hyacinth, Grossdoddy gave me a willow whistle he'd made, Topsy pushed against my hand for a pat, there was the scent of honeysuckle and blossoms, the sound of frogs near the river. Salome said to me, "You are so quiet now, why don't you talk?"

"I was thinking how peaceful it is here," I said.

David nodded. "That's what I often think."

"In the world I'm going back to we are always fighting for peace."

—*Maclean's*, April 1, 1950

THROUGHOUT THE MANY YEARS since I went to live with the Martins we have become good friends and spent much enjoyable time together. Though their rules and beliefs and lifestyle are the same as they've always been, there have been other changes in their lives.

Bevvy and David now drive to church in a *dachwaegle* and sit on the front benches with the old folks. They no longer live in their ancestral stone farmhouse—David's well-tilled fields will inevitably become a housing development. They are comfortable in a neat little house in the country beside the large, modern home of their son Amsey, who has ten children and drives a big black car with no chrome to his very successful business in town.

Salome and Lyddy Ann live on farms of their own with their husbands; their younger children attend Old Order parochial schools, and their older ones are thinking of being married.

"But the land where our people always lived is too near the cities and costs too much for our young people. When they buy farms now they have to go so far away that we'll not have much time with our great-grandchildren," Bevvy laments. "Quite a few now are living around Mount Forest, they've got two churches there already, but it's fifty miles away and that's too far for us to drive with a horse."

"Ach yes, but we'll get there," David says. "We can hire a car. And you'll see our young people will get along; they'll get along the same as we always did."

6

the
1950s
Writing

E DNA STAEBLER'S HANDS-ON, in-the-field approach became her
trademark as a journalist. Journalism was the mainstay of Staebler's writing and publications during the 1950s.[1] Her articles
appeared at regular intervals, and to research them she travelled often
and far at a time when many women of her background were house-
bound. Staebler's reputation as an independent and adventurous woman
was consolidated through assignments that ranged from the Mennonites of Waterloo County to the Hutterites of Alberta; from the Six Nations
Iroquois of Brantford to the African-Canadian community of Nova Scotia; from Old Order Amish to the residents of the Ile-aux-Coudres in
the St. Lawrence. She also made a solo trip to Europe in 1954, Staebler-
style, with no advance planning or reservations and no fixed itinerary.
For three months, she travelled through Europe, visiting parts of France,
Spain, Italy, Switzerland, Austria, Germany, Holland, Belgium, England,
Scotland, and Wales. Travel and writing brought Edna new friends—
and lovers.[2] As her twentieth wedding anniversary drew near, Edna
was clear-eyed about the problems in her marriage (May 13, 1954). At the
same time, she wondered whether Keith's delinquency sometimes served
as an excuse for not writing more (September 19, 1957). Despite her success as a journalist, Staebler continued to fret about her writing and to
berate her efforts. In later years, Staebler recognized that "They were
good pieces—talking of the life of people in Canada who had had no self-
expression and were perhaps misunderstood by other Canadians. And
I made good friends among them—Hutterites, Indians, Negroes, French
Canadians, Mennonite, Amish—and I gathered a wealth of material

which I've never used" (March 13, 1961). She saw herself, however, "dully plodding at only the assignments for *Maclean's*, as if they were all of life, all that was important. I've had to feel their importance to keep at them and to get them down, but I've dawdled too long. I've not concentrated. I've not thought deeply enough in a long time" (January 29, 1956).

Staebler's experiences in Neil's Harbour diverted her from introspection. Diary entries from the 1950s, however, show that she was still prone to the inward eye. They reveal a complex and often contradictory personality. "I think I'm always afraid of and always trying to escape from being enveloped in mediocrity," she wrote (March 23, 1958). At the same time, despite her unconventionality, Staebler continued to care about her reputation as "Edna Staebler, the respectable citizen of Kitchener, a 'well-known' Canadian author" (August 29, 1954). Her life, Staebler decided, was made up of fragments "unless I can bind it together with my work. I need to do that to give it security and purpose and I need to *pay* for my life, to give it back by writing about it" (September 2, 1954).

Further to the undeniable success of her first *Maclean's* articles, Staebler joined the Canadian Authors Association in 1951. She also became a member of the Writers' Union of Canada and attended its first conference in Ottawa in 1974. Staebler met and befriended many Canadian writers, including Pierre Berton and W.O. Mitchell, Claire and Farley Mowat, Margaret Laurence, Marian Engel, Sylvia Fraser, Rudy Wiebe, and Harold Horwood ("My Writing Life"). In addition to writers, she met the dynamic and influential publisher Jack McClelland, who would be instrumental in Edna's progression from magazine to book publishing. But that lay ahead, in the next decade. For now, in the 1950s, notwithstanding her lack of confidence in her writing, Staebler was enjoying freedom and professional satisfaction, qualities that were fairly rare for a woman of her time and place.

Notes

1 Journalism also dominated her publications in the 1960s when she branched out into *Chatelaine* magazine and various newspaper articles. See the bibliography for a list of Staebler's magazine publications.

2 Alphonse Ludaescher, a Swiss chiropractor, noticed Edna aboard the Queen Elizabeth II and accompanied her on the train to Paris. Edna subsequently visited Alphonse in Switzerland and twice again on trips to Europe in 1956 and 1958. As with other of her men friends, she maintained a correspondence with Alphonse over the years. In later life, Staebler would ask: "What would my Mennonite friends think if they knew I'd had lovers? They'd be disillusioned, shocked, even tho the affairs took place fifty years ago before I knew Eva and Nancy" (August 10, 2000).

top left 1950s. Edna on "Barge Canal" assignment; *top right* 1950s. Keith and Edna; *bottom* 1957. The Cress sisters (left to right): Ruby, Edna, Norma.

From the Diaries

March 16, 1952[1]
"On our way to South Carolina," we say. Somehow saying, "South Carolina" sounds smarter than saying Florida. It sounds as if you know where you're going instead of going where everyone else goes.[2]

March 20, 1952
Seeing so many Negroes living so poorly makes me wonder what they think. Do they simply accept their lives, knowing they'd never be different? Or do they dream or hope that someday life for them will change? Or are they quite content? Seeing them serve people in the dining room last night I felt they must be very humble or resentful.

November 24, 1952
Perhaps happiness is something that comes by itself in a natural way like growing. Slowly, slowly things happen to a person, they are accepted with serenity as the outgrowth of things that have gone before. Each thing that has happened helps us to understand and take calmly the things that come after. It is even thrilling and exciting and secure to know that one's life has a pattern that, in a way, keeps repeating itself and so gives one a clue to handling it in a way that is not too painful or disrupting. Each time there is less and less bewilderment and frustration, the shock is less intense. This morning I've even had to make myself sit here and write this. It seems in a way not very important at all. I'd much rather be working at the story I've been trying to write for the past three weeks. It's much less necessary to think about and talk about than Yvonne Craig lying near death in the hospital in Guelph.[3] I feel that I don't really have to think very much about my living at all, I just let it go and it keeps on. There is no point in dramatizing and feeling tragic and sorry for myself because it hasn't worked out like a fairy tale or even The Happy Marriage. I am happy. I have so many things to do and think about and love and enjoy. Life is so full and interesting and wonderfully exciting and beautiful. My only frustration is not being able to tell about it well enough and quickly enough.

I don't mean I think life is all sweetness and light. I know, too, it is bitterness and tragedy and darkness. But all of it is interesting, and most of it is beautiful. Even in what appears ugly and sordid, there is sometimes beauty, perhaps the beauty of vitality or the beauty of death.

And I am a part of all this. A part. I am not a whole. I am like one day's newspaper in the millions of papers that have been published everywhere through the years. That is all, just one day's newspaper, a few not very big headlines, stories of men and women, comics, trivialities, stupidity, a smattering of politics, homemakers' hints, advertisements, quite a few, I'm afraid.

January 3, 1953

I've just made the unpleasant discovery of a lump in my left breast—damn it.[4] I suppose now I'll be one of those false-fronted women. I've always been proud of my bosom and enjoyed wearing sweaters. I thank God I've reached an age and a stage in my life when I'm more interested in writing than I am in attracting men. Only yesterday morning while I was making my bed, I wondered vaguely if I wished for a lover this year and was quite honestly pleased and surprised that I had no desire for anything but good writing. (4)

May 13, 1953

At one time he [Keith] used to malign me, constantly criticize, and say things to hurt me, make me lose face and faith and courage. He tried to undermine me and destroy me. He'd tell me people were afraid of me because I was clever, that they were uncomfortable when I was around, that I was always trying to be different, and didn't belong. He was snarly and defiant and secretive if I asked him the simplest questions, he'd tell me to mind my own business and he'd do whatever the hell he pleased. He was earning the money and he'd do with it what he liked.

But to other people he'd say he was married to the most wonderful woman in the world and they'd envy me because I had such an adoring husband and feel sorry for him because I didn't tell him how much I loved him. No, I felt sorry for myself and hated him. I hated him for his duplicity and his mean, greedy way of using me. I hated his cowardice, his drunkenness, his self-pity, self-deprecation, and his weakness. And I pitied him. I longed to help him. I tried to comfort him, and to tell him to live a happy way. I worried about him. I tried to build him up, to love him. And I stuck with him. And I went through hell. (11)

June 17, 1953

Why do I want to write? To be published, to get cheques, to be greeted by good writers as an equal, to be mentioned in W.A. Deacon's fly-leaf, to be reviewed favourably in the *Atlantic Monthly* and *The New Yorker*?[5] Of course I want that. And because I want that, I write nothing. If I want that, I'll have nothing to write about. My work will only be myself looking in a mirror.

Having something to write about, something that needs very much to be told, that is the first thing. Knowing something well and feeling deeply about it. Observation and feeling, you (Dr. Robins) once told me.

And I have not been feeling. I've been afraid. I've been holding myself back, carefully rationalizing about everything so I couldn't feel and be hurt. And I have written nothing. I've been insulating myself from life because I've not been letting myself love. (17–18)

July 27, 1953

I often long to dream and live in the illusory world of poems and novels, books of philosophy, a world I once loved and believed in and still do in part. But I can't somehow keep in it. I must go about and be with real live people and learn directly from them and become them. If I try to "keep up" with my reading, I will have no time for my writing or even my living. Yet I have so much to learn from books, and so little time to learn. I long to go back to the sea, to fill myself with its beauty and greatness, to be with the people I love who live by it. But if I do so I won't finish my story. I won't get my writing done. And that I must do. Oh Lord, I waste so much time, precious, precious time that slips so swiftly away from me.

Later, after reading one of Anne Wilkinson's poems and thinking about whom I must write for—it would be tempting to try and write only of beauty, to write the things I know people like Norma [Edna's sister] and Est [Esther Breithaupt, Edna's friend] and K's mother would love.[6] And love me for writing! It would strengthen the defence of their world, and it is a world that needs defending and fighting for. But I know it is only a part of the real world. It is a real part and a most necessary part, but only a part. I must not forget that. I must write as honestly as I can about all parts of the world as I have been privileged to see them. I must not keep Norma and Est and K's mother in mind when I write, but people like Dr. R, and those whose experience is broader and whose understanding is greater. (24)

September 18, 1953[7]
Dr. R. once said creative writing is feeling and observation, love and observation. That makes all things clear. That makes good work possible. Only if I love enough, have enough feeling for things and people, can I want to write about them. Only if I lose myself utterly in my love for them can I write well about them. Only then can my writing be worth doing. I must have something to write about. I must first of all LOVE. (30)

September 28, 1953
Today I feel like hurting somebody. I'm so damn bloody tired of being so damn bloody good and strong and tender and kind. Today I'd like to stick pins in babies and sprinkle tear gas on cats and kick men in their behinds and punch women's breasts. God, what a feeling. And all I'll likely do is go down to Loblaws and buy margarine and rice crispies.

Why am I in this hellish mood? Because I haven't done any damn writing today, and I haven't done any good writing for weeks and I haven't had anything published for a *year*. (30)

November 2, 1953
It's damn near time I stopped being a piddling, timid, exhibitionist ninny and got some work done. Some real work, honest, solid, constant, and unafraid. Something about real people in conflict with life. I've been trying to avoid pain for a very long time; I've been trying to be happy. The moment any unpleasantness has come, I'd quietly switch my thinking to something else, I wouldn't let myself suffer. The moment I'd find myself getting into any depth, I'd quickly shuttle for the shallows—afraid. Happy? No. Just skimming the surface. Not suffering because I've been afraid to let myself feel other people's suffering and so I've not been living. (34)

November 3, 1953
I have wakened in the night, or perhaps I have not been really asleep, and now I know the Answer as I MUST know it *all the time*. It is one word only—*love*. All else is chaos and confusion. Love is singleness of purpose and honesty and direction. Love is listening and seeing and knowing. Love is simple and sure and peaceful. Love is wisdom and understanding. Love is joy and beauty. Love is life and hope and work and magic and faith and light and shade and colour. Love is everything, it is the kingdom and the power and the glory. Love is God. Amen. (35)

November 5, 1953

Guilt—horrible word. Guilty because I don't *work*. Remedy—WORK. I use my writing as an excuse for not doing all sorts of other things, like being kind to old people and calling on the sick and going to meetings and seeing Mother and being an indifferent housekeeper and not entertaining, but I don't *write*. Then I do nothing, I am nothing, and I feel guilty as HELL.

December 5, 1953

If I would stop wanting to be happy and expecting to be happy and trying to be happy, I might be more content. I tell myself I must immerse myself in my work. I must lose myself and I can and I do at times, and up to a point. But underneath, and cropping out every so often, is a powerful longing for affection, for someone I can put my arms around as mothers do children. It is not a longing for passion, tho' occasionally that comes too and occasionally I have been indiscreet and foolish and afterward fearful and miserable. And yet, long after I have not been regretful because I have had the experience and if I had not yielded I would have had nothing. Perhaps in that lies my answer, to welcome experience, happy or sad, good or bad, to live no matter how, but to LIVE and not be afraid. To face things squarely and do what I can about them, instead of meekly creeping into my little shell and insulating myself from them.

January 23, 1954

Another cocktail party at the Hughes's [Conny and Freddy, friends of the Staeblers]—dull brown in shade. Older, fatter people than last week. I left in the middle to go to a lecture and movie on forest life and when I got back all the food was gone. Now K is mad because I went up to him while he was playing piano and said, "Let's go home." And now I'm so bloody damn sick of a lot of things and people that I'd like to leave tomorrow on a long, long trip where I could see mostly nothing but sea and sky and birds flying and boats.

"Tuesday"[8]

I spoke, then, to two English ladies. One said she wouldn't give the Germans house room. The other expressed great delight at the Canadians' love of England and made the unfortunate remark that we were loyal British subjects. I immediately informed her that we were not; we were

Canadians, loyal members of the British Commonwealth, not subjects, an obsolete term. I said we are like a child of Britain that has grown up.

August 29, 1954 [9]

All I need to learn is how to make up my mind, for good or ill, and then stick to it. You'd think my decisions about writing were made in cement, completely unchangeable, whereas writing is the most fluid thing. Until a piece is being printed, it can still be changed. So what have I got to worry about? The trouble about writing of my trip has been my usual one of having had interesting, rather foolish adventures that it just wouldn't do for me, Edna Staebler, the respectable citizen of Kitchener, a "well known" Canadian author, to admit to. Either I'd have to write under a pseudonym or change my character, and another character probably wouldn't have the crazy combination of naiveté and sophistication that Dr. Reaman says I am blessed with.[10] If my character were not married, she'd be too innocent and too experienced. Maybe I should just write her exactly as me and see what happens, my thoughts, my fears, my reactions. If I do that, maybe she'll have some sort of funny, dumb, serious, sensible character. Since my own thought of myself might be quite different from anyone else's thought of me, I might create a complete disguise. Actually, I had not much thought of myself at all while I was travelling. I was always looking around me and thinking about other things, other people, and so it could be in the book, a complete looking out and around me, not *at* me.

August 30, 1954 [11]

The start I made yesterday is no good. It is stiff posturing, again the elocutionist. I think the only way I'll overcome it is by changing my narrator to someone else, some character other than my own self. Only then could I write freely and unself-consciously, as it is so much easier to become an actor on a stage than to get up alone on a stage without any sort of disguise or excuse for being a bit unconventional and uninhibited. One can give so much more to a character than one can allow oneself. But of course the character has to be created, thought into deeply. The work must become a piece of art.

September 2, 1954

I think my whole trouble is this: I want to write deathless prose spontaneously. I'm lazy; I don't want to work at my writing. I don't want to suffer over it. I want to whip it out GOOD. And why? Because if I could work quickly, I could get so much more work done. I could tell so much more of the millions of things to tell. I wouldn't have to so carefully CHOOSE. I wish I could just simply and easily write about things that I see and people without the need of giving form to my work. I'd like to just show life and love and beauty as I find them, as anyone could find them if their eyes are open and their hearts are listening.

But who would print such stuff? They'd say these are only anecdotes. This is only life, it isn't art. These things are not poems or stories or novels or essays—not news. No one would read this stuff.

There are times when my life seems so dramatic and alive and wonderful that I should record every minute. But I don't. Then other times it seems to be hopelessly dull. No it doesn't. When I say that, I'm simply using words. I'm being trite. My life is never dull, tho' sometimes I am rebellious about wasting time talking about dull things like what so-and-so did yesterday and what so-and-so wore and what her house was like. I get tired of repetition of uninteresting details about people who are staid and conventional. It's like counting a bushel of beans, those little white, all-the-same-looking navy beans. But those same beans could be richly brown and wonderful if served in a brown crockery bean pot. So there's the answer, I suppose. Even dull people and events, if they are cooked up well and flavoured with the prose writer's art, could not only be palatable but rich and delectable fare. God help me. I can't stand my unproductivity. I love living, I love fun, I am happy. I can be diverted from depression like a child. But my whole life is made up of fragments unless I can bind it together with my work. I need to do that to give it security and purpose and I need to *pay* for my life, to give it back by writing about it.

But I must stop this posturing, this pretending to be what I'm not. I must write honestly and humbly. Of course my work won't be clever but it can have colour and feeling. Above all it must not be empty, affected, or trite. God help me; help me to see things with clarity and with compassion, understanding, and humour. I must stop trying to be GREAT. I must only try to do the best that I can. I must TRY. I have not been trying. I have only been agonizing, not making up my mind, putting down a few words, knowing they were not well said, then leaving them to read or talk endlessly on the phone. I have not honestly tried. I have not written and written. I must let the thoughts come, let the words flow, good or bad, let them out and work on them afterwards. If they don't come out, I'll be constipated. That's what I'm suffering from now: acute and chronic mental and spiritual constipation. It sounds horrible and it is horrible. There's only one cure for it and that is a cathartic. But what is the cathartic for me? Perhaps just the easy painless business of sitting here and putting words on paper. That's all. I don't need to be pushed over a cliff and be picked up in pieces and put together again all made over. I don't need to go thro' some purging and dramatic experience that is going to expel all my doubts, my fears. John Gray even said to me that he believes I'll write good books one day but something has to happen to me first.[12] I think I've been waiting for that thing to *happen*. Instead of quietly, calmly letting it happen to me as I think it can happen and will happen now if I keep on writing, writing, writing, and stop worrying about whether it is saleable. (79)

September 5, 1954

And now brothers and sisters, what are we going to do with our writing time today? It's time to make up our minds. It should be so perfectly simple to pick a thought and stick to it till we've pulled it out of our minds. Perfectly, perfectly simple. We just have to do it, that's all.

Oh, but we don't want to. It might be hard work. We might have to think and that would hurt us. We'd rather just relax and not bother or fiddle around like this putting any old thing down on paper, always half hoping that perhaps when we're dead someone will find it and say, "this should be published. It's interesting and it's lively." BUNK. But it's true, whenever I write anything, whenever I have written anything from the time I STARTED A DIARY WHEN I was sixteen years old, I've had the furtive silly thought in the back of my mind and I've written some horrible stuff—dull, inane, sloppy, sentimental, and pretentious.

Often I've been plagued by the fear of insincerity. I wouldn't be quite sure if I had written honestly of my feelings, or if I'd written for effect. Though mostly I think I was sincere at the time of my writing and appalled later by what I had written. I never read back in my journal. I can't bear to. I did once in my old sixteen-year-old one and it was so utterly thin and trite that I hated to own up to it. But I've kept it. It's in the drawer of my desk right now, just in case I might some day want to use it. What for? I'll never know. I was afraid to express any emotion in it, afraid that someone would find it and know what I felt or the very bad things that I did, like kissing someone in a car at night. I would never have admitted to my physical sensations. Anyone reading it now would have thought I passed through my adolescence like a statue of Virtue. Perhaps I should read back and see what actually is there.

But this isn't getting me anywhere. It's just postponing writing, real writing about something interesting that might sell. Always have to keep that selling in mind or I'll lose my reputation. I won't be a writer if I don't sell something and prove that I can be literary. (85–86)

September 10, 1954

During these early morning writings, my unconscious mind is supposed to reveal itself before it is influenced by anything I read or hear from any other source. But mine doesn't seem to be very bright or concentrated. It flutters around from one thing to another just as nimbly as it does in the middle of the day or night. (407)

November 1, 1954

I like walking along the streets at night and looking into people's windows. Not going up close to them and peeping, just glancing in as I go by on the sidewalk. I wonder what the women are thinking about when they sit alone on their chesterfields. And the men. One woman not far from here had her head bent as if crocheting. Another, I think, was reading a book. One house I saw tonight had a dresser on its back wall with all its shelves filled with china animals—birds, pigs, dogs—a shocking sight. (422)

September 17, 1955

I don't know. God help me, my writing isn't any good either. But damn it, I'm going to stick with it. Sherwood Anderson said he couldn't write unless he had a woman to love him.[13] I seem to need loneliness and unhappiness to force me into it. Often I impose loneliness on myself. It is so easy to just run around [illegible] with people, winning their favour and approval, instead of doing what I want to do, what I must do, and having them disappear, and then defending myself against them. Why should I bother? The only true friends I have are those who believe in me and wish me well and try to help me. Only great people are capable of being great friends, and there aren't many great people. (43–44)

January 1, 1956

The worst day of the year, I hope, always. I said all the wrong things, did all the wrong things, or rather didn't do any of the right things. Instead of working, I phoned Mother for an hour. I ate candy and nuts and cookies instead of going out for a little ride to please Mother. I watched TV. I hate myself. I talk too much and I think too little and I don't do a God damn thing—four months and I've not yet finished my Negro piece ["Would You Change the Lives of These People?"]. I'm ashamed. I hate myself and I go around thinking I'm so damn smart, so much smarter than all the other people. I'm a nitwit, a nincompoop, a cabbagehead, and a fraud. God help me. I've got to learn to believe in something again, to believe strongly and firmly and eagerly. I have to recapture the rapture and magic and faith that I do know are there if I give myself time to think of them, instead of smothering my flame with phone calls and TV and chocolates. God help me. God help me to *live* in 1956 and to make it live in my writing and God help me to write and write and write. (436)

January 29, 1956
God help me, if I could only put life down as it is, glowing, palpitating, expectant, eternal, refreshed, rejoicing, funny, tragic, lovely. God help me, help me, there is so much to write, and I write so very little and so very slowly. Help me, God, to write better, faster, and more abundantly, not just to make money, but because there are things to say that should be said and I should say them and say them well and beautifully. God help me, I've been slipping badly, I've been selfish, I've been losing my vision, I've just been plodding along looking at the ground around my feet and no distance at all beyond them. I've lost sight of my star. God help me to find it again and to keep moving steadfastly towards it, writing, recording all as I go on my way. I remember the time when I felt life to be so beautiful, or so enjoyable, or so interesting, or so full of meaning that I regretted not being able to record every passing moment. But lately, during the past few years, I've been dully plodding at only the assignments for *Maclean's*, as if they were all of life, all that was important. I've had to feel their importance to keep at them and to get them down, but I've dawdled too long, I've not concentrated. I've not thought deeply enough in a long time. If I could and would let myself keep looking into the heart of things at all times, I should be able to write well and more quickly. But I've been skimming the surface for a long, long time. I've been lazy or superficial or afraid, like that verse in the Bible, I've forgotten it exactly, about he who seeketh to save his life shall lose it, but he who loseth his life shall find it. I've been like a hermit who tries to keep himself warm at a dim little flame by carefully watching it and feeding it little bits of dry straw instead of going out into the great world and the warmth of the sunlight and looking and seeing and loving and learning and understanding and *giving*. God help me, help me,

help me to stay in the sunlight, the sunlight of life and experience and compassion. Help me to put it down, to give it again and again, clearly and beautifully and effortlessly. Please God. And now, let me sleep, and tomorrow let me begin, let me be able to work tirelessly and well, for Thy sake. (457–58)

January 24, 1957
When I think of all these things and these people, and the time I waste, the talent I waste, I feel deeply ashamed and afraid. I know I can write. I have much to write about. I have editors, publishers who want my stuff, and I fiddle around with my cat and the newspapers and talk on the telephone and lie on my bed and dissipate my thinking and throw my life away. (516)

September 19, 1957[14]
Wrote a letter—which comes first: the chicken or the egg? If I am a strong character, could I keep writing *despite* my situation? Do I make K's delinquency my excuse for not writing? Would I work and accomplish if I didn't have him to worry about? I wonder and I feel guilty and I don't accomplish.

January 19, 1958[15]
Tried to write a bit today. Sat at my window and tried to write a couple of paragraphs about what I could see. There was feeling in what I wrote but no story. Nothing that went anywhere. I feel wasted again. I do none of the things I could do so well with people because I save myself for my writing, but I don't write.

March 23, 1958
I must think more about the compulsion to learn, to win freedom by learning more, understanding more. Also, I must think more about my basic beliefs—my faith. I can't seem able to believe in God as a personal, orthodox ruler. I can believe in the power of love, good will, honesty, qualities of human character and behaviour. I think I'm always afraid of and always trying to escape from being enveloped in mediocrity. I should write a book about someone who tries to get away from her hometown and family, but marries someone in town and is kept there for good. Why? What tie of duty, what great weight of guilt she carries? Her longing to escape makes her hate her captors and her guilt for that thought makes her slavishly dutiful.

June 28, 1959[16]
Ian [Scandlers, new editor at *Maclean's*] told K that there are only twenty people in Canada who can write for *Maclean's* and I'm among the top ten and why the hell don't I WRITE?

Notes

1 Box R3-4. Diary Trip to Florida 1952.
2 Staebler accompanied Keith and their friends Charlie and Marnie Henderson on this trip to Florida.
3 Yvonne Craig (1916–52), wife of John Craig, gardener.
4 Happily, this was not a cancer development.
5 William Arthur Deacon (1890-1977), Canadian literary critic and cultural nationalist, remembered for his humorous *The Four Jameses* (1927) and for his encouragement and promotion of Canadian writers.
6 Anne Wilkinson (1910-61), Toronto-born poet and diarist whose work has been collected in *The Poetry of Anne Wilkinson and a Prose Memoir* (1990) and *The Tightrope Walker: Autobiographical Writings of Anne Wilkinson* (1992), edited by Joan Coldwell.
7 My Journal for 1953.
8 Box R1. Travel Diary Europe 1954.
9 Box R3-6. Diary January 7, 1946–September 5, 1954.
10 George Elmore Reaman, author of *Trail of the Black Walnut* (1957, reprint 1993), was another friend with whom Edna discussed writing and literature.
11 Journal 1953–1954–1958. Lent by author. There are two sets of journals included in this package, which accounts for discrepancies in pagination. Page numbers are therefore approximate.
12 John Gray (1907–78), publisher and author, influential president of Macmillan's publishing firm from 1946 to 1973, during which time the company expanded to become one of the largest and most successful in Canada.
13 Sherwood Anderson (1876-1941), American writer, author of over two dozen books, helped usher in the generation of authors that included Hemingway and Faulkner. *The Sherwood Anderson Diaries* 1936-41 were edited by Hilbert Campbell (U of Georgia P, 1987).
14 Box R2-1. Diary 1957.
15 Box R2-1. Diary 1958.
16 Box R2-1. Diary 1959.

the
1960s

Must Work

PUBLICLY, EDNA STAEBLER has been matter of fact about the end of her marriage, which occurred at the outset of the 1960s.[1] "In the winter of '60–61 while Keith was in an alcoholic rehab centre," she related in her Writers' Union speech ("My Writing Life"), "I stayed in Neil's Harbour and wrote a story for *Chatelaine*. When I came home, I was told my college friend and confidante had persuaded my husband to marry her!"[2]

Privately, however, the legal end of the Staebler marriage was a blow for Edna. It was, as she put it, "a helluva year. I wrote my misery in my journal" ("My Writing Life"). Divorce was not common at the time, Staebler pointed out. "There was much talk and uncertainty.... For the first time in my life, I was completely responsible for myself. I could no longer blame delay in my writing on Keith's binges. I'd been married twenty-eight years, had never lived alone, never paid household bills. At fifty-six I thought I was old and probably couldn't make it on my own. But I had to" (ibid.).

The Staeblers' house and cottage were in Edna's name. She sold the house, winterized the cottage, and made it her new home. The cottage at Sunfish Lake on the outskirts of Waterloo became a place of enormous joy and happiness for Edna. "Friends came to see me," she wrote. "Pierre and Janet [Berton] and their six children and Pierre's mother came several times in a summer, so did other *Maclean's* editors, other writers and a male admirer.[3] I was never lonely; I had two cats and a phone. There was always something to watch on the lake: ducks, geese, herons, small birds at the feeders, raccoons, squirrels, deer, the changing sky and the water. I was never bored" ("My Writing Life"). At the outset of her new life, however, Edna often felt fearful and distressed, as her diaries from the 1960s indicate. Once again, writing helped her through trying times, although Edna repeatedly berated herself for not writing more. "The only thing that makes me feel I have any direction is the need to work every day at my writing," she wrote August 10, 1961. Writing combined with her family work ethic and personal religious beliefs to form vital guideposts during this period.[4] "I must sit at my desk and start writing—*every morning*. God help me—I must think more about God and good things," Staebler instructed herself (March 23, 1961). If she felt that she should "make God the first thing in [her] life" (March 23, 1961) during this difficult period, Edna was nevertheless not inclined to make religion the focus of her life. "Not all my life. I must not become like Mrs. S, who retreated from life by spending all her time with her books and her God so she lost touch with reality" (March 23, 1961). Edna had explored and developed her ideas about religion throughout the 1940s, recording her thoughts on the subject in diary entries during that the decade. "I believe religion is so deeply and undoubtedly personal," she stated August 15, 1948, "that no man can tell another what he must be. It is something that cannot always be expressed in words." She did not believe in original sin, Staebler declared. She liked to think that "the source of all things is God. So men are fundamentally good, but through ignorance at times do things that are evil" (August 15, 1948). Her life was directed, she wrote, but at the same time a "Power" was available to her with which to be joyous, creative, and insightful (March 3, 1946). "I am convinced of a Power which motivates, which drives us, which governs our lives," she had written April 14, 1946. "If we can submit to it eagerly and fully and fearlessly, we should become creative and powerful in our own way." Twenty years later, Edna's explorations of religion were ongoing. "Is God merely an attitude?" she asked in her diary April 18, 1965. If so, "then prayer is useless, except that asking or speaking to God is a way of speaking to, exhausting, reminding, changing oneself." This was a practical religious understanding for Edna as she confronted major changes in life following divorce from Keith.

With her life headed in new directions, Edna's thoughts about writing addressed new concerns. Her diaries document a growing concern with form (April 16, 1961). This was a dimension of writing that eluded Staebler, for whom diary writing came so easily. She grappled with the question of genre and which seemed best suited to the kind of writing she preferred and found most natural. "I want merely to tell and I have so much to tell, really. My own life has been exciting and varied. Many strong and wonderful people have come into it. But how could I give it form? I can't just spill it out bit by bit. Where would I begin?" (August 5, 1961). Was autobiography her genre, Staebler wondered. "Maybe it's so hard for me to write because I really want to write about myself, my experiences, and not the objective things that I try to write about other people," she considered, "but I'm afraid to write about me and my experiences lest I reveal myself as a weak, unattractive, poor proof of a person" (August 3, 1961). More accurately, writing for Edna seemed to stem from a powerful "urge to record everything" (February 28, 1962). There was as well an element of joy in writing. "I think I just wanted to write for the joy I would find in the writing, and if I had it, perhaps I could give it," she mused December 17, 1961. She was not interested in fame and glory, Edna declared. Rather, her goal was "to write honestly, beautifully, with power. The power of quiet, moving conviction or humour. I'd like to be able to move people's hearts, to give them a better view of what I have seen, greater insight, compassion, generosity, and love" (July 20, 1962).

Love is a recurring theme in Edna's diaries of the 1960s, not altogether surprising in the aftermath of her divorce from Keith Staebler. Even as she explored her longing for affection (September 14, 1962), however, Staebler recognized the flaw in needing affection and approval in order to feel that her pursuits were worthwhile (September 9, 1963). Such needs were especially detrimental to her pursuit of writing, she decided, and there was "much more urgency and reason for [her] to get on with [her] writing … [than] … caring about approval" (March 5, 1963). Indeed, more important than longing for affection was the "longing to share" (September 14, 1962). Sharing might even be the secret of life, Edna mused. And for her, writing was an excellent way to share. This only increased the importance of writing and why she should be doing it more and better. "There are so many things I could write. My life's been so full. I lack only discipline. I am so lazy," Edna admonished herself (November 1, 1960). "I must work. I'd like to be able to discipline myself to work every day at my writing" (April 16, 1961).

Work would pay off. In the course of the 1960s, Staebler achieved publication in book form. The book in question was not the one she aspired to write following her visit to Neil's Harbour. Nor was it the novel or short stories that took shape in her early morning thoughts only to dissolve when she sat down at her typewriter. But it was a book all the same. *Sauerkraut and Enterprise* (1967) was published on the occasion of Canada's Centennial year, at the request of the Kitchener-Waterloo University Women's Club. The club saw the tremendous potential in collecting and publishing Edna Staebler's various essays on the local area. The book immediately sold 10,000 copies and was reissued two years later by McClelland and Stewart. Meanwhile, in 1966, Ryerson Press approached Edna for a book on Mennonite cooking.

Edna had learned to cook in the years immediately following marriage, but she was the last person to boast of her abilities in the kitchen. In her view, her Mennonite friend, Bevvy Martin, was a far superior and excellent cook. Bevvy's "cookbook" was handwritten and composed primarily of lists of ingredients. Edna set about working with Bevvy and her recipes, testing them and writing instructions and anecdotes as she experimented. Two years later she delivered a manuscript to Ryerson. *Food That Really Schmecks* proved to be a phenomenal success.

Published in June 1968, *Food That Really Schmecks* was already in second printing by September of that year, and it would sell more copies than any other book published by McGraw-Hill Ryerson (Ross 204). The combination of Mennonite recipes and Staebler stories struck a perfect note with cookbook readers. *Schmecks* made Edna Staebler a household name and led to two equally successful sequels, *More Food That Really Schmecks* (1979) and *Schmecks Appeal* (1987), as well as the *Schmecks Appeal* cookbook series (1990–96).

The 1960s, which had opened on such a difficult personal note, closed with a crescendo of professional success.

Notes

1 Married October 14, 1933, the Staeblers were officially divorced February 1962.
2 Helen (née MacDonald) Kergin. She and Keith Staebler were married twenty-one years.
3 Edna makes special mention of Sheila Burnford, author of *The Incredible Journey* (Boston: Little, Brown 1961), an enormously successful tale of two dogs and a cat whose instincts guide them home, and Margaret Laurence, widely known for her "Manawaka series," *The Stone Angel, The Fire-Dwellers, A Jest of God,* and *The Diviners.*
4 A sense of work ethic surfaces throughout the diaries, reflecting the values of an individual and a family of mixed Mennonite and German background, as well as a community and a generation that experienced the Depression.

∾

🔲 *top left* 24 October, 1964. Edna after speaking at the Walper Hotel, Kitchener; *top right* 1969. Edna at Gerry Noonan's following a visit to one of his classes; *bottom* 1960s. Edna in her new home at Sunfish Lake.

From the Diaries

May 22, 1960[1]

I have been thinking of communication, how necessary it is to everyone. I used to write in my diary every day before I was married—stilted, nice reporting of what I did, where I went, and how I felt about things, always with a reserve and a thought for what posterity might think if they ever got hold of it. I think I never wrote my true feelings or what I did in my most emotional moments.

Why have I stopped writing in my diary? After I was married I suppose I told K all the things I ever recorded and no longer felt the need to get things down. Then, too, I was busy. I usually wrote in bed, morning or night, and sharing a bedroom with him made that impractical. Besides, my life was no longer only my life, it was all shared with him. Since that early time I have had spurts of writing in times of great stress when I've been worried and agonizing and self analyzing. Also I've talked too much and too long on the phone with Mother and Norm, telling them all my activity and some of my troubles.

November 1, 1960

There now, that's five pages in forty minutes, easy going. I should be able to do eight in an hour, 240 pages in a month if I'd write every morning, and that's long enough for a novel. Just an hour a day, an hour that is normally wasted. I'd have all the rest of the day to work on other things—articles, short stories, another book. If I'd really *work* at it, I could be prolific and I'd be happy, or at least I'd be rid of the horrible gnawing that bothers me almost all the time because I'm frittering my life away and not using my God-given talent. But what shall I write about? That is what stops me. That is so foolish. There are so many things I could write; my life's been so full. I lack only discipline. I am so lazy; I won't keep my mind at a thing. I just let it wander all over the place. I must try to keep it in check, get it started on the one line and keep it there. Many writers say they do their best work in the morning. What if I scribble away here for a month and have nothing that's any good at the end of that time? I've lost nothing and I might feel better because at least I'd have tried and I'd have established a good working habit.

Maybe tomorrow I'll try to write the story of Fred [Kruger], just get it down, any old way. From beginning to end as it happened. At one time that was a force in my life. I loved telling people about it. But perhaps I've worn it out. I've told it too often. Anyway, it wouldn't hurt to tell it again in writing. I must buy more paper. (41–42)

March 13, 1961[2]
I wrote my book and from it wrote an article which I sold to *Maclean's* and that easy victory resulted in my being given assignments which took me to different places and people across Canada. That gave me a measure of success and confidence and frustration, too, because I didn't ever feel that what I wrote was good enough and I would try sporadically to write something else, a short story or a book about the adventures of Mally [Edna's cat] and they were no good. So I'd scurry back to do a piece for *Maclean's* again, and they were good pieces, talking of the life of people in Canada who had had no self-expression and were perhaps misunderstood by other Canadians. And I made good friends among them: Hutterites, Indians, Negroes, French Canadians, Mennonites, Amish, and I gathered a wealth of material which I've never used. I've been horribly lazy. I've wanted everything to come easily without working for it and I've blamed K always because I didn't get any writing done. Every irregular thing he did was an excuse for me not to do any writing.

March 16, 1961
This morning I thought, as Marnie [Margaret (nee Paisley) Reider, Edna's friend] has told me, I don't have to be and I'm not like the average woman alone in the world, widows who no longer are needed and who fritter their lives away in teas, bridges, TV, and reading novels and having their children in for supper. I've got a real purpose in life. I must learn to write well and to keep on learning more all the time about life and God's love and the world. I'll have lots of time now, and no other responsibilities except Mother and I'd like to write a really good piece or a book on how a woman can live happily and without being lonely because I want to do it, to prove that *it can be done*. Not frantically striving and boasting about how glorious it is to be free but with poise and serenity and quietly living and *knowing*. God help me to *be still and know* and to look forward to each new day with anticipation. I must know, of course, that there will be setbacks and discouragements and difficulties that I'll have to face, but I must remember that God will give me the strength to face them.

March 23, 1961

I must sit at my desk and start writing *every morning*. God help me. I must think more about God and good things. I must make God the first thing in my life. Not all my life; I must not become like Mrs. S[taebler] who retreated from life by spending all her time with her books and her God so she lost touch with reality and had little understanding of people, was really afraid of them. No, I must not spend all my days at Hidden Springs or all my time here with my notebook or my books on recovery and constructive thinking.[3] I must read them everyday but then I must practise them—practise, practise, practise. All accomplishment comes from that, and so, no doubt, does happy and successful living. God help me to do it. I have every chance now. No more excuses.

March 26, 1961

I must trust God. I must know it is all in His Hands and I must start now to live my new life—write letters to the friends I've neglected so long and then work at my writing....

I think I should stop writing here and perhaps write a novel, or is what I think here material for one? I find now that rehashing is distasteful to do, a sort of duty, not a compulsion. I think now I want to get on with life, not to look back at it. (322)

April 16, 1961

I must work. I'd like to be able to discipline myself to work every day at my writing—hours and hours, every morning, some afternoons, some evenings. I'd like to write about what I've lived and learned, so other people could share it. I'd like to write truthfully and beautifully and with quiet power—things that people would always remember.

I'd like to see more of the world, of people, and tell about them. But I don't know what form my writing should take—novels, short stories, articles, essays, books of non-fiction. In this God must guide me. I've been so inhibited and floundering and unproductive for so long.

August 2, 1961

I'm so much healthier and happier now myself. Each day brings me more joy and relaxation and friendship and I love it and am beginning to dream of a future here, there, anywhere. The whole world is mine and I love it. I am not afraid of it and I have faith and a feeling of anticipation and awareness of beauty and love all around me. So many people seem to like being with me and I with them, and each day brings me more. There seems so much to do and *to be*.

August 3, 1961
Well, I just got up and went to the bathroom and while I was there I thought maybe it's so hard for me to write because I really want to write about myself, my experiences, and not the objective things that I try to write about other people. In other words, from the prayer of St. Francis, I want to be understood rather than to understand.[4] I want to do the easy thing, to express me, so I will be understood, but I'm afraid to write about me and my experiences lest I reveal myself as a weak, unattractive, poor proof of a person. So I try to write about other people. But because it is hard work I do it reluctantly, sparingly. And, actually, I have time to do both. All the hours when I waken early in the morning and lie in bed muddling and rehashing, I could spend in writing at something I like.

August 5, 1961
Why don't I, instead of sitting here just thinking idly on paper, why don't I try to write something I perhaps could share with someone, send to an editor and have some hope about? There'd be no harm in trying. It would be better for me than this, give me a feeling of some accomplishment, make each day start with the thought of something to do and something good done by the time I'm ready to get out of bed.

Mazo de la Roche wrote only one and a half hours a day.[5] She didn't plan her stories, just wrote in longhand whatever came to her, let the characters dictate, let them have their own life—purely fictional but yet real. Why don't I try that? Why am I tongue-tied, so afraid? I'm tied to my own life. Everything I can think of writing has to have happened to me. I can't seem to let go, to create. I want merely to tell and I have much to tell, really. My own life has been exciting and varied. Many strong and wonderful people have come into it. But how could I give it form? I can't just spill it out bit by bit. Where would I begin?

Perhaps I shouldn't worry about that, just put down each morning whatever comes to me in any order and then later, much later, perhaps never, edit and change and work at it during the day. Let this be my remembering and writing time, and then after breakfast I could work at whatever I needed to.

August 6, 1961

I've been thinking all I ever do is convince myself over and over again, day after day, year after year, that life is interesting and loveable and should be recorded. I must write about it, then when I've come to that comforting conclusion, I get up out of bed and I putter or do whatever else I care to do, or I read a book about writing, on *How to Get Things Done*, or *Wake Up and Live*, or *Becoming a Writer*, or *If You Want to Write* by Brenda Ueland, or *Mental Health Through Will Training*, and I feel quite self-righteous and on the right track.[6] But I don't *do* a thing. I don't *write*. And now, right this minute, I'm doing it again.

August 10, 1961

I am not satisfied with my life. It lacks continuity. I'm more or less drifting in limbo, going nowhere. The only thing that makes me feel I have any direction is the need to work everyday at my writing. That alone gives me a feeling that I have something to do today and tomorrow and tomorrow and the day after that. People come into my life and go out again. They are concerned about me but they have their own lives to live and must live them. The attention they can give to me is momentary or daily or weekly or monthly, or not at all, and that's natural and as it should be. I must now look after myself. Nobody else can or will. *It's up to me.* Whatever I do with my life must be my own choosing. I alone am responsible for what happens to me, if I'm happy or sad, creative or dead, vibrant, loving, or dull and full of self pity and fear and resentment. The answer is obvious—I must work at my writing. I have a job to do now and I must no longer dally. There is no excuse. People come and go here. Many of them are N[orma] and R[uby]'s friends. I don't have to be with them and I can work here in my room without interruption if I *want* to. I *must*.

November 15, 1961

I must believe in the future, one day at a time. I must work hard and love working. I must reach out and give to as many people as I can. I must give them my attention. I must constantly give love and attention. With God's help I could now have great peace and confidence and love. Life— God has brought me so much. My life has been gloriously full of joy and sorrow. People have often wondered how I've managed to stick with K all these years without breaking under the strain. It is because I have loved life and literature, people, beauty.

[...]

Love is the only defence of life. And if one has love one has all. God, keep me loving. Keep me aware of love and life and help me to give it back in my writing. Let me never waver. Help me always to see love in all people and to show it clearly and compassionately that love may grow in the world and warm the hearts of all who read my work. God, help me to work more swiftly and easily that I may produce more and more for the world to know. Keep me steadfast and interesting, let me make people laugh and love and have greater understanding and compassion because they have read what I've written. Help me to make my work warm and lively and honest and beautiful because that's how it should be to give my readers what I want them to have. Help me to grow that I may help them to grow. God, there is so much for me to do. Let me never be idle. Let me be a constant, free-flowing channel of Thy love and help me to be patient, help me to accept what I cannot change. Take my bitterness from me and all my distrust and fear.

God, keep me loving. Let me love, love, love every minute. I have always said I didn't see how one could be constantly happy, not in the face of others' unhappiness or tragedy or sorrow. I do not ask for happiness. I ask for love—abiding, constant, ever present in my heart for all things and all people. Let it glow like a flame that can warm all it comes near.

December 17, 1961

I wish I'd be working on a novel, or even short stories, or essays, or anything that would be writing for the joy of writing, as I wrote my Neil's Harbour book. Since I did that I've never recaptured the relaxation and pleasure of writing. I've always worked at it. I've always had assignments to be done, done in a certain way. They've tied me, or I've let them tie me. Yesterday Ralph Hodgson [Edna's brother-in-law] was talking about *The Catcher in the Rye*.[7] He was enjoying it very much and laughing about it and reading out bits of it and being really thrilled with it and unable to leave it and I said how wonderful it was to get a book like that that could take you out of your everyday world, could absorb you and delight you and transport you, and I began to wonder how I could do it, how I could write with enjoyment a book that could be so enjoyed or that could be of help to someone as books I've read have been helpful to me. But no, I don't think I really thought that. I think I just wanted to write for the joy I would find in the writing, and if I had it, perhaps I could give it. Why don't I do this? (1,032)

January 1, 1962[8]

I really want to write about Canada. There's so much to see here and to do and people to meet. I love being with people, listening to them talk. I hope I'm getting over my need to impress myself on them by much talking, as I've done so often. I need only listen to enjoy them, enrich myself and learn much and make them feel better too.

January 7, 1962

(6:50 AM) This is the time I should be spending on writing a book, a short story, or an essay. Why don't I? Because if I did, I'd have to *think* and thinking is a very difficult process at this hour of the day. I am so lazy. The path of least resistance is such an easy one to follow—warm, cozy, safe, peopled with such well-meaning friends.

January 12, 1962

Letter yesterday morning from Bill S[trickland] in Neil's Harbour. He said there were a number of things in my piece about Jean that he didn't like.[9] I think possibly the fact of their isolation. He said, "we have paved roads and phones and lovely homes with everything modern— we are not isolated." I knew people down there would object to that. They don't think they are isolated. They don't know they are. I suppose because they can think themselves out. They can get out and bring in whatever and whenever they please. For us here in the busy, crowded heart of Ontario, they, in the northern tip of Cape Breton, an island, seem lonely and far away and cut off from us. But for them the world emanates from their doorstep.

I suppose for them, as for everyone, the heart of the world is where they are. Everything radiates from them and their thoughts go out from that spot. That is their point of view. For someone living on the sixth floor of an apartment in Toronto, Neil's Harbour looks tiny and far away and isolated. For someone in Neil's Harbour, Toronto is an unknown confusing mass.

February 16, 1962

Last night at the class I talked to Marg McKinnon.[10] She and so many others read a lot. They seem to be sharp and to know so much. I don't read enough because that makes me feel guilty too, because I should be writing instead. She said that is her trouble too.

Dr. Boyd talked of the various kinds of writing and how some writers can do different kinds: prose, poetry, essays, journalism.[11] I said I suffered from not knowing what kind I should do, if I should do one thing and it's hard to do I think I should be trying something else. But I don't try it. What is there to prevent me? I could have all the time I'd need to try all kinds of writing. There's no crime in failing. I could try a form every day and still work on my articles, or I could write a book or a story every morning before I get out of bed. I could work at it for two hours.

February 28, 1962

The wild and wonderful thoughts that race thro' the mind when one cannot sleep are amazing. I wish I could put them all down. Why? I'd never read them again. But some of them are so much fun or exciting or terrible or interesting or thought provoking. It's a shame they should be so open-ended. Why have I this urge to record everything? Why does life sometimes seem so exciting that not one moment of it must be lost, and then other times it is so puzzling or dull or frustrating that I feel as if I have a tangled skein in my head and it never will be unravelled.

What do I really want to do with my life? Not what do I think I ought to do, like helping the poor and the suffering, but what do I really want to do? Until I decide that I'll keep on doing and being nothing.

Do I really want to be a great writer? If so, why? And what do I want to write? Do I really think I could be? Have I what it takes? I know I have not. When I read the truly great things, I know I could never write anything like them. Novels by Tolstoy or Proust are like canvases by Rubens and Leonardo DaVinci. They are big and full and they have tremendous capacity for detail and complexity. They have genius. I am no genius. I have only a limited talent. But I should make the most of that talent. Maybe that is my answer, simply to make the most of my limited talent. But what is my talent? I can write fairly clearly, with feeling, and I'd like to write simply and beautifully something that would be remembered, a single pearl on a chain or the first star in the sky or the word of a poem or the face of a lovely girl in the street or the sea in a storm. That is too difficult, could be complex, why don't I do it? Why don't I write what I'd like to write? Why do I procrastinate? Can't I do it? Is that my talent? (1,156–57)

July 11, 1962

I look at Sunfish Lake and I love it and I think I should write about it. But there is no story here, not a real drama. And yet there are people and all of them have a story, and there is the lake itself, a tiny jewel in the land.

Thoreau immortalized Walden and it is still selling.[12] Why don't I do it? (1,268)

July 20, 1962
Do I want to be famous and have no private life? Do I want to be something?

I'm sure I don't really. I'd hate to be recognized wherever I'd go, or be given public adulation. I'd always feel afraid I couldn't keep up the image. I wouldn't want to.

No, that isn't it.

I would like to write well enough to feel honestly within myself that I'd really done my best and deserve the praise that I'd get from other writers and editors and critics who'd know good work if it existed.

I'd like to write honestly, beautifully, with power. The power of quiet, moving conviction or humour. I'd like to be able to move people's hearts, to give them a better view of what I have seen, greater insight, compassion, generosity, and love. (1,303)

September 14, 1962
The Search—might be a good title for my life since most of it seems to be spent in trying to find understanding, which is rather like the waves in the sea, constantly washing, receding or quietly, patiently lapping, for a very short while, unless there are storms.

There is usually a calm in the morning. That's when the fishermen go out and that's when I most quietly contemplate.

There are many things that I must ponder:
1) I want to think much about loneliness, to face it squarely and honestly, without any panic.
2) I want to think out carefully and fairly my piece on Jehovah's Witnesses.[13]
3) I'd like to think about Jack Bechtel and know how he translates what he feels and thinks into forms and colours with paint.[14]
4) I want to be honest and sensible in the longing I have for affection.
5) I'd like to be able to have enough insight and compassion for other people so that I wouldn't be mad at them, especially so that I wouldn't say things about them that I'm usually sorry for.
6) I'd like to know myself well enough to forgive myself and to get rid of my guilt and my laziness and to be truly creative in a way that is honest, moving, beautiful, or humorous, and always interesting.

7) It would be good for me to think more about people I meet every day, to be sensitive to them, to listen not just to their words but to their hearts—this above all.

8) I want to be closer to nature, to know more and care more, to feel closer and more of a part. If I did that I could never be lonely. I could live alone here at sf [Sunfish Lake] without any fear. I must let myself have more awareness. I must read and learn more about many things that are part of the universe. I must learn to love God.

9) I must learn to translate my thoughts and feelings to paper. I want so desperately to share them. In a way, I suppose that's the secret of life—that longing to share. Partly it's a desire to be rid of the burden, to have someone else take it for me, to let someone else do it, whether it be taking my responsibility or taking my blame.

September 23, 1962

I've always been moved by poverty. I've always felt concerned and anxious to help people who need help. I've thought long and seriously of their problems but I've also been selfish, refused to be generous, except a little bit with people I've been fond of. I've really not done very much. My main excuse has always been for myself; I talk always about *wanting* to share things, my home, my knowledge, myself. But how much have I really given, I wonder? Or is it impossible to give without also receiving, and which comes first? Are the two entirely reciprocal? Do I only give so I will receive? And what's wrong with that if it is a law of life and inevitable and impossible to be otherwise? Why worry? Why not just live, love, and work? The main thing for me to do is to *work*, to share my loving with my writing.

October 6, 1962

I feel guilty because I don't work and I suppose it is logical, man must work. There must be a law of giving and receiving and what we give we get. If I don't give anything I get nothing. If I give sunshine and happiness to people I'm with, it makes me feel good. That's why I enjoy being with them. If I am alone, I must also give and I can do that only if I work at my writing. If I am happy within myself I must give it out or I can't be happy. So again the answer is *write write write*. Not just here; this is selfish, not giving. This is conscious analyzing and getting me nowhere, what I do here is convince myself ad nauseum. The time I've spent writing this drivel, I know I could have spent working on J.W. [Jehovah's Witness article], and getting it done.

November 18, 1962

Why don't I start the book I've been talking about for ages? I keep putting it off. During the day and early in the morning here in bed, I keep
thinking about it, keep thinking of ways I could start it, of how I could
treat it. Only it always seems there are so many, many ways, so many
books for so many times of my life and so many of my different selves.
I must choose one and start to write it. I must not call it work, merely
writing, therapeutic writing. I tell myself I want to forget the past. I
must not indulge it and review it by writing about it. I must live in the
present, think only of it and enjoy it. But still my mind does slip back constantly and I try to retrieve it.

November 22, 1962

It must be something from my experience that I consider worth writing,
either because it is interesting, revealing, novel, or something big enough
to be shared. Doesn't this require a certain confidence in myself? I had
it when I started my book in Neil's Harbour. I was so sure of it and of
me. Then when all hell broke loose in my marriage I questioned everything that I thought I was sure of. For years and years I've been floundering. Will I regain my composure, my faith? I've not got it yet, but
I'm trying and I hope it will come to me, clear and unwavering, that
then I will write of it, or should I write while it comes? I can write objectively about other people but not about me and my life and affairs. Is that
what I want to write about? I feel in a way that it should be. My life's been
so rich, so full, so varied. But writing about it takes me into the past and
I want still to live and experience and write about now. I don't want to
just sit here in my little room and interpret the past. I long to be seeing,
doing things, travelling, meeting people, talking about ideals, love, making love, but writing too, always writing, every morning, all morning,
wherever I am, detaching myself, recording. Is detaching the answer? I
can't seem to do that. Meet people and appraise them and listen to them
and recreate them. I can't do that calmly, [or be] cool and intellectual. I
must feel with them, become them, be emotionally involved with them.
But when that happens, I'm usually lost or upset and bewildered, or
hurt and exalted. And then I can't write, but tell myself I will later when
the fury or fancy or fog has passed.

January 18, 1963

Experiences from my life? Hasn't it been a failure? Why write about
that? Except as a warning—a life not to be followed. Then why tell about

that? Do I really believe it has been a failure? Am I not constantly rationalizing and trying to convince myself that it hasn't been? Am I not always trying to build up my self-esteem so I can love myself or go on to love life? Do I love it? I seem to spend most of my time doubting myself and hating my weakness and my faltering, indecision, my lack of accomplishment and utter selfishness, egotism, my, me, me, me, me.

God help me. If I could learn to write well, with less agony and less frustration, and carry over into my living, I'd be so much better. If I could write much and well every morning and be free then to love and do things for and with other people, perhaps write again in the evening, if necessary, so long as I wrote satisfactorily every day, and then did other things with a free, open, unmuddled, unselfish mind, I'd be fine. I'd be happy. I'd be free. God, help me to learn and to do what I've learned. Help me to know for sure and to use what I know and to give what I can. Help me to write what will help other people, as I've been so often helped by what others have written. God, teach me to love, to love what I know, to tell it, to so love the world that I must give it, to so love the people who live in the world that I'll want to feel responsible for them and help them in the best way that I can. God, open my eyes, my heart, and my mind. Help me to give and give freely, with beauty and quiet confidence. Thy will be done.

January 25, 1963

What is my freedom? The right to do what I want when I want? Is that freedom? Then I have it, but it doesn't make me happy, because I don't do what I want. What the hell do I want? And if I want it why don't I do it and go after it? I tell myself I want to be a good writer, to write books. Then why don't I do it? What if I should add another mediocre book to the millions already in the world? Am I capable of writing a really good book?

I lack motivation. I don't love enough. If I love anything well enough to want to express it, to share it, then I might write a good book. That is the key to all my uncertainty, all my dreaming and living. I must love enough. If I can't find enough to love in my daily routine, I must love something else that I want to share, and the routine, the loneliness of every day that passes will no longer exist. I'd have lost myself, be absorbed and be happy in the thing I am lovingly writing about. That must be my answer, to write lovingly. About what? About me, and my life, and my struggle to find love and understanding. No, my struggle to love and to understand.

March 1, 1963[15]

In my work, my writing about people, I try to present them as objectively as I can, to show them as accurately as I see them, by revealing them in their dialogue and their action and in my choice of anecdotes and recounting of other references in their lives. I try to be honest, to show them from all sides and as lovingly, compassionately, uncritically as I can. In that, am I being subjective? Because I am myself and certain things about them appeal to me personally, those are the things I express, the things I give my reader. And that's inevitable. I must make a selection of what I consider significant detail. Another writer might choose quite different things that would express his feelings or thoughts about the same people. Is pure objectivity possible? I suppose not. What about factual writing, can it be pure? Maybe it can. I'm always more interested in trying to abstract the truth than the fact. In some of my pieces, I have deliberately manipulated facts to illustrate truth, and there is some danger in doing that because the people one writes about might not understand that, [might] say one is being dishonest. All very interesting. I must think more about it. (1,702–703)

March 5, 1963

When I work on a piece I think of what I am writing. I don't know about trends and schools and methods. I write. But I should know, I'm sure. I've lived so long in the little world of my own problems that I don't have very much else except the few isolated experiences I've had with the people I've written about. It's time now for me to emerge, God willing, not too late. But I wish I were twenty years younger.

However, since I'm not, there is that much more urgency and reason for me to get on with my writing and do less of living, in the sense of having and going to parties and being approved and wailing and caring about approval. What matters if I am popular or not? Who cares? I can't expect everyone to like me, to be uncritical of me. It's my work that matters, and how well and honestly and sensitively and creatively I can do it. If I can be satisfied with that, my living will take care of itself. I don't need to care if people like me or my hats.

I've been thinking about the different kinds of writers we have here in Canada, as many kinds almost as there are people. Some create; they are so alone in their own little world that the people they write about are mostly imagined, like Mazo de le Roche and Janie. There are the others, like Bill [W.O.] Mitchell and me, who live with the people they write about and get to know them very well and put them on paper, real people, translated, tho' Bill's are so creative and mine are actual.

But why worry? Why try to generalize? The important thing is to do it the best way I can, in my own way, tho' maybe I should learn some more of other people's ways instead of blundering along in my own way of trial and error. I waste so much time in agonizing over things, in getting started. I must learn to just write, get things down any which way, then work at the best way to say it.

I'm almost bursting now to get started again. I must work on something. I've written nothing for over four weeks and I'm beginning to feel empty and muddled and horrible. (1,707–708)

March 13, 1963
Yesterday morning I suddenly realized that the reason I have had such a hard time with my writing is because I've resented it, made it a chore, instead of loving it and loving to do it and looking forward to doing it, wanting to do it more than doing many, almost any, other things. I must love my work. If I do I'll be happy. I'm so lucky to have the talent. I must love using it. I used to love writing when I worked on my NH book. I'd get at it every chance that I could. It took me back to NH and the people I loved there and I lost myself in it completely. I loved thinking of words, the right words, and of the right way to express what I felt. It wasn't work, it was an abounding joy. That's how it should be, and could be, and must be now if I'll let it. I must write with love. And that's how I approached my work yesterday morning and it seemed to come clear. (1,717–18)

September 9, 1963
I must do something constructive. I must get out of my rut of family, Sunfish, Maurice, introspection and sloth, eating too much and feeling inadequate.[16] I'm vegetating. I should be out working with people. I should be working at my craft. I don't think I'm really a writer. I'm too friendly and too lonely to live by myself and just write. I must have the approval and affection of people to feel that what I'm doing is worthwhile. I doubt if I'll ever write a novel or anything about my personal experience. I wouldn't feel it was worth it.

November 8, 1963
And why? Why write here at this hour of the morning that is really the middle of the night? It has no virtue. It is self-indulgence. Why do I

keep scribbling here almost day after day about myself? Who is to read this? Why waste my time? In a vague way I suppose I am hopeful that some day my diaries will be discovered to be something special. But are they? What do they convey? A hodgepodge of conflicting thoughts. Do they lead anywhere? Is there any conclusion? Any help in there for anyone else?

[...]

Have I nothing to say? Only if I get excited enough about something can I write about it. And right now I'm in contact virtually with no one but me and M. So I write here. I seem always to want to put something down, to record life as it passes, but that is not writing creatively. That is pure self-indulgence. It isn't disciplined work. It is sheer laziness.

[...]

Joan [Mackenzie] wants me to write a travel-guide book of Canada, to go write about little villages and scenes all over the country.[17] A truly big project, and experience too, but it could be productive, it is needed. It could be fascinating to work on. I would become interested if I'd get started, get off my fat fanny here at the lake and start looking outside of myself. (2,020, 2,022)

December 1, 1963

What should I be writing? What would really satisfy me? Am I being totally egotistical and self-centred if I want to write of my life, my loving of life? Could I do it in a readable form? Would it be published? Why this constant niggling to write something of me, me, me. My mistakes, my overcomings, my goings-on, my growth, my recordings. Is there any pattern, any love in my life? Can I grow or am I dying? Am I becoming any better or am I worse? Have I any cause to love myself? Why must I hate myself? Why do I feel guilty, inadequate, unlovable? Why am I sometimes unloving as I am when I think of me, me, my laziness? (2,038)

January 21, 1964

God, help me to do it today. Help me to write several pages that I can be satisfied with. I believe that I can. I know that I have it in me to help me to get it out and on paper. Faith without words is dead. Let my faith not be dead. God, make me work. Make me accomplish, not just sit here and muddle and stew and get nowhere. Please, please, God, I need to write something. There's no reason now why I shouldn't be the happiest, most creative, and productive woman in Canada. I have the time and the place and no money worries. (2,080)

February 5, 1964
God, help me, what is wrong with me? Why must I write? Why can't I just love and enjoy things and people? Why must I justify my existence by writing? And why not write about my experience? But deep in my heart I know this is nonsense. Man must work to be happy; he must work at what he has a talent for, at what basically he loves best, and I suppose for me that is writing, yet why do I resist it? Because it's hard work? Because the only writing that's easy is what I write here, or writing letters—undisciplined. (2,089)

March 26, 1965[18]
I read *Tropic of Cancer* by Henry Miller last week.[19] He writes well and with power and with honesty too, I've no doubt. But such a life. Such a distortion of values, such contempt for women, who for him are just bodies to be used. But his imagery is vivid; this is writing that parallels surrealism in painting. As I read it I kept wanting to tell my story, my life, to express me in the same way, but differently, my way, with different experiences and motivation and faith and fulfillment and defeat and success and my own inadequacies and guilt and ideals and fortunes, and life all around me, or people I've known and loved—or not loved. Should I try to write that? What purpose would be served? Is my life worth revealing? Have I a firm enough faith to be of any value? Am I faltering, and would I just be wasting my time? Or would trying to tell my life story help me to find something that now I merely question and side-step or deny? Am I too lazy? Is that why I don't write? Or am I afraid? Afraid I'd reveal myself as a hollow, shallow, insincere, unloving, selfish bitch? Should I try? God, help me to try. Why should I keep reading, always reading, to add bits and pieces to my knowledge, which I don't really need, which I soon forget. Is it all wasting time? Why do I always want to take courses, to learn more and more? Is reading and listening to lectures a form of rationalizing? Assuaging the guilt I feel constantly because I'm not thinking, deciding, writing, creating?

I remember that ever since I was very young and suffered agonies of embarrassment and inferiority and ignorance, I used to think that if I could only *know* enough, understand enough, I could eventually be happy. I seemed to be always reading in the hope of learning something that would give me the secret of eternal bliss. And sometimes I'd find it, and I'd be happy for awhile, with a sort of incandescent glow, but then something would happen and I'd be dragged down and wouldn't know how to cope with the horrid reality. Perhaps that's my trouble. I've always lived in a little world of dreams and ideals that I, and no one else, could ever live up to. But though I know this to be true, I still keep on trying and trusting and hoping and following that glow, that illusive flicker of dream, of light, of faith. What is it? Why is it?

Should I try to write about it? About my struggle to find it, to believe it, to make it reality? Or is that what I've been doing here, in this old notebook of mine all these years, but especially the last four years when I've been alone and forced to face things more honestly and courageously? But what does this show? Could what I've written ever be of any help to anyone else? Is that why I'd like to write, to help someone else? Why do I feel guilty all the time because I don't write? I needn't feel guilty if I don't write for money, or for prestige, or merely to give me something to do. No. My guilt is valid only if my non-writing is a withholding of something—knowledge, inspiration, or whatever that might be useful, helpful to someone else.

A few weeks ago I was asked to speak about writing to a group of teenagers. Only three eager, shy, ungainly, young, very young girls showed up and I talked and talked for a couple of hours. M said what a waste, all that time and effort for only three little girls. I should have had a real audience. But I didn't feel that way about it at all. I felt that if I'd said anything that might have helped those three youngsters who came because they really wanted to learn something, it was more than worthwhile. Maybe that's how I should approach the writing of a book, a revealing book. The only catch is that it might never be published, might never even have an audience of *one*, and all that time, all that effort, that might be spent on something else that could be worthwhile. What could I do that would be worth doing? Articles, all sorts of articles about things and people. Is that enough? Is that what I should do? In my viewpoint, my character, if I have any, should come through. I suppose in my selection of things to write about, to tell, the things I observe, I give my dream away. I suppose, actually, in anything I write I do that. I don't have to spell it out. I don't have to say, "this is what I believe," this is what happened to me. This is how I was made. I don't need to reveal the I. It will show through whatever I do, if it's worth showing or not.

Perhaps I'd just better forget myself, forget trying to tell about me, about my experiences, and write, write, write. Always, often, forever—about the world, the people around me.

Balls, here I go again. Noble me, trying to get out of it. I have plenty of time for both kinds of writing. I just need to *do* it. I'm just lazy, or scared that I can't do it, scared I'll show somebody that I can't—myself? Maybe—or a publisher? So what? What have I got to lose? I could write here in my book, every night, or every morning for one hour, or for two or three pages, just to see what might happen. But will I? No. I live in indecision. I'm bugged by indecision and indecision means postponement, indecision is *fear*. "Better make a wrong decision than *no* decision." I always make *no* decision till the right to choose is taken from me and I'm forced into something, and serves me right if it's something I don't like. God, I'm a coward, a lazy, loafing coward. That's what I'm afraid of, *me*, a lazy, loafing coward, a thief of time and experience—life.

So what? What am I going to do about it? Probably nothing as usual, just talk, talk, talk, to try to inflate myself, or write here about it, as if that had some virtue. I can tell myself I *wrote*, yes, I wrote six pages in my notebook.

April 18, 1965

I often think about writing a book or something about What is God? My own search, evidence, doubts, theories, if you'd call them that. Is God merely an attitude? Is God within an attitude of loving? Is that enough? That puts all the onus on *me*. I have to do it, feel it, think lovingly and all will be well with me. But what if I'm so ill, or beat, or despairing that I can't be loving? Is there such a thing as *can't be*? Should I at all times be able to be loving? And what about prayer? Is it meaningless?

If God is merely an attitude then prayer is useless, except that asking or speaking to God is a way of speaking to, exhausting, reminding, changing oneself. And what about praying for help for someone else? Or help for something that comes or is needed from outside oneself? The latter may be again changing or conditioning one's attitude, "taking it" if the desired thing or condition is not forthcoming. What about praying for someone else, someone who is ill or needs help to resolve something? Could my petitioning God bring it about? Does it merely make my concern [illegible]? I don't think so. To pray for someone else's health and to see the person slowly losing the battle is dispiriting. Should one presume to pray? Is this kind of prayer even answered? I've read that it is. But why isn't it always so? Why do so many people who are prayed for die anyway? Or suffer anyway?

March 26, 1966[20]
Beginning to worry about cookbook. How in hell am I to collect enough recipes and write interestingly about them?

January 26, 1967[21]
Worked on book. I'm always happy when I'm working. I should do more of it. It makes me feel good.

January 13, 1968[22]
Did some good work in the morning. M came about five for dinner and we watched a movie on TV at night. A waste of good time, but M needs to relax. I guess it doesn't hurt me to do the same, but sometimes I resent it.

January 22, 1968
Took my MS [manuscript] to Ryerson's. They're quite lackadaisical. I'll probably have trouble with them—my impatience.

May 4, 1968
I have a horrid feeling in me about my book because of the delay and because the cover is to be BROWN.

May 6, 1968
Wrote a letter to Art Steven, art director at Ryerson's, to protest the *brown* cover and the design he's planning for my book. I'm really mad about it.

June 20, 1968
Thrilling day. Letter from Jack McClelland saying they'd like to reissue my *Sauerkraut and Enterprise* next spring, and that he thinks it's delightful, a remarkable piece of work, a minor classic, and that it will sell for a great many years to come. I'd like to frame his letter.

February 6, 1969[23]
A little newcomer to my patio, a plump little song sparrow. Sat in living room and watched birds all morning, and this aft from 5:00–5:45 the little newcomer was out there alone, eating, eating, eating. He seems to be a stranger, all by himself amongst the others.

September 25, 1969[24]

A book—about what? Something vital, something meaningful, something real. M would like me to write a big book. He thinks I have a special gift of communication with all kinds of people. I must talk to them, get their ideas and put them down; try in my own limited way to bridge the gap between the young and the old, the tycoon and the hippie, the washed and the unwashed, I suppose. But how do I do it? I'm not a sociologist. I'll have to do it in my own way. I'd like to make it interesting and loving and fun and simple, honest, finding my way as I go along.

On the night of Mardi Ann [Robinson, a Sunfish Lake neighbour]'s wedding, a young man, Peter Massell who is going to college to learn how to teach English, said I must write a book that really *gives* something. He said he, and other students who know my work, want to know more about what I think. He said, "Bare your soul. Tell us what is in your heart. Let us know. That is what literature is made of. Don't be afraid to write what you know. We want to know it. We need to know it. We're looking for answers." He said that at the moment (he's twenty-three), he has a lot of theories and he's trying to put them into practice. He doesn't know if they'll work. He must try, and they may be all wrong, but he must try.

What answers do I have? Has my life been a success? Is success desirable? Have I been happy? Should I try? What has made me happy? I know I'm miserable if I'm not working, producing, writing. But I'm disturbed and tense and unsure and miserable too when I am working. I'm happy when I'm doing all sorts of things—baking, swimming, being with people, but only if I am spending part of my time working as well.

This past year I've been idle. I've enjoyed many of the things I've done but I've written nothing and I can't go on any longer that way. I've been getting more and more restless and guilty and starting to *blame*, but knowing that it really is my dissatisfaction with *me* that is the root of the trouble.

Where to start? What to start at? A history of Waterloo County? That is not my answer. M says it's too limited. It will be done anyway by somebody. My book must be about live people. It must be *now*.

I've been feeling too protected, living in this lovely place, sheltered, isolated, my horizon no farther beyond me than the wooded hills at the end of the lake, and M here beside me. For a while, perhaps, I've needed this healing process, this convalescing, but now I must get out and beyond in my thinking and learning. God help me.

I'll just be experimenting at first, listening, asking questions, making notes. M reminded me of how I resisted writing the British Mortgage story.[25] I knew nothing about it and was sure I couldn't do it. And the cookbook, what a long, drawn-out struggle for unity that was. And I never did feel satisfied with it, yet it is selling well, people do like it, and the Br. Mtg. story was acclaimed my best, though I don't think it was.

So, I must get started. I must ask questions and I must find answers. I must have a purpose and I must get to work. I'm rife, anxious, eager. God help me.

October 21, 1969[26]

Went to meet *Margaret Laurence*, writer-in-residence at U of T.[27] Dinner at Doc and Eula May Myers, then Margaret spoke at the University Women's Club open meeting.[28] She was very nervous before she went on, more or less read her very interesting speech about how her life on the prairies had influenced her writing. Back to Myers for a drink, then home in the snow. We talked and *talked till 5:30*—then bed. She is getting a divorce at Christmas in England and finds it a shattering experience.

Notes

1 Box R3-1. Notes 1959–60.
2 Box R3-2. Diary February 11, 1961–62.
3 Hidden Springs Centre, a Christian rehabilitation farm located near Brantford. Following Keith's treatment at the centre in late 1960, Edna learned of his relationship with her friend Helen (née MacDonald) Kergin. To help cope with her distress over Keith's request for divorce to marry Helen, Edna herself sought treatment at the centre for a period of time.
4 Widely credited to, but in fact not originating with, St. Francis of Assisi, the prayer reads as follows: "Lord, make me an instrument of your peace. / Where there is hatred, let me sow love. / Where there is injury, pardon. / Where there is doubt, faith. / Where there is despair, hope. / Where there is darkness, light. / Where there is sadness, joy. / O Divine Master, grant that I may not so much seek to be consoled as to console; / To be understood as to understand; / To be loved as to love. / For it is in giving that we receive. / It is in pardoning that we are pardoned. / And it is in dying that we are born to eternal life." The first known printed copy of the prayer was in a small twentieth-century Italian prayer book. From Italy, it is thought to have been brought to the USA by Cardinal Spellman. See Regis Armstrong and Ignatius Brady, "Frances and Clare, the Complete Works," *The Classics of Western Spirituality* (New York: Paulist Press, 1982).

5 Mazo de la Roche (1879–1961), Canadian writer whose 1927 novel *Jalna* inaugurated a hugely successful series of fifteen sequels, and became the basis for the 1935 film of the same title as well as two television productions in 1972 and 1994.

6 Dorothea Brande, *Becoming a Writer* (New York: Harcourt, Brace, 1934). Brande was also the author of *Wake Up and Live*. Brenda Ueland, *If You Want to Write: A Book about Art, Independence and Spirit* (New York: G.P. Putnam's Sons, 1938). Abraham K. Low, *Mental Health through Will-Training* (Boston: Christopher House, 1950).

7 J.D. Salinger's popular 1951 novel whose adolescent protagonist, Holden Caulfield, observes the adult world with a critical eye. A decade later, Salinger published *Franny and Zooey* (1961).

8 Box R3-2. Diary January 1, 1962–February 1963.

9 Jean Williams, daughter of Edna's hosts in Neil's Harbour, Clara May and Henry Ingraham. The article in question was "The Village that Lives One Day at a Time."

10 Student in a writing course that Edna took in 1962.

11 Evelyn Boyd, the writing course instructor.

12 Henry David Thoreau (1817–62), American author best known for *Walden, or Life in the Woods* (1854), one of two books he published during his life, which describes his two-year experiment in self-sufficiency living in a hut at Walden Pond, near Concord, Massachusetts. Little noted in its time, the book has since been hailed as a literary masterpiece.

13 Jehovah's Witness. Staebler was working on an article for the *Toronto Star* weekly magazine. See bibliography for publication details.

14 Kitchener artist. In January 1962, he was commissioned to create a mural for the Kitchener Public Library lounge.

15 Box R3-2. Diary February 1963–June 6, 1964.

16 Maurice Hearn, "M," a close companion to Edna following her divorce in 1962.

17 One of Edna's friends in the Canadian Authors Association.

18 Box R3-1. Diary June 7, 1964–May 21, 1973.

19 Henry Miller (1891–1980), American novelist and essayist whose autobiographical *Tropic of Cancer* (1931), a frank account of an American artist's Parisian adventures, was banned for many years in Britain and the United States.

20 Box R2–1. Diary 1966.

21 Box R2–1. Diary 1967.

22 Box R2–1. Diary 1968.

23 Box R2–1. Diary 1969.

24 Box R3-1. Diary June 7, 1964–May 21, 1973.

25 *Maclean's* editors had suggested that Staebler write a story on the British Mortgage and Trust Company in Stratford, which was under investigation.

See her article "Stratford's Dark Day" *Maclean's* 17, 10–12, 34–36. January 22, 1966.

26 Box R2-2. Diary 1969.

27 Renowned author of *The Stone Angel* (1964) and *The Diviners* (1974) among other novels, Laurence was writer-in-residence at the University of Toronto from the fall of 1969 to spring 1970. She visited Staebler at Sunfish Lake.

28 Professor Robert Myers of the University of Waterloo.

the
1970s

Something to
Write About

FOLLOWING THE OVERWHELMING SUCCESS of *Food That Really*
Schmecks, publishers were eager for another cookbook from Edna
Staebler. Jack McClelland, who had reissued *Sauerkraut and Enter-*
prise with McClelland and Stewart in 1969, expressed renewed interest
in her manuscript on Neil's Harbour. With tourism on the rise on a
newly paved Cabot Trail, the book presented possible sales potential.
In April 1972, more than twenty-five years after she had first started
working on it, *Cape Breton Harbour* was published. That same spring,
on March 8, 1972, Edna's mother died.

Staebler had worked hard to bring her book to final form. The manuscript required structural changes, character development, and short-
ening. The finished text, *Cape Breton Harbour,* was favourably reviewed
(May 4, 1972 and August 12, 1972), sold well, and earned Edna new fans,
including George Dowse, a young man who turned up at Sunfish Lake
in June 1975 (June 27, 1975). Edna was dissatisfied with the marketing
and distribution of her book, however, and accompanied by her Mennonite friend Eva Bauman, she undertook to promote it herself in local com-
munities. Meanwhile, she worked towards a sequel to *Food That Really*
Schmecks. Writer friends, Harold Horwood in particular, cautioned that
a second cookbook might typecast her as a cookbook author and limit
her identity as a writer. But Edna still had lots of recipes and anecdotes
to share. She set herself a high standard. The second book had to be at
least as good as, if not better than, the first, so that no one could say
she'd been able to do it once, but not twice ("My Writing Life"). For six

years Staebler tried and tested recipes. *More Schmecks,* published in 1979, was a bestseller. McClelland and Stewart sent Staebler on a coast-to-coast promotional tour. She did dozens of interviews and signed hundreds of autographs. "I stopped feeling guilty about having written it instead of a novel that might have been mediocre and sold only two hundred copies," Staebler told the audience at the Writers' Union meeting in May 1997.

Staebler had attended the first annual meeting of the Writers' Union in 1974. There, and at subsequent meetings of the union, she met and made friends with many other writers, such as Farley and Claire Mowat, Sylvia Fraser, Marian Engel, Margaret Laurence, Harold Horwood, and others. Despite her new community of writers, in her diaries Staebler wrote of lingering self-doubt, guilt, and dissatisfaction with her writing. "Why do I simper and feel apologetic about *Schmecks?* Because it isn't *literature?* Who the hell am I to think I could produce *literature?* I'm too damn conceited, too snobbish, that's what's wrong with me" (February 7, 1974). Staebler's stern self-interrogation and unblinking summary of her life on March 6, 1975, generated stiff insights: "What is there in all that [life summary] to feel guilty about? Nothing but my reluctance to admit my non-fashionable, non-society, non-wasp background. Afraid I'd be scorned, looked down on. I'd heard my wasp friends deriding people who were Mennonite, or factory types, or whatever that was prosperous, merchandising, or professional" (March 6, 1975). Nearing seventy, Staebler seemed to be reaching a stage that she once discussed with Margaret Laurence: "Margaret says she had to come to terms with her past—and I guess Alice [Munro] did too. Many writers seem to write about their childhood and youth—get it out of themselves. They come to understand themselves better by writing it out. Maybe I would, maybe I should do that—just for me. Get it out, get it down, get rid, then read it over and if there's anything then that might be good enough to interest anyone else, write it once, work on it, then maybe one day I'll have another book" (April 15, 1975). The present volume is arguably that book.

Edna's diaries for the 1970s appear to end with an entry on March 13, 1976, in which she again berated herself for not writing. "What the hell's wrong with me?" she demanded. The balance of the decade seems to have gone unrecorded or missing. Despite the success of her cookbooks, widespread recognition of her writing talents, and happy moments at the outset of the 1970s, the decade ended on a dismal note for Edna Staebler.

Note

1 Harold Horwood (1923–), Newfoundland-born writer and politician, founding member of the Writers' Union of Canada and union chair 1980–81. A memoir of his writing life, *Among the Lions: A Lamb in the Literary Jungle*, was published in 2000.

top left 1979. Edna at her desk with her books and her cat, Cecily. *top right* 12 October 1976. Edna at Sunfish Lake; *bottom left and right* 1978. Edna and Kath Reeves at Sunfish Lake.

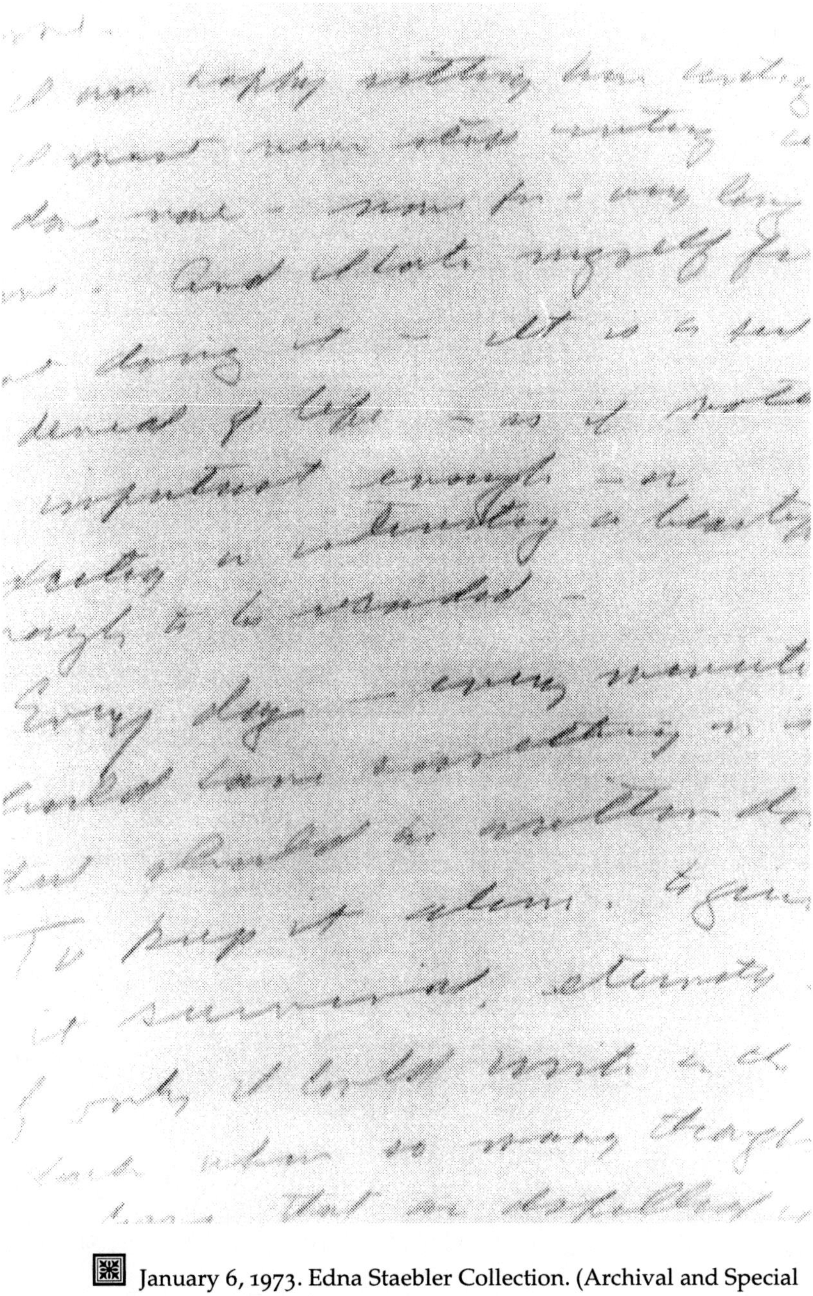

January 6, 1973. Edna Staebler Collection. (Archival and Special Collections, University of Guelph Library)

From the Diaries

March 2, 1970[1]
Worked on Neil's Harbour book. Good practice, but I haven't much hope for its publication, should have been done twenty-five years ago.

May 24, 1970
Edna Knarr, cousin of Dorothy Stevenson, my *Schmecks* fan from Arizona, invited me to have dinner with them at their new house in Colonial acres. Very nice, but I did all the talking—showing off.

July 29, 1970
According to Dorothea Brande's book on *Becoming a Writer*, one is supposed to write every morning before uttering a word or doing anything else, anything that comes into one's head from the subconscious.[2] But I don't seem to learn anything. I seem to wake up completely and could put down anything at all that I choose to think of. I'd like to avoid having this become a mere diary of events but that is what my mind seems to dwell on—what happened yesterday.

For a very long time I've written nothing in a notebook about what has been happening to me or my thinking and I feel guilty about it. Every day passes without a record of growth or regression and I fear so many times that I am making no progress, just plodding along, quite content mostly, running around having fun with people and Maurice, so it seems on the surface. But in my heart I am not satisfied. I keep making the same old mistakes over and over again, feeling the same anger and niggling guilt because I'm not writing, blaming other people for what is really my own lack of will, or deficiency.

October 26, 1970
Mother cried when she went to bed, said she prays every night that she won't wake up in the morning and she wants her own—not strangers—to look after her in her old age.

October 28, 1970
M came for dinner and after we corrected typescript of my book. He can't imagine who would buy it and I'm beginning to wonder too, though there are some well-written parts.

January 15, 1971[3]
Sixty-five—now I am a Senior Citizen—a little old lady on Old Age Pension. Fearful thought. Incredible! I don't like it, or feel it, but I think there might be a psychological reaction.

February 28, 1971
Woke at four. Got up and actually got four pages typed ... brought in my mail. McClelland and Stewart letter re: book. Needs more characterization and structural changes. Damn it—discouraging.

July 27, 1971[4]
A beautiful sunny morning and I am awake to the horrible knowledge that I am an absolute *fake*. I've at times known this before, but today the fact seems to be hitting me from every angle, in every aspect. I am essentially *bone lazy*. I will do anything, anything to avoid working. I almost said sitting down and working, but there is nothing I do more easily than sit down. So why not work? I sit and read, knit, mend, talk, sit, and do anything but work. If I am averse to sitting at my typewriter, when I am not really comfortable unless I am absorbed, don't notice being uncomfortable, why don't I just sit with paper and pencil in my hand and work anywhere? Put thoughts down on paper, instead of reading bits and pieces of whatever I can lay my hands on? What am I hoping to find in my reading? A new way to write, a new way to live? Facts about the world that I should know, or be branded as ignorant? I must read all the damn magazines that I subscribe to. Why? They begin to clutter up the place and I must read them, then stack them neatly away, and maybe eventually get rid of them. I have time to read few books because I must read my magazines and I deplore not reading books. I love reading books. How absurd can I become? It seems that I make my entire life a vast contradiction and *failure*. Why don't I get wise to myself, stop fooling and wasting? Why? If I really worked hard and steadily, ceaselessly, I would have confidence. I would have the thrill of achievement and the feeling that I have a right to say something, to be listened to. As I am now, I cannot legitimately criticize anyone because my own life is a sham. I appear to be successful. I live well on K's money. I rarely turn out a bit of writing and get myself a bit of praise and recognition, a cookbook, a few magazines articles, and I *call myself a writer*.

I do anything I can to avoid writing. I putter, I tidy my house, I talk on the phone, I make lists, I think of things I must do. But I don't always do them. Now and then I entertain friends, but not as often as I should or would like to, because I am nursing my guilt over not writing. God, I'm insufferable. I don't deserve the good life I have here in this beautiful place. I make up excuses. I blame Mother, Maurice, the weather, everyone, everything, because I don't get any work done. It's always someone else's fault, though I know it's only my own. This morning I hate myself. I criticize Nancy and Jimmie.[5] What are they doing? What are they contributing? They read, they travel, they talk, but to support their reading and talking they are now working in factories every night from nine to six and slugging it out all through the summer. They are earning the money to support the way of life they have momentarily chosen. I tell myself they are not producing, no art, no literature, everything goes in. I see in them my own image and it makes me feel more and more guilty.

Apparently I do have talent, at least some limited ability to put words on paper in a readable way. But so little, so rarely. Between bouts of work I worry that my talent is lost through neglect. I'm sure my mind becomes fuzzy, stale, and stagnant. As I grow older, I am less *aware*, less delighted, less absorbed, and enthusiastic. In a terrible way I am slowly dying. I am becoming *less*, taking in less, giving out less. I am not learning, and if I am not learning I am not living. Only as I learn and record what I learn, and give out what I learn, do I *live*.

September 27, 1971[6]
Margaret Laurence said when I visited her that we are trying in our writing to do the impossible, maybe that's why we try. We enjoy the challenge. She said no one can put a person on paper, not the whole person, the real person. No one can put a bird on paper. I said what we put down can be made real only by the imagination of the person who reads it. When I read Marg's book *The Fire-Dwellers*, I immediately thought of Kate Reid as the woman, and all through the book I pictured Kate Reid in the part.[7] It seems that always the transition from the unknown to the known must be made. It must always seem Real, because the writer in his imagination can make that leap. He must strive to give enough and be clear enough to give his reader enough to recreate the Reality.

I find it difficult to describe the appearance of people. I could use all the stock phrases, descriptions, but they don't give the essence of a person. What I'd say about one person could be said so glibly of another who might actually be quite different.

September 28, 1971
A letter from my editor telling me there will be a section of illustrations in my book with elements from them as chapter headings—very attractive, and expensive no doubt.

October 30, 1971
Beta Sigma Phi girls came for tea, only thirteen came instead of the twenty-five I expected—nice young (in thirties) women, all very proper and dressed up—one in white kid gloves. They brought sandwiches and I did the rest. And why? So they could sit and "gab." Not very interesting really. And I was so tired after I just sat here in my chair and fell asleep. No Hallowe'ening tho' I was decorated for it.

November 1, 1971
The book won't be out now till March—they hope. Jack is taking great pains to make it a very special book. They want me to write a dedication, title, and chapter headings.

November 16, 1971
Dinner at night with CFUW Exec [Canadian Federation of University Women] for Jack McClelland who spoke to a good crowd at the K[itchener] Library on the Committee for an Independent Canada.[8] Frightening. Had drink with Jack after and talked about book. He hopes to make mine attractive as a gift book that may sell for many years. I hope so for his sake almost more than my own. I'm so pleased to see it in print, that is enough for me—if it sells well, I'll be surprised and pleased.

December 20, 1971
Toronto all day at M&S going thro' drawings with Jennifer [Glossop] to use for chapter headings. Tried to persuade Jack to change title to *Stranger in Harbour,* but no luck.

December 23, 1971
Phoned in copy for book jacket—the end of NH [Neil's Harbour] writing—God help it.

March 8, 1972[9]
Mother died today—at two PM. We were there, she just breathed and slipped away—as she always said she wanted to. "I'd like to go to sleep and just not wake up," she'd often say.

March 10, 1972
Cleaned out mother's dresser drawers today and cried when I remembered that I was the last one to put on her glasses and take them off her—the last person she saw and spoke to, as I was with Daddy—forty years ago.

March 18, 1972
My *Schmecks* fan Elizabeth Wilmot was coming from Toronto and wanted to come out to see me. I met her at the mail box, she's very nice—thirty-ish and anxious to do a book on railway stations she has been photographing all over the countryside.[10] She seemed glad for the advice—hope it helps.

April 8, 1972
My books came today—great excitement for me. Beautiful cover, but I'm not happy about the inside drawings, printed in brown. The chapter heading sketches, tho' lovely, have heavy, oddly-shaped frames around them which detract. But it's wonderful to have Neil's Harbour in a book.

May 4, 1972
Picked up at four to have my picture taken for book review done by Jean Johnston.[11] She called to say she thinks it's a classic, really wonderful. But it wouldn't do for her to say so in the paper??? She said it was magnificent.... Hurray.

May 11, 1972
On my way in to my party yesterday there was a letter from Marge Fowler enclosing a long review of my book that had been in the Halifax *Chronicle* and other N.S. [Nova Scotia] papers—a nasty mean snide review by Lorna Inness—deploring the fact that another person from Upper Canada had described the Maritimes as it used to be, not as it is now with TV and cars and villages with business and artists, etc., standardized, stereotyped, typical—no credit at all for a sincerely loving book about interesting individuals.[12] I'm furious and would like to write a nasty letter back to the editors of the papers. The N.S. gov't spends millions trying to attract tourists but if any of them dares to write about the joy he (or she) has found there, he is given the axe.

May 30, 1972
Beautiful review in *Quill* done by Helen Hutchison—she says CBH is beautifully written and a very good book and E.S. is warm, loveable, unobtrusive, and a lady.[13]

July 12, 1972
I'm horribly disgusted with myself, bone lazy, accomplishing nothing. No work of any kind—hate myself. Feel miserable—then why in hell don't I *do* something?

July 31, 1972
M not happy about me having Kath here this summer, he feels deprived.[16] I feel so sorry for him, he's slipping and he knows it and is desperate and negative about everything and everybody and very bad to be with and to combat. Tries to force things and I can't let him do it or I'm smothered. I feel guilty, selfish. I'm just not capable of devoting my life to a man as a man wants. If I don't give in and do everything M's way and with him, he feels hurt. I feel guilty, but resentful. I want my cake and to eat it too—can't be done. There is no fifty-fifty relationship—it's got to be willingness to go 100 percent of the way or nothing and I'm too selfish to do that.

August 12, 1972
Gerry N[oonan]'s review of CBH is in the July/Aug. issue of *Canadian Forum*—a full page.[15] He's pleased and so am I. He thinks the book should win the Gov. General's award but there is no category for it. Nice of him to think so.

August 22, 1972
Anna Porter from M&S called me yesterday AM and asked me if, for 6 or $7000, I'd rewrite a book on ethnic groups in Canada that was written in '67 for the Dep't of the Sec[retary] of State and is very dull reading. It's a reference book, four hundred pages long. It seems the answer to my current problem—immediate, hard, concentrated work on a book that is well worth doing and would be widely distributed by the gov't to schools, libraries, and all gov't dep'ts here and abroad. It is a reference book. Anna says it is boring and could be much better done by me and they have no alternative in mind if I don't do it.

September 8, 1972
If I did the ethnic group book I'd want to meet people from each group, forty-eight groups, and that would mean a month's work in each one, likely, four years and the writing, etc. If I simply edited the present book it would be a chore. The typing alone would take me a month and I'd merely be rewriting someone else's work, not improving it much, really. And for what? 6–$7000, my name in the public and someone else would have done all the work really, a hack (book) job. But an important book and one that is needed and should be done well and I could do it now, no delays—a needed, important book, and if I don't do it, what will I do?

November 13, 1972
Spoke to Gerry Noonan's creative writing class at WLU—more sociological than craft, but enjoyable and challenging. Had lunch with Gerry and Dr. Roy and a man who teaches film making.[16] Went to Coles bookstore and found CBH tucked away on book shelf while locally printed books had the most prominent spot at the front of the store. I nastily objected, then felt horribly ashamed.

November 25, 1972
Spoke to Gerry Noonan's creative writing class from 1:00 to 4:00. I find this very stimulating, because I got so much attention, no doubt, and it makes me feel knowledgeable and important—false premise and often I think of all sorts of things I should have told and some I shouldn't. Good, attentive group—asked many questions.

January 6, 1973
I am happy sitting here writing. I must never stop writing. I've done none, none, for a very long time. And I hate myself for not doing it. It is a sort of denial of life, as if nothing is important enough, or exciting or interesting or beautiful enough, to be recorded.

Every day, every minute should have something in it that should be written down. To keep it alive, to give it survival, eternity. If only I could write in the dark when so many thoughts come that are dispelled if a light is turned on.

April 28, 1973
Drafted a letter to McGraw-Hill about my contract—it's bugging me, yet why should I care? I have enough money. I won't make a fortune anyway, so why not forget it, admit defeat, and get on with something else?

May 6, 1973
Can't sleep—should get up and work on that income tax muddle that has
been plaguing me for months, weeks, and constantly during the past
few days when I've actually been working hard to solve its mysteries.
I hate involving myself with money. It seems so grating, digits and digits, paper work and scheming. But I suppose it is necessary if one wants
to be free from the worry of *not* having it, or enough of it.

All the fuss about my McGraw-Hill contract. I'm glad I wrote and
told them how I felt about that, even though they've answered only
with a phone call to my lawyer, conceding my request to have their foreign rights rescinded, but not giving me what I really want, a regular 10-
15 percent royalty on *Schmecks* sold by McGraw-Hill International. I
must make that contract myself if I can. I wonder if an approach through
Victor de Kayserling, the promotion director who seems human and
interesting, [might help]. I think I should write to him and ask him to
intercede for me if he can.

July 13, 1973[17]
Drove to M & S, saw David Scollard, ex-managing editor. Told him my
grievances about getting no promotion for CBH. He made notes. Said
he'd tell Jack, and at 12:20 said good-bye to me. And I went out without being offered lunch or a cup of coffee. To hell with them. I feel
slighted and rejected. Only one answer—get to work and write something better for somebody else. Now I have infinite opportunities.

September 26, 1973[18]
Every morning when I waken I should write. I could do a good two or
three hours work before the rest of the world gets on the telephone to
interrupt me, instead of lying here in bed muddling in my mind so, set-
ting the pattern for the day's thinking. I could accomplish something
that might make me feel virtuous at least, and maybe wonderful.

But what? I must get a start, any old start, that is the truth. I want
that start to be magnificent, immortal. I don't want to write just any old
thing that I know I'll have to do over again and again.

But why not? Isn't that what I've always done, over and over again,
till eventually I give it up as the best I can do? And what more can I
do? Not magnificent, not immortal, since I'm not, but the best I can do.

How do I write conversation that sounds real? Because it is real.

When I am with people who have a different way of speaking English than my own way, I am often delighted by the unusual inflection,

the turn of phrase, the similes, the strange metaphors. I listen intently. As soon as I can unobtrusively do it I make notes, trying to reproduce the sounds I have heard. An inflection baffles me. How can one write the rise of a person's voice at the end of a sentence? The rhythm of a person's speech, the rise and fall of the voice? How can that be suggested? I don't know. I can easily record the dropping of *g* at the end of words, the grammatical quirks, the addition of *h*'s at the beginning of words or their obliteration. A *ch* sound instead of a *j*. Vowel sounds are often hard to capture. *Ou* might become *ow* to [illegible].

The resultant misspelling of words to recapture sounds might be confusing or annoying to the reader so it must not be overdone, used only occasionally to suggest that it is constant.

The writing of dialect for me is painstaking. I watch every word and every person who utters that word because everyone might have a slightly different way of speaking, a different vocabulary. Speaking is an individual thing. To reproduce it requires the most careful listening, not once but many times till one *knows* a person so well that one can become that person in reproducing what that person says, or might say. It must be so consistent with the character and personality that the person himself in reading it would have no quarrel with it, even though the reproduction might not be the actual words that were spoken, might be created by the author long after the actual or supposed conversation took place.

When I write the words of an old fisherman whom I've listened to many times, I see him in my mind, and in my mind I hear his voice. I know what he would say, how he'd say it, quite a different way, perhaps, from another old fisherman of a different temperament.

November 24, 1973[19]
Found Margaret Laurence's and had very good conversation and casserole in the house she is renting from an Indian professor—478 Regent St. Took her a bottle of Scotch, at her request, and she drank one-third of it, [of] almost 40 oz.—too bad. She told me about her new novel and read a bit to me, it sounds beautiful, over four hundred pages. She's slightly into Women's Lib—we are sisters. She's a wonderful woman and says this is her last novel.

November 25, 1973
Margaret slept till noon. I crocheted and left at three and drove home. She's such a super person, has many friends and is so generous and car-

ing about all of them. I worry about her drinking, but she can't do it too often or she wouldn't produce as she does. She says she's done what she had to do and now she's finished. She always knew what she had to do and did it. She told me to pray.

January 14, 1974

Happy Birthday to me [January 15]. Why do I resist birthdays? Sixty-eight is almost a venerable age, but not quite. I still don't feel old or impaired in any way. If I keep walking every day I don't even feel stiff.

But it's the downhill part of life from now on. That is rather depressing. But not yet. I'd like to feel that I could still keep on climbing. Actually, I suppose climbing is tougher. Going downhill implies lack of effort, just sliding, resignation. Maybe that wouldn't be so bad if we could accept it that way. *But not yet.*

If one believes, as people once did, and some still do, that when one dies one goes to heaven, I suppose every day that comes closer to that end would be welcomed. If we really believed that after death would be far better than life, we would surely move towards it and endure everything with equanimity because something better would soon be coming.

I wonder how many people really achieve that? I'm damn sure I'll be like Mother and resist every bit of the way because I don't want to be old and infirm. I dread it. But I don't want to worry about it yet, not yet. At the moment, I'm sixty-eight. I don't feel old. I think now that when one is eighty one might start feeling old. I hope not before that. If I can keep my teeth and my eyesight and hearing and hair and good legs and stomach, I should be all right. God help me. I'd better get busy, though, if I'm going to write many more books. I should be able to. All I have to do is sit and think and put things down. Of course, they probably wouldn't be published. Why do I *resist* writing?

January 19, 1974[20]

Read Harold [Horwood]'s book—really thoughtful and moving.[21] I wonder, is it really so marvelous or do I think so because I know Harold and read him into it? But I think I'm right. I think it's *really* good.

January 31, 1974[22]

Puttered and worked on letters all day. Cold, strong wind. Walked out for mail at five. Got letter from *Reader's Digest* telling they are still considering CBH as a possible book condensation. So excited about it that I didn't sleep till after 2:30. Must not let myself, but how?

February 7, 1974
Why do I simper and feel apologetic about *Schmecks*? Because it isn't *literature*. Who the hell am I to think I could produce *literature*? I'm too damn conceited, too snobbish, that's what's wrong with me. I want to *excel*—a helluva disease. I must stop it. I must let myself *fail*. I should try to write a *lousy* book.

February 22, 1974
Felt mostly dissatisfied with myself all day. The end of winter is always like this. I should go away at this time and I stay here thinking I'll *write*, but I don't do a damn thing but feel guilty and miserable and sorry for myself and blaming M, or me, and hating myself.

March 2, 1974
Am I a has-been, and must I face that and lie down and die or stick to my crocheting? And my notebooks? Why do I want to write another book? To keep my mind alive, that's why. What do I *want* another book to do? To give people enjoyment, make them laugh, make them feel good. To do that I must laugh at myself, as I was, as I am, as I might be. No agonizing, no taking myself so damn seriously. I'll never reach any literary heights or get any accolades. But so what? Good old *Schmecks* has probably given more people more pleasure than half the Gov. General's award winners rolled into one. And that's not all to my glory but because it is also a collection of darn good, gut-filling recipes. (199)

March 15, 1974
I must know I have it. Have what? A life. I have lived. I have seen and heard and felt and known, and not known, as everyone has. But the difference is that somehow in my bungling, faltering past, I've learned a little about recording it on paper. And if I don't use that gift, I'm a fool and I'm lost and I'm dead. I've gone beyond the Vanishing Point. Amen. Bless dear Bill Mitchell, Dr. Robins and Pierre [Berton] and Margaret Laurence and Harold Horwood, Jack McClelland ... and all the wonderful people who've come into my life to help me know that I've lived—that I *live*.
    Now come on, Cress, get going. No excuses. It's time now for *action*.

November 11, 1974[23]
Black. Woke up too early. Head full of fuzz. What can I accomplish? Why must I accomplish? Because of my deep dissatisfaction with myself,

I think accomplishment is the only thing that can give me satisfaction. Accomplishment of what? Writing, of course. But why must it be writing? I knit, I tidy my house, I write notes, I pay bills, I talk on the phone, I have the family for dinner, I speak to groups of people, I enjoy all those things. But the one thing that I can do and no one else can is the writing of things that come only from my experiences, and I'm not doing that. So I'm not doing what I should do and that makes me feel guilty and unhappy about myself.

Then why in hell don't I sit down and do it? I have time. I have comfort. I have everything I need. Then why not get at it? Why keep postponing? (207)

November 12, 1974
Decided I must not let myself stay in this slump of feeling horrible because I'm not writing. I have so much to be contented with. I must keep up my spirits with joyful thoughts, and maybe one day I might even write something. Meanwhile *don't worry*. (217)

December 31, 1974[24]
Last day of the year. A good year, fun and interesting and full of friendliness and nice people, but not productive for me. I don't feel right about it. Success has changed me. I seem to get much adulation and I bask in it and do nothing now to earn it. Resting on my laurels, they tell me, and I don't want that, but do nothing about it.

February 6, 1975
Spoke at Kitchener library today, nervous when I drove in, maybe no one would come to hear me. But they had to bring in a lot of extra chairs. Lynn Matthews gave me a wonderful, warm introduction.[25] I talked about the Peterborough conference,[26] the publishers' dilemma, books by local friends, and my own books. Read pages from CBH which they seemed to enjoy. They gave me a beautiful corsage of white and pink roses. I was truly overwhelmed.

February 17, 1975[27]
Read Peg Bracken's books today.[28] She is *so good*, but I remember despairing last time because I'd never be able to do anything as good, and of course I haven't. But her line is *hating* to cook. Mine is finding joy in it, and I mustn't forget that. Must stress the idea of love and adventure, that's why I'm writing it—to give what I feel about doing it myself. I'd

do much, much more of it if I wouldn't get so fat doing it. I'd love to cook up a storm every day and *gorge*.

March 6, 1975
In so many ways I've always been hypocritical, always pretending, scared to be honest, scared to be found out. What have I done that's so drastic? So wicked? Why should I be so guilt-ridden? Am I a monster? What am I scared people will find out about me? When did the guilt start?

Probably when I hated my baby sister because she was so pretty and got more attention than I did—having had all of it for four years before she arrived to usurp me. I remember being taught that it was wicked to hate, that terrible things would happen to people who hated. I couldn't even say I hated watermelon without being scolded for it. That's it. I was probably full of hate that I didn't dare talk about. I was a solitary child. I read a lot. I played by myself, didn't like dolls much, rather skated alone, went to the library often, stood on the sidelines when groups of kids formed or played games. Was never chosen for baseball because I always batted out and could not catch a ball. Was always given the minor role when I played dress-up dramas with Lib Ruddell and Frances Bean, who had two older sisters with beautiful clothes.[29]

Also, as I grew older I was ashamed of my parents. They weren't in society, didn't dance or play golf, or read books. I corrected their grammar. They came of local stock. Daddy's people were Mennonite pioneers. I didn't want my friends to know that. During the First World War, I suspected they were pro-German and I was scared of that too. I was thoroughly British in all my sentiments. Mother kept saying they weren't pro-German, they were simply against war, hating, and destroying. I listened to all the war propaganda and thought whatever the British did was great or inevitable.

I wanted to be British. I resented my Mennonite-German local mixed ancestry. I rejoiced when I found out that one of my great grandmothers was Irish. I spoke of it often. I almost developed an Irish accent. I loved everything Irish. Then French. Daddy's people way back came from Alsace. Aunt Rachel told us. I liked that too, tho' I know nothing of Alsace. But it was French and the French were allies of the British and romantic, marvelous, artistic, sophisticated people. As I grew older I liked to identify with them.

So, my guilt? I suppose I was always afraid I'd be found out, that my background would not be acceptable to my friends, my wasp friends, and they'd drop me, ridicule me. They were such snobs, and I was the worst snob of all because I had to work so hard at doing the right thing. I made many mistakes which humiliated me, showed my ignorance and my lack of breeding—God—*breeding*. My parents were decent, hard-working, gentle people, not ambitious beyond making a good living, which Daddy did. They were really *good* people, went to church every Sunday, but never talked about religion. They fed us well, dressed us very well. Mother loved clothes, had parties for us, gave us spending money to keep up with our friends. But wouldn't let me go to Fanny Purve's dancing class when my friends went. That was a great trial. I couldn't be one of the elite if I couldn't dance with them. I was so awkward.

My happiest times were when I was alone and reading, identifying with the heroes and heroines I read about. I loved the romantic adventure, mystery, later religion. Always purity and love and goodness. I always wanted to be *good*, not goody good, just nobly good. I never could understand kids who wanted to be bad, to do what they weren't supposed to do, that they had been told *not* to do. I was obedient. Mother made sure of that. I was scared not to be obedient. I was scolded if I didn't do the right thing at the right time. If we were bad, we were put in the kitchen pantry in the dark with the door shut, closed in there with shelves of pots and pans and I can't remember for how long, time stretched interminably when I was young. We were never beaten. Mother couldn't bear to have anyone hurt physically. Daddy spanked our bottoms if we'd been very, very bad. There was the threat of the *strap*, but I don't remember ever *getting* it. Yet I seem to recall the sight of Norm and Ruby being spanked with his bare hand and them crying, more from hurt feelings than hurt bottoms, I'm sure.

Now, what is there in all that to feel guilty about? Nothing but my reluctance to admit my non-fashionable, non-society, non-WASP background. Afraid I'd be scorned, looked down on. I'd heard my WASP friends deriding people who were Mennonite, or factory types, or whatever that was prosperous, merchandising, or professional. Daddy was brought up on a farm, then he worked in a factory, became an apprentice, and eventually a registered mechanic. He opened a little repair shop in Waterloo beside Mother's Aunt's house. He designed and made an emery grinder that sold fairly well.[30] Then he investigated the manufacturing of springs for the upholstering trade, Kitchener-Waterloo being the furniture towns of Canada. He designed a machine, devised a way of tempering springs, enamelling them, and he was in a new business and a good business. Not fabulous, but good, and he worked hard.

And his hands were dirty, black, ingrained, and Mother used to make him scrub them. She also got him to join the Kiwanis Club and he became a Mason and a Shriner and a member of the Craftsmen's Club, where he went every Saturday night to play cards, often buying us a treat of salted peanuts at Woolworth's on his way home.

Daddy never read a book—ever. He'd been given one of the Elsie books as a prize award when he went to the public school in St. Jacobs.[31] No wonder he never read a book after that, tho' I'm sure he never read that sappy thing. Even I couldn't read it and it was a girl's book.

Daddy did read the Kitchener newspapers. There were two at our time and he switched from one to the other as their policies suited him, or gave up when they offended. He also read *The Globe* and *Saturday Night*. Really read them and talked about them, and so did Mother. I think she was keener than he, always read the papers thoroughly and clipped things from them for us to read and paste in her scrap books.

March 31, 1975 [32]
I've been so low in my mind lately because I accomplish nothing, no writing, a few letters, that's all. The constant growing and self-consciousness. Read old diaries—repetition. Pretty damn stupid, and the letters I wrote are incredible. I'm sure I thought they were marvelous when I wrote them.

April 15, 1975 [33]
I've had so many marvelous experiences in my life. I'm so darn old. Surely I should be able to get them down and give them significance and colour and interest and reason for being. But why must there always be a reason? Many writers say they want only to entertain. Shouldn't that be enough? Must there always be a moral, a motive? Other writers say they write for themselves because they must. Margaret [Laurence] says she had to come to terms with her past, and I guess Alice [Munro] did too. Many writers seem to write about their childhood and youth, get it out of themselves. They come to understand themselves better by writing it out. Maybe I would. Maybe I should do that, just for me. Get it out, get it down, get rid, then read it over, and if there's anything then that might be good enough to interest anyone else, write it once, work on it, then maybe one day I'll have another book. It doesn't have to be a big book, maybe one hundred and fifty pages. But it must be a good book, well written, maybe serious, maybe fun, maybe both, as life is. And the cookbooks could be done gradually and enthusiastically as well. Maybe

then I'd have two books. Why not? People want them. I must write them. Instead of reading novels all the time and talking and boasting and pushing myself as I think I am doing now, trying to bolster myself up, make myself bigger than I am. One's potential is only revealed by one's accomplishments. Boasting about the very little that I have done isn't going to produce anything more or convince anyone that my work is any good. It is good, it isn't great, and there sure as hell isn't enough of it. (289)

June 27, 1975[34]
I'm being very quiet this morning so I won't waken George! George Dowse, a young, long-haired, black-headed stranger asleep in my guest-room bed.

He wrote me a letter perhaps two years ago telling me he had discovered *Cape Breton Harbour* in Britnell's bookstore window in Toronto and it had meant so much to him that he hoped one day he could bring it to me for an autograph.

He wrote once again after that and there was a note from him recently telling me he'd be coming soon and enclosing a few clippings of columns he had written.

His first letter somehow made me think he was an old man, living alone, but the columns he sent made me know very definitely that he was young and searching and sexy.

I didn't answer the letter. I was afraid that if I encouraged him to come here to see me, he'd be disappointed. The Edna of my Neil's Harbour book was young, perhaps twenty-five. I didn't want him to come all the way from Toronto to find an old woman. Not that I think of myself as an old woman, but I'm sure he would think so.

On Wednesday he phoned me. It was about 5:00 PM. He was in Kitchener at the bus depot. He hadn't a car but was willing to take a taxi out here to find me.

He hitchhiked and someone who knew of me brought him right to my door, a slight, long, black-bearded young man with thick, long, black hair, wearing blue and white running shoes, blue jeans, a jacket, white turtleneck jersey, carrying a camera case. As he came down the path, I could see he had finely-chiseled, beautiful, deep eyes with fine features and fair skin, all very pleasing.

And while he drank the tea and ate the biscuits I had quickly baked for him while he was finding his way here—I thought I must give him some compensation for coming so far, and a good smell in the house might make my age less intolerable—he told me he left Cape Breton fifteen years ago, had never returned, and my book had brought CB to him in such a vivid, enthusiastic way that it had in a way changed his life.

He lives alone in a one-room apartment in the heart of the city, had been driving a taxi and taking a journalism course at a community college hoping to go on to university, but was refused entrance. He had spent the past year-and-a-half in his apartment reading, reading books that he felt were important for him to read: philosophy, history, *War and Peace*, and Hemingway.[35] He is steeping in Hemingway and often quotes him, as well as many other authors he has read, but Hemingway is *the One*.

And of course he is writing, and getting rejection slips, a boxfull so far, and he's working on a book about his home town, a dying fishing village in Cape Breton. (491)

September 14, 1975
God, there's so much to do and to write and to read in this world. I need almost another life to live. I seem to want to know all of it, to experience it and love it.

March 13, 1976
My head is still stuffed with that horrid sticky stuff. I feel low. No work done all week. The feeling that it never will be done, the book never written, just limping along, piled up sheets of paper and cookbooks cluttering the room, and if the book even does go a bit by bit, it won't be any good.

Who am I kidding? Actually I've been "working" on this thing for over a year. I was copying recipes last winter. Had over 400, now I have over 600, many of them useless, nothing written about them, most of them not tested. No theme developing in my head, no characters for the book. No fun. In other words, there just isn't a book. I'm just kidding myself. And who else? Two publishers waiting for a first draft and I have nothing to show them. March 31 was my self-imposed deadline. I'm no nearer to it than I was a year ago, not really. I have *written nothing*. Typed out recipes that I've not tried, yes, but what good are they? Anyone could do that, anyone who can type. And even my typing is terrible. I'm not going to England, not going abroad this spring because I haven't reached my deadline. I don't deserve it. And time marches on.

What the hell's wrong with me?

November 15, 1979
To Halifax... to be interviewed by Lorna Inness. The only person who did a nasty review of CBH. I was apprehensive—didn't know how she'd react, but she was very friendly. Didn't mention CBH—and nor did I. Grand interview.

Notes

1 Box R2-2. Diary 1970.
2 Dorothea Brande, *Becoming a Writer* (New York: Harcourt, Brace, 1934). Later reprinted by J.P. Tarcher, 1981.
3 Box R2-2. Diary 1971.
4 Box R2-1. Diary June 7, 1964–May 21, 1973.
5 Edna's nephew Jimmie (Norma's son) and his wife, Nancy.
6 Box R2-2. Diary 1971.
7 Margaret Laurence, *The Fire-Dwellers* (Toronto: Macmillan, 1969). Kate Reid (1930–93), celebrated Canadian actor and regular member of the Stratford Festival.
8 The Canadian Federation of University Women was established in 1919. The bilingual CFUW/FCFUW is a self-funding voluntary, non-profit organization with a membership of over 10,000 women university graduates. Members are active in public affairs and seek to improve the social, economic, legal, and educational status of women.
   Founded by Walter Gordon and colleagues to promote Canadian independence, and launched on September 17, 1970, the Committee for an Independent Canada (CIC) recruited Jack McClelland and Claude Ryan as co-chairmen. By June 1971, they were able to present then prime minister Trudeau with a petition, signed by 170,000 Canadians, demanding that foreign investment and ownership in Canada be limited. With the help of local leaders, a number of CIC goals became law, such as Canadian content regulations on radio and television. The CIC was disbanded in 1981. Staebler's comment here about being "frightened" no doubt refers to her concern, shared by many Canadians at the time, of increased foreign (notably American) investments and ownerships in Canada.
9 Box R2-2. Diary 1972.
10 Wilmot did complete her book project: Elizabeth A. Wilmot, *Meet Me at the Station*. (Agincourt: Gage Publishing, 1976.)
11 Jean Johnston, "Staebler Novel Paints Earthy People," *Record* (May 6, 1972).
12 Lorna Inness, "Books, Authors," *Halifax Chronicle Herald* (May 6, 1972), 42. Staebler took as a harsh criticism Inness's comment, or rather caution, that readers not take the portrait of the Neil's Harbour Staebler knew in the 1940s as representative of the harbour and its residents in the 1970s.
13 Helen Hutchison, "New Paperbacks," *Quill & Quire* 28, 4 (April 1972).

14 Kathy Reeves, a friend from England who came to stay with Edna each summer. Her husband, Bill Reeves, had been stationed in Goderich during the war
and, like other men in the service, had been a guest of the Staeblers.

15 Gerald Noonan (1932–2000), professor of English at Wilfrid Laurier University and a devoted friend to Edna. See her entry February 7, 2000, for her
reflection on their friendship. "Cape Breton Harbour," *Canadian Forum* vol. 51
(July/August 1972): 43.

16 Flora Roy, Noonan's colleague and long-time chair of the Department of English at Wilfrid Laurier University (1948–78).

17 Box R2-2. Diary 1973.

18 Box R3-3. Diary December 28, 1973–76.

19 Box R2-2. Diary 1973.

20 Box R2-2. Diary 1974.

21 Possibly Horwood's second novel, *White Eskimo: A Novel of Labrador*, published in 1972, or his first novel, *Tomorrow Will Be Sunday*, published in 1966.

22 Box R2-2. Diary 1974.

23 Box R3-3. Diary December 28, 1973–76.

24 Box R2-2. Diary 1974.

25 Lynn Matthews, chief librarian at Kitchener Public Library from 1971–93.

26 A conference on the "State of English Language Publishing in Canada" was
hosted by Trent University in Peterborough, January 24–25, 1975. Publishers,
librarians, teachers, and writers, including Margaret Laurence and Edna
Staebler, attended. Hugh Faulkner, then secretary of state, addressed the
conference, which led to the foundation of the Canadian Book and Periodi-
cal Development Council.

27 Box R2-2. Diary 1975.

28 Author of *I Hate to Cook Book* (New York: Harcourt Brace, 1960) and *The Complete I Hate to Cook Book*.

29 Lib Ruddell, childhood friend. As mentioned in chapter 3 (notes), Ruddell,
who had married Gerry Eastman, had an affair with Keith while Eastman was
at war. Frances Bean was another friend from childhood; she married Fred
Breithaupt.

30 Emery is a coarse material used for polishing metal.

31 The "Elsie [Dinsmore] books" were by American writer Martha Findley
[pseudonym Martha Farquharson] (1828–1909). The twenty-eight-volume
series featured a God-honouring young girl named Elsie who approaches life
and its problems with a passionate love for God.

32 Box R2-2. Diary 1975.

33 Box R3-3. Diary December 28, 1973–76.

34 Box R3-3. Diary December 28, 1973–76.

35 *War and Peace* by the Russian novelist Leo Tolstoy (1828–1910). Ernest Hemingway (1899–1961), American short-story writer and novelist whose more
famous works include *The Sun Also Rises* (1926), *A Farewell to Arms* (1929), *For
Whom the Bell Tolls* (1940), and *The Old Man and the Sea* (1952).

9

"Cape Breton Harbour"
1972

The opening chapter of Cape Breton Harbour *provides a sense of Edna's creative non-fiction writing style. Readers will recognize whole passages from her previously published* Maclean's *article, "Duellists of the Deep" (1948), reframed by the more immediate, personal, even emotional first-person narrative voice that Edna adopted in her creative non-fiction account of summers spent in Neil's Harbour. The book has stood up well to the test of time and remains an engaging portrait of 1940s Cape Breton.*

∽

Stranded

Thursday, August 9

Now I'm really shaken. I've let myself be abandoned in the bleakest little fishing village on the north coast of Cape Breton Island.

I don't even know the name of the place; until an hour ago I didn't know it existed. I can't find it on the map of Nova Scotia, the tourist guidebooks don't mention it, there are no signs on the road pointing the way to it. It simply appeared on a sudden bend of the coast after we had been driving through forest from Ingonish, the spectacular village twelve miles south of this one on the Cabot Trail.

"Dramatic!" I exclaimed at first sight of the lonely clearing, "A stage set for Peter Grimes!" Kay muttered, "A desolate dump." Shirley suggested running in to look for souvenirs.

We turned off the dusty trail to a narrower road kept from the rim of a precipice by a snake fence. Across a bay on a rocky point the white sides of a red-capped lighthouse were outlined by the blue sky. Far below us a strip of beach separated the dark water of a pond from the shimmering silver of the North Atlantic. On our left a scattering of bare-faced wooden houses staggered up a hill that hadn't a tree. Straight ahead, against a background of ocean, a mass of fishing shacks clustered round a couple of jetties along a stony shore. Bleached, windswept, barren, the village was almost surrounded by the sea.

We stopped at a tiny store where Kay and Shirley thought they might be able to buy long-visored swordfishing caps as mementos of our trip. Glad to be left alone I stayed in the car and brooded. I had been arguing with my companions. We left Halifax two days ago to spend a couple of weeks in Cape Breton but because the popular, posh Keltic Lodge at Ingonish couldn't give us accommodation we were rushing back to the city. And I didn't want to go back.

Kay and Shirley live in Halifax, only 300 miles away, and could return to Cape Breton quite easily. I had come 1,300 miles by train from Ontario for a holiday by the ocean, and I resented giving it up because I couldn't have a room with a bath. All my life far inland I'd longed to visit a rocky coast, to watch towering waves, to hear them roar; Ingonish is majestic, the swordfishing no doubt exciting: I wanted to stay there, to exult in the sea and the mountains, to talk to the natives, to go out in a boat and catch fish.

Suddenly, far from the shore beside me and silhouetted by glitter, I noticed a little boat with a figure at the top of her mast. A man ran out to the end of her bowsprit; for a moment he was suspended, he lunged forward from the waist with an arm extended, poised, recovered, then darted back to obscurity in the hull while the figure on the mast dropped to the deck. The men had speared a swordfish!

Immediately I knew what I would do. I dashed out of the car and ran to the store. In its dim light I could see Kay and Shirley trying on caps. Behind a cluttered counter was a big-boned woman with a sharp nose. I asked her, "Do the men here go swordfishing?"

"Yes, miss, all but the old ones that go out for cod and them that don't fish, like my man and the preacher and..."

"How do you get out of the village if you haven't a car?"

Her nose went up and she looked at me over it. "We has got a car! Only three people here got one, the doctor and us and Gladdie Buchanan. I won't take the bus, 'tain't fit to drive in..."

"There's a bus?" I was gleeful. "Where does it go?"

"To Sydney. In winter it don't run at all and you can't get out by sea neither, the drift ice comes in an'…"

"Is there any place here to stay?"

She looked surprised. "You mean overnight?"

"A week or two."

I heard Shirley gasp. The woman turned from me. "I won't take you. I got nothin' against you but I always say it's chancey takin' strangers."

"Is there no tourist accommodation?" I persisted.

"Mrs. Pride's got a cabin but it's full for the night. Laurie Malcolm sometimes takes a boarder but she couldn't take all of you."

"We don't want to stay," Kay almost shouted.

"It's a good place, there's plummin' and only four here got that."

"Where does Laurie Malcolm live?" I asked.

"With her mother and sister. Her and Katie is old maids, held their noses too high, fishermen was scared to go after 'em."

"Which is their house?"

"White one right behind this, the way you come in."

"Thanks." I turned to the girls, "Won't you stay?"

"Lord no, not in a fishing village!" Kay seemed outraged.

"It's not beautiful like Ingonish but I'm going to try it."

"You can't stay here alone," Shirley objected. "What will your sister say if we don't bring you back to Halifax?"

"Let her stay if she wants to," Kay was annoyed. "We're not her keepers."

The woman leaned over the counter. "She'll soon leave," she said confidently, "there's nothing for her to do."

"I'll find something," I answered and made a dignified exit.

The Malcolms' house had sharp angles, a gable running from front to back and a lower gable going into the big one from the side. I opened the gate of the picket fence, startling a flock of chickens in the yard as I ran up a path to a narrow verandah that crossed the front of the house.

My knock was answered by a faded grey woman, about sixty, who looked so prim that I wished I'd worn a skirt instead of shorts. When I told her what I wanted she asked no questions, she simply said, "I'll take you."

I ran to the car and joyfully announced that I was staying. Neither Kay nor Shirley said a word. I opened the door of the back seat and dragged out my luggage. "Thanks for taking me with you, and please tell my sister I'll write." The girls didn't answer; their profiles were as fixed as those of sovereigns on a coin. Standing in the ditch beside them I felt like a mendicant.

Kay's arm moved. The car shot forward. Its wheels spat dust. I was left at the side of the road alone.

As I watched the car disappear, I said to myself, "Good riddance. I'll have a wonderful time here. I'll go swordfishing and swimming and dancing, I'll ..." I glanced at the lonely village; there wasn't a person in sight.

Slowly I gathered up my belongings and carried them to the white house. This time a different woman came to the door; she looked a bit younger, had greying red hair and black eyes that flashed. "I suppose I'll have to let you in," she said, opening the screen, "my sister Laurie never turns anyone away. I wouldn't have taken you, it's too much extra work," she grumbled as she led me upstairs to a little room almost cut in half by a sloping ceiling. Pointing to an oak wash-stand holding a large pitcher and basin, she said, "You won't need that, the bathroom is down the hall. The pump isn't working because the water in the well is too low so you can't use the tub; if you want a bath you'll have to tell us and we'll give you a pail. And another thing" she lowered her voice, "we don't flush the toilet unless it's absolutely necessary; for the sink we take a dipperful of water from a bucket on the floor."

"I won't waste any," I promised, "I'll bathe when I go swimming."

"Swimming?" She looked startled. "This is not a tourist resort; we don't care to see people expose themselves."

"I'll wear my beach coat."

She glanced sharply at my legs. "I hope it covers you," she snapped and bustled down the stairs.

Now I suppose I should go out and explore the village. But why? I can see all of it from where I'm sitting on the iron bed by the window. There's nothing but the lighthouse, sea and rock, the dirt road, faded houses, fishing shacks, and scorched grass. All I can hear is the surf, a cow bell, and the clucking of the hens in the yard.

I certainly won't stay here a week; I won't even unpack my bags. The red Malcolm woman is hostile, the fishermen might be filthy old men and I wouldn't be safe in their boats, the glitter on the sea is menacing; it makes me feel as the Ancient Mariner did after he shot the albatross. I hate it and I want to go home. My family doesn't even know I've left Halifax where I was spending the summer with my married sister; if anything happens to them or to me I couldn't be found way up here on the edge of the world. I'm lost!

I ran down the stairs, knocked on a door where I heard voices, and went into the kitchen; a very old woman was sitting on a rocker by a black cookstove at which the thin grey woman who said I could stay here was stirring something in an iron pot. "May I make a collect phone call, please?" I asked. "I want to talk to my mother." The old woman didn't even turn to look at me; the other one said, "We don't have the phone."

"Could I use the one at the store?"

"There is none; there's no telephone line on Cape Breton's north coast."

No phone! No communication! I'm trapped in a vacuum!

Stunned, I climbed up the stairs to my room and wrote a letter telling my family I'll be leaving wherever I am in the morning; I forgot to ask the name of the village, the postmark will have to tell it.

I should never have left Halifax, but throughout my summer-long vacation there I'd had no more than a glimpse of the sea beyond the grey city harbour. When an acquaintance of my sister mentioned two girls she knew who were going to Cape Breton and wanted a third to share their expenses, I leapt at the chance. I was so anxious to stay on the coast of the wild North Atlantic, to go round the remote Cabot Trail, that I'd have travelled with chimpanzees—and probably been less irritated by their chattering than by the prattle of my erstwhile companions about golf and their chances of meeting a millionaire at Keltic Lodge.

I wonder what kind of story they'll tell my sister. I'd better write her. But why bother? I'll be in Halifax before a letter could reach her.

Dammit. Instead of going back comfortably by car—as I might have with Kay and Shirley—I'll have to take the rickety old bus over the road I've already seen. I'll miss the most scenic part of the Trail over the mountains. I wonder if I could get out of here by boat? I'm so mad and muddled and scared I don't know what to do.

One thing I am sure of. I'll never leave home to go adventuring again. This is the first time and the last. From now on I'll stay with my family and do all the things they want me to do: play bridge and golf, go to cocktail parties and teas, to beauty parlours and boutiques. I might even marry George.

But now I am being silly. I'm safe here with these spinsters and I have enough money to get home. I'll just have to pull myself out of this slump and accept whatever I'm in for.

I got out the copy of Tolstoi's [*sic*] *War and Peace* that increased the weight of my luggage by two pounds. "Well, Prince, so Genoa and Lucca are now just estates of the Bonapart family," I started. I stopped half way down the page and started again. How could a Russian soiree have interest for an outcast in a desolate fishing village? I tried a third time and read a bit farther. Then lulled by the sound of the surf and a cowbell, I slept till they called me for supper.

In a small room with a round stove and a corner cupboard, the two women, listening to the news on a battery radio, sat silently at either end of a table; my chair faced the doorway to the kitchen where the old woman was eating alone. "Mother hasn't eaten in the dining room since father died," Miss Laurie, the grey one, told me. "We always have dinner at noon but we thought you might like Neil's Harbour fish for your first meal here."

I was hungry but when they served me oily black-skinned fried mackerel, warmed-over turnip and spongey grey boiled potatoes of last year's growth, I could hardly swallow.

"Why don't you eat?" Katie, the younger one, asked me when the newscast was over and her own plate was empty.

"I'm sorry but I—I can't."

"Oh?" Miss Laurie sounded concerned.

Katie was huffy. "Don't you like fish? You'll have to eat it if you're going to stay in Neil's Harbour. We don't have much else."

I couldn't hurt their feelings by telling the truth. I said, "I like fish, but I—I think I'm homesick."

"Are you going to cry, dear?" Miss Laurie looked anxious.

"Oh no, I wouldn't do that."

"Then you're not homesick," she smiled. "You'll be all right soon."

It was a good thought; I enjoyed the steamed pudding that followed. Katie gave me a second helping and told me to go to the wharf where tourists like to watch the boats come in from fishing.

I walked down the road towards the lighthouse. Past the silver shingle shacks (the women called them stages) was a wooden wharf where the rear ends and bare feet of children were more prominent than their heads as they leaned over the edge, and a wispy little grey-haired man was piling up wooden boxes. "Good evening," he said to me, "you just come?"

"This afternoon."

"Never seen you round nowhere."

"I was in my room."

He smiled eagerly, "You stayin' fer a spell?"

"No, I'll be leaving on the bus tomorrow. I'd rather get out by boat, does anything from here go to the St. Lawrence?"

"No, *Aspy* goes the other way."

"What's *Aspy*?"

"You don't know the *Aspy*?" He looked at me in amazement as I shook my head. "She's very himportant vessel, freight and passenger steamer comes up from Sydney on Tuesday and Friday with everything we needs. Goes back Wednesday and Saturday."

"Then I'd have to wait two days."

"You in a hurry?" he drawled. "Could go to North Sydney on fish boat, comes every day to fetch fish; she ain't a passenger boat, smells awful of fish, but she takes folks onto 'er that wants a ride bad."

"That would be perfect. When does she come in?"

"Any time now, you can speak to her skipper."

"Cheers!" I said to myself, "I'll be travelling on the ocean, I'll see the coast from a boat; that is far better than going tamely over the rest of the Trail in a car. It will be an adventure!"

I looked around. Entering the bay was a vessel with a sailless mast and a bowsprit like a diving board with a metal sort of pulpit on the end of it.

"Here comes the *'lizabeth*," someone shouted. "Gotta fish."

By the time the boat reached the dock there were perhaps twenty children, three dogs, and ten men chattering excitedly in a dialect I could not understand and presumed must be Gaelic since Cape Breton was settled by Scots. The children, tanned scalps showing through sun-bleached hair, were dynamos in well-washed jeans or calico dresses; the dogs were shaggy Newfoundlanders; the ruddy-faced men, like broad-billed birds in khaki caps with visors six inches long, wore rubber boots, thick trousers, and flannel shirts; shyly conscious of the presence of a stranger, they turned away when their curious glances met mine.

As the *Elizabeth* scraped gently alongside, a rope through a pulley on a post at the end of the dock was tossed to the men aboard. They did something with it that I couldn't see, then three men on the wharf heaved ho. A monster was stretched from the deck to the top of the fifteen-foot pole! I was seeing my first swordfish. It was stupendous! The body was round; the skin dark purple-grey, rough one way, smooth the other like a cat's tongue; the horny black fins stood out like scimitars, the tail like the handlebars of a giant bicycle; but the strangest thing was the broad, pointed, sharp-sided sword, an extension of the head, an upper bill three feet long! As the rope was slowly released, the men guided the creature down to the dock where it lay like a rolled-up rug.

A little boy knelt near the head; with a hook he ripped open the glazed membrane of the huge round eye that was uppermost. Out of the cavity ran clear, slurpy liquid. The child put his hand into the socket, pulled something out of it then looked up at me. "Want heyeball?" he asked, thrusting his fist towards me.

Ughghghghghghghghghghgh! I couldn't touch the fishy thing. Everybody was watching. What would I do? "Let me look at it," I hedged. He opened his hand and I saw a perfect sphere, clear as glass, about an inch and a quarter in diameter, reflecting colours like a bubble.

"Take en," he said.

I still hesitated, "I haven't any money with me."

The child shook his head, "Don't need money."

"You mean it's a present?"

He grinned shyly and nodded. I couldn't spurn a gift. I held out my hand. The boy placed the crystal gently on my palm. It felt cool and tender as a piece of firm jelly or a gumdrop that's had the sugar licked off it. "What should I do with it?" I asked.

"Take en home and put in sun and it'll turn roight hard," someone answered. "Be careful not to break en." I held my treasure reverently; it didn't even smell like fish!

Another boy cut out the bloody eye socket, looked inquiringly at me, then grinned and tossed it into the water.

"How much would the fish weigh?" I asked anyone who could hear me.

"Ower six hundred pound, I reckon," a blue-eyed fisherman answered. "He's some beeg."

"What does it taste like?"

"Don't know, never et 'em, we just ketches 'em and sells 'em for folks down in States," he said. "Don't fancy to try none o' the big ugly things meself but some round 'ere cut off a bit near the haid and taked it home and cooked it; they say hit's got a roight noice flavour to it, loike pork, not strong atall. Americans must loike'm or they wouldn't pay so much for 'em. We's gettin' thirty-two cents a pound today."

I did some mental arithmetic. "No wonder you're so happy to catch one."

He grinned. "We be, but they's awful scarce." With a saw in his hand he knelt beside the fish. "Want sword?" he asked me.

"Oh yes. Don't you need it?"

He laughed. "We just throws 'em overboard."

The rough grey sword was heavy and felt like bone. The cut end showed bloody marrow that exuded fishiness. How popular I'd be with it on a train in a day or two! A fisherman saw me sniffing. "Stick in ant heap and ants'll clean en out for you," he offered.

"How long will it take?"

"About six weeks."

The man next sawed off the head, then the fins, the broad black tail and the fan-shaped crimson gill plates; as each piece came off the young-sters threw it into the water where flashing white birds darted at it before it sank to the shadowy creatures hovering in beds of waving kelp. With a knife the underbody of the fish was ripped open. I wanted to yell, "Let me out of here, quick," but the faces all round me were bland as blancmange. I couldn't insult them by running away, so I stayed where I was and watched all the stuffing being pulled out of that huge cavity: like a gourmet in a nightmare I saw long white links of sausage, steamed puddings, buckshot, sets of false teeth, lumps of pink lard, clots of black jelly, and bright red claret splashing over everything—includ-ing my legs.

The carcass, washed with salt water pumped up by a gasoline engine, was hoisted on a carrier and taken by four men to the scales. Everyone gathered round to learn the score—six hundred and eleven pounds, marked with indelible pencil near the tail and on a bill which would be paid to the owner of the boat on Saturday night.

The *Elizabeth* having moved to her mooring, another boat landed a fish. One by one the lucky boats came to the end of the dock; the others went straight to the anchorage, the men coming ashore in dories that had been fastened to buoys in the water. Twenty boats had gone fishing, five swordfish had been caught, acclaimed, and lowered by tackle into the icy hold of the fish boat that had come alongside.

When I spoke to the skipper about giving me a ride he said I was welcome to leave with him when he comes back at three o'clock tomor-row afternoon. I thanked him and said I'd be ready. But almost as soon as I said it I wasn't sure that I wanted to go. Swordfishing was exciting, the fishermen were interesting, the children were captivating. I was enjoying myself!

A group of little boys leaned over the side of the wharf trying to catch small black fish with a line and bare hook; others darted here and there with swordfish tails and guts before they tossed them overboard. A tow-headed, tiny little girl, her white dress dotted with fish blood, got into everyone's way. The only child I heard being scolded was a boy with the face of a cherub and a mass of golden ringlets falling over his ears. Another boy, perhaps twelve, smiled every time I looked his way but when I spoke to him he jumped over the side of a boat, hid behind the cabin and peeked at me with one eye. A plain little girl they called Martha held an eyeball carefully in a bit of cloth. "Why do you put it in a cloth?" I asked her, afraid I might be ruining my prize by holding it on my bare palm. Martha hung her head, hunched her shoulders and turned away.

A plump teenaged girl in a jumper smiled at me then came close and said in a whisper, "Don't they talk funny here?"

"Are you a stranger too?" I asked her.

"From Louisburg. It has swordfishing but it ain't like this place, it's historical," she said proudly, "got an old French fort that tourists come for. I been staying here at my aunt's a couple of weeks, having a right good time; the fellows are keen," she grinned. "What are you doing tonight?"

"I don't know, what is there to do?"

"Nothing, just walk up and down the road. Come with me if you ..." she stopped herself, "if I don't have company." She giggled, then added vaguely as she walked towards the shore, "I might meet you somewheres along."

The excitement on the dock had died down. The fish were cleaned, the people were straggling away; the sun was slipping behind the highest hill across the bay.

I went back to my room to put on wool slacks and my Grenfell jacket, styled like an army officer's tunic; when I pull the belt tightly round my waist, my shoulders straighten and I feel brave.

As I passed through the Malcolms' kitchen on my way out of the house, the old mother noticed me for the first time. "Where are you going?" she asked.

"For a walk," I told her.

"Looks like a fine evening," she said. "I wish I could walk." She tried to rise from her rocking chair, then sank back into it with a sigh. "My legs won't let me go," she whimpered. "I've had three broken legs and no one does anything for them." She looked accusingly from one daughter to the other. "Even the doctor won't come to see my legs any more."

"It's rheumatism, Mother, there's no cure," Katie said gently. Then turning to me, "Don't pay any attention to her, she imagines things."

"I want her to know," the old woman scolded. "It is awful to be old. When I was young I loved to walk, I'd go for miles and miles along the shore and never tire. Now I can't leave this chair, I'm weak, and no one cares for me. If I were back in Newfoundland where I was born I'd be happy and still young. Now I am a stranger in a cold unfriendly land and no one comes to fetch me home."

The road that comes into Neil's Harbour from the Cabot Trail runs near the top of the cliff till it reaches a store marked Alec Maclennan's, where it branches: the right fork, slipping narrowly between the fishing stages, runs out to the lighthouse point; the other fork, after passing the Malcolms' house, angles left and runs beside the sea.

I followed the left branch. On one side boulders lay between the narrow grass strip of the roadside and the water; on the other side, beyond a few square houses and a steepled Presbyterian church, there were grassy banks and rocky slopes with spruce trees growing in the shallow earth.

As I sauntered along, people in pairs passed me and said hello. Men walking briskly alone muttered goodnight. Groups of boys sitting on the bank flattered me with wolf whistles; groups of young girls giggled and called hello—I didn't see the one from Louisburg. As I passed a tiny store perched on the sea's edge a man standing in the doorway said, "Hello dear"; realizing he meant me, I walked faster. Where the space between the road and the water grew wider there was a shingle-covered school, an Orange Lodge Hall, and a little white Anglican church; beyond them a shore of great stones made the road bend away from the sea. I didn't go farther because darkness had come.

Straight before me when I turned back towards the village, the Light at the end of the Point was glowing with a yellow flame. As I walked towards it I heard talk and soft laughter coming from the night. Dark figures approached and passed by me. Sometimes there was a chorus of whistles. Once I heard footsteps close behind me and a man's voice saying, "Come with me, dear." I didn't look around, I ran till I reached the houses near the corner. Their angles, sharp against the deep dark blue of the sky, were blacker than midnight, blacker than void. In all the village I could see only five yellow patches of light. But through the windows of the Malcolms' kitchen, a faint glow came from a lamp left half way up the stairs for me.

≈

"The Great Cookie War"
1987

The Great Cookie War involved the food giants Nabisco and Procter and Gamble, and a recipe for Rigglevake cookies included in one of Staebler's books.[1] The recipe was at the centre of the conglomerates' struggle for patent rights to a "crisp and chewy cookie" that represented millions of potential market dollars.[2] Recounted with a healthy dose of deadpan humour in an article that Staebler wrote for Saturday Night *magazine in May 1987, "The Great Cookie War" is a tale of lawyers from New York, Washington, and Ottawa, film crews from* The Fifth Estate, *and reporters from the* Wall Street Journal, *all scrambling to her cottage home at Sunfish Lake on the outskirts of Waterloo, while columnists for* Harper's *and* Forbes *magazines and radio hosts from Saskatoon to San Diego vied for interviews—everyone eager to talk to the by-then nearly eighty-year-old Staebler. CBC radio's Peter Gzowski was a fan and Staebler was a guest on his popular program,* Morningside. *Staebler's account of "The Great Cookie War" reveals her as a strong journalist even at age eighty. In trademark Staebler style, she included the story in her cookbook* Schmecks Appeal *(1987), where it makes a unique and interesting addition to the cookbook genre.*

~

MY INVOLVEMENT IN THE GREAT COOKIE WAR began on May 7, 1984, when Don Sim, a lawyer in Toronto, phoned and asked if he could come to see me. He sounded very pleasant, said he had enjoyed my magazine articles and the five books I had written, and knew several people in Kitchener-Waterloo who were my friends.

"But why do you want to see me?" I asked him. I knew I didn't owe anyone money and I was sure I hadn't done anything that would make someone send a lawyer after me.

He said it was too complicated to explain on the phone and besides he'd like to keep it as a surprise.

We arranged for him to come a week later. I gave him the rather complicated directions for finding my winterized cottage on Sunfish Lake, a small, secluded, privately owned kettle lake near the northwest corner of the city of Waterloo. The lake was left by a glacier 12,000 years ago. Surrounded by wooded hills, it lies near the Mennonite farmlands of Woolwich Township, where my Mennonite great-great-grandfather was the first permanent settler.

At nine o'clock the following Tuesday morning the lawyer knocked at my door. I opened it and saw a giant of a man, six feet five inches tall and weighing over three hundred pounds (I learned later). In awe I said, "My, you're a big man," and wondered which of my chairs would hold him. Fortunately he chose a love seat near the fireplace where he chatted amiably for half an hour about my writing, and his career in Toronto.

He told me he was the head of Sim, Hughes, a firm specializing in patent, trademark, and related legal matters. He and the other nine lawyers in his firm also have degrees in engineering or science. (Later, lawyer friends told me that the legal profession considered Don Sim the most brilliant and highly respected lawyer in his field in Canada.)

And all the time he talked I kept wondering why he was sitting in my living room.

Finally he told me. "I've come to see you about a recipe in your book with all those delicious Mennonite recipes."

Suddenly I remembered something. I said, "Is it the Rigglevake cookie recipe in *Food That Really Schmecks*?"

"How did you know?"

I told him that a year ago a lawyer representing Nabisco had called me from Connecticut to ask about the recipe. He had wanted me to phone him back when I had the answers to all his questions, but I had friends from France visiting me at the time and it wasn't convenient. He didn't call me again so I presumed it wasn't important.

"It is very important. Cookies are big business." Don Sim was emphatic. "Last year Canadians spent $400 million on cookies and in the U.S. that amount would be over $2 billion. Nabisco controls about 80 per cent of the cookie market in the world. They own Christie's, Peak Frean's, Dad's, Béton in France."

"Do you represent Nabisco?"

Don Sim threw up his hands and shook his head. "Nabisco is the enemy," he said. "My client is Procter and Gamble. They own Duncan Hines who have only recently gone into the cookie business. They started in the States and are now building a large plant in Brockville, Ontario, where they will soon be turning out a million cookies a day."

"Are they using my recipe for Rigglevake cookies?"

"No, no, not at all. For six years their food scientists worked on a formula that would make cookies that were soft inside, crisp outside, and would stay that way for months after they were packaged. To protect their product P&G patented their formula. But Nabisco and several other American companies started making similar cookies. Procter and Gamble is now suing them for infringement of their patent."

"But what has that to do with me?"

"I'll come to that. When P&G started making cookies Nabisco hired people to read thousands of cookbooks with cookie recipes to find one that had a recipe with two separate doughs, one crisp, the other chewy, and in your cookbook *Food That Really Schmecks*, on page 193, they found Rigglevake cookies."

He took a copy of *Schmecks* from his briefcase, and read: "Railroad Cookies:

Light part:	Dark part:
1 cup sugar	1 cup brown sugar
1 egg	1 cup butter
1 cup butter	1 cup molasses
1/2 cup milk	1/2 cup water
2 teaspoons baking powder	2 teaspoons soda
1/3 teaspoon vanilla	1/2 teaspoon vanilla

He looked at me. "And then in your delightfully vague way you say, 'Enough flour in each part to make dough easy to handle.'" He closed the book. "Now where did you get this recipe?"

I told him it had been given to me by Bevvy Martin, an Old Order Mennonite friend who had let me copy it from the little notebook in which she had written her mother's and grandmother's recipes. The name Rigglevake was a Pennsylvania Dutch word for railroad. Why they were called that Bevvy didn't know.

"Would you ask her to make the cookies for me?"

"No. I couldn't. She's eighty-three years old and quite frail since her husband died a few months ago." I'm protective of my Mennonite friends; when students, media people, and others ask me to introduce them I refuse.

Ever since I lived with Bevvy Martin's family and wrote about the lifestyle of the Old Order Mennonites, I have treasured their friendship and respected their ways which may seem strange to people who don't know them. They won't own radios, television sets, or musical instruments. They will ride in a car but won't own one. They use electricity and tractors but won't have telephones. They won't go to court or to war. They refuse old age pensions, family allowances, and medicare, but pay all taxes and have their own schools. They wear no cosmetics or jewellery, not even wedding rings. They shun everything worldly and fashionable that might make them vain and take their thoughts from the Lord. They speak Pennsylvania Dutch and have a look of quiet contentment.

"Where did Bevvy Martin get the recipe?" the lawyer asked me.

I told him she probably got it from her grandmother whose grandmother may have brought it from Switzerland three hundred years ago when the Mennonites emigrated to Pennsylvania to escape religious persecution. After the American Revolution some came to Ontario to remain under British rule. Although there are more than 160,000 Mennonites of various sects living from Ontario to BC, there are only about 3,000 members of the Old Order. They cling to their homesteads near Kitchener-Waterloo, and their white clapboard churches stand on their own farmlands within a buggy ride's distance—except for a settlement that has begun around Mount Forest, Ontario because the burgeoning cities have forced them to move.

Don Sim was persistent. "Will you find out for me from your friend how old the recipe is, what kind of molasses she uses, how much flour?"

"You're asking the same questions the Nabisco lawyer did. Why do you want to know?"

"The legal technicalities are too complicated to explain but I can tell you this: my client wants to know if Rigglevake cookies are crisp and chewy. Would you say they are?"

"I don't know; I've never made them."

"Do you know anyone else in the Old Order community who is familiar with the recipe?"

When the lawyer from Connecticut had called me I'd told my Mennonite friend Eva about it; Eva is forty and lives fairly near me; I go to see her quite often. She knew the recipe; her mother and grandmother had made the cookies at Christmas time but she herself had never tried them because they were fussy to make.

"Do you think she might make them for me? We'd certainly pay her well for her time and materials."

"I could ask her." Every morning and evening Eva machine-milks twenty-one cows. She makes all her own clothes and those of her three young daughters, and one little son. She is always ready to give her husband a hand in the barn or the sugarbush. Her large house is spotless and tidy. Every day she cooks for at least seven people, very often for thirty. In the summer she picks fruit from the trees in her yard, hoes, weeds, and harvests the bountiful garden bordered by well-tended roses and hollyhocks. She processes all the food that fills three large freezers, cans and preserves the fruits, meats, and vegetables in hundreds of jars that stand, shining and colourful, on shelves from floor to ceiling along two basement walls.

I thought Eva might like to earn some money—if she didn't want to make the cookies she could say no.

"How much would she charge per hour?" Don Sim asked.

"Eva's faith, family, farm and food are her greatest concern; I'm sure she never thinks in terms of dollars an hour."

"Would you think twenty dollars an hour was reasonable?"

Twenty dollars—for making cookies which Eva does so easily and often for her four children. I tried not to show my delight. I said calmly and as if I were considering the amount; "Yes, I think that would do; she might make them for that."

"I'd give her a bonus as well," he said. "Would she accept that?"

"What for?"

"Just to make sure she'd be working for Procter and Gamble and not Nabisco."

"What else would you expect her to do?" I didn't want to commit Eva to anything she wouldn't approve.

"There's the slight possibility of a demonstration. Would she do that?"

"I don't know, certainly not if it involves a camera; she's an Old Order Mennonite and the making of a graven image is against their fundamental beliefs."

"No, that wouldn't be necessary. She might have to show a few people how she makes the cookies. Would she do that?"

"I'd have to ask. Many of the Old Order are quite withdrawn but Eva and Hannah enjoy meeting people."

"Who's Hannah?"

"Eva's sister, two years older; they dress alike and people often think they are twins. Hannah has three teenage children and lives on a farm about two miles from Eva. They do everything together; you're more likely to get Eva if you ask Hannah too."

"No problem, ask her to make the cookies and we'll pay her the same. Tell them to keep track of all the ingredients—especially how much flour they use and how long it takes to make them. Let me know as soon as you can, if they'll do it and when they are done I'll send someone to get them."

I could hardly wait to tell Hannah and Eva the good news.

I knew the Old Order Mennonites had little or nothing to do with lawyers, but baking cookies was quite a usual thing for their women to do. I didn't know why P&G wanted the cookies and I didn't care. I was only glad my friends who work so hard had a chance to be earning money so easily.

After lunch the same day I drove the four miles of gravel road from my house to Eva's. She lives in a white brick house with seven bedrooms, an attached doddy house (grandfather's house), a great weathered barn with a silo behind it, a corn crib, an implement shed, and a drive shed for the black topless buggies that provide Eva and her family with transportation.

I found Eva in the yard near the back stoop; she was vigorously scraping the varnish off a door resting across two sawhorses. She greeted me with her usual joy.

"I've come to tell you something," I said, "but I want to tell you and Hannah at the same time."

Eva's dark eyes sparkled. "Good. I'll put on a clean apron and go right with you."

She ran up the cement steps into the house and, in a few minutes, came out wearing a clean apron over her printed cotton dress made in the traditional style of the Old Order: a basque waist under a pointed plastron, called a cape, and a long gathered skirt that almost hid her black stockings. Her curly dark hair, centre parted, was almost hidden under her stiff helmet-like black bonnet, which fitted over the dainty white organdie head covering, which she was never seen without because St. Paul in the Bible said women should cover their heads when they pray, and Old Order women might pray any time.

Though the Old Order won't own cars, they may ride in them. We drove through the village of Heidelberg and a mile beyond it to Hannah's farm. Hannah, dressed exactly like Eva, was happy to see us and put the kettle on the stove to make a cup of tea while we sat around the kitchen table.

When I told the young women about the lawyer's visit and what he wanted, they were delighted. They didn't ask why he wanted the cookies. They looked up and read the recipe in the book. Eva said, "We'll practise first and see how they turn out before we make them for him." I called Don Sim the next morning. He said he'd come himself the following Thursday to pick up "the product," and would I ask the ladies to make a couple of schnitz and shoofly pies for him as well. I had to drive to Eva's to tell her. She said she had never in her life talked to a lawyer. I told her he was fun and she would enjoy him.

As arranged, Don Sim came to my house with a member of his law firm, Gordon Zimmerman, a sensitive young man, a lawyer and chemist who had been brought up in Waterloo and understood the ways of the Old Order.

Don Sim brought me a colourful Italian pottery cookie jar filled with shortbread. While we chatted in my sunporch we watched ducks and a family of Canada geese swimming on Sunfish Lake.

"When I was a little girl living in Kitchener, my father used to come here to fish; I always wanted to come with him but my mother wouldn't let him take me in a boat on this bottomless lake. Now I swim in it every day and paddle my own canoe."

We drove to Eva's; Hannah had already arrived in her horse and buggy and the young women greeted us with welcoming smiles. We sat on plain wooden chairs and a bench around the long plastic-covered kitchen table; there were flower plants on the sills of the uncurtained windows. Eva's four-year-old, Harvey, sat beside his mother smiling shyly but not speaking. Eva explained that he wouldn't understand English until he started going to their parochial school.

She gave us a cup of tea and passed a plate of Rigglevake cookies. Made of two separate doughs, one light, the other darker, they were round and flat and looked like pinwheels.

"These I made to practise," she told us. "Yours are all packed." She indicated several boxes on the kitchen counter. "My children liked them really well." She patted Harvey's head.

"Mine did too," Hannah said.

"I hope you kept track of all your time for the practice cookies as well." Don Sim reminded them.

"We have it all written down." Eva handed him a paper. He said he'd send them cheques through the mail. "And we'll no doubt be wanting you to bake more cookies for us a bit later on."

As the men drove me back to my cottage they expressed their delight in the Mennonite ladies. "They're like no one I've ever met before," Don Sim said. "They're so natural, so graceful, and they have so much poise. Being with them makes me feel happy. "

The next evening at a dinner party I told about the lawyers and the Mennonite ladies. One of the guests, a business man, said, "What are you getting out of it? I hope P&G is paying you plenty?"

I said, "No, why should they? I'm enjoying the experience."

"Don't you realize they're using you, your reputation, your knowledge, your contacts, your time? You're being involved in industrial espionage."

The very next day, before I had time to think about it, a cheque for $500 came in the mail from Don Sim; he said it was to reimburse me for the time I had taken and the research I had done since our first meeting in May.

Early in July I read in the Kitchener-Waterloo *Record* that Procter and Gamble were alleging that a Nabisco employee had illegally entered a Duncan Hines manufacturing plant and gained access to trade secrets the year before; P&G wanted the courts to order Nabisco to stop infringing its patent and to award unspecified monetary damages.

Next day I had a phone call from Bryan Dare, of Dare Foods, a Kitchener company making cookies that are sold round the world.

He said, "Edna, I hear you're involved in The Great Cookie War."

"I seem to be but I don't understand why. Do you?"

He said he could explain it to me.

He came to my cottage that same evening with a carton containing packages of crisp and chewy cookies made by Nabisco, and Duncan Hines (U.S.), as well as packages of Dare's—enough cookies to last me for several months.

Bryan explained that if a recipe has been published it is in the public domain and cannot be patented. Therefore, if P&G's patent described cookies that were already in a published recipe, patent should not have been granted. "Nabisco claims your recipe is described in P&G's patent."

"But they're not using my recipe," I said. "They're not making Rigglevake cookies."

Bryan explained that P&G didn't base their patent on the ingredients. It merely described cookies made of two separate doughs which when baked were crisp and chewy; it even mentioned pinwheel cookies several times. If the case came to court, Nabisco would try to prove that

Rigglevake cookies in my book were crisp and chewy. P&G would try to prove they were not.

But I was still floundering. "Why not let anyone make any kind of cookies they like?" I asked. "They must all be at least slightly different."

"Because millions of dollars are at stake," Bryan told me. "If crisp and chewy cookies become popular and P&G can stop the other firms from making them because of infringement of patent, it could mean millions to them."

Near the end of July, Gordon Zimmerman asked me to tell Eva and Hannah that P&G wanted more cookies. He and Don Sim would call for them in a week if it was convenient.

That same afternoon I got a phone call from New York, from a lawyer named Anne Barschall, who said the law firm of Kenyon and Kenyon for whom she worked represented Nabisco. She would like to come to Canada to see me about the recipe for Rigglevake cookies in *Food that Really Schmecks.*

I told her I could probably tell her anything she'd like to know on the phone. She said no, she wanted to meet me in person and, if possible, have me bake the cookies for her.

I told her I wouldn't do that.

"Could you find anyone in the Mennonite community who would do it?"

I knew I couldn't ask Eva and Hannah because they were promised to Procter and Gamble. Also I wasn't sure how committed I was to P&G and didn't want to involve myself illegally with both companies.

I said, "I can't promise anything."

The woman was very insistent. "Will you find out and call me back collect?"

"I could do that."

"When?"

"In a week."

"Why not sooner?"

"I'm busy right now. I have a house guest," I told her, but actually I wanted to wait till I'd had a chance to discuss it with Don Sim, who would be coming on the following Tuesday.

When Don came and I told him about Anne Barschall he didn't seem at all surprised or perturbed. He said, "Let her come. You'll enjoy the experience and she'll learn something from your lifestyle and that of the Mennonites. It might do her good."

While we sat around Eva's kitchen table, drinking tea and eating sticky buns, Hannah told us she was so curious about the crisp and chewy cookies that she had bought a package of Christie's (Nabisco) to see what they were like. "The children thought they were wonderful," she said, "but I didn't think they tasted quite natural."

Don Sim said, "Wait till Duncan Hines (P & G) get their product on the market in Canada this fall. I'm sure they'll be better." He grinned. Then he explained that when cookies are put in the oven to bake, the sugar caramelizes, and if you eat the cookies immediately after they are baked they have a special texture. But after the cookie has cooled the sugar reverts to its former crystalline state and the texture is not as great as the fresh warm cookie. P & G's formula was devised to retain that original texture for months. He was sure the recipe for Rigglevake cookies in my book could not fill that requirement.

Next day I called Anne Barschall in New York and told her she could see me the following week. After several more phone calls it was arranged that she would stay at the charming Jakobstettel Guest House in the village of St. Jacobs, which is in the middle of the Mennonite countryside and just six miles from my cottage.

She arrived after midnight and had to waken the housekeeper of the Guest House to let her in.

Next morning she called me and I told her how to find Sunfish Lake. Though the way—over gravel roads through forest and along a narrow lane in a cedar swamp—is tricky, she found it without any trouble.

Anne was a big girl, about twenty-eight, not fat but tall, rather pretty, with dark curly hair, glasses, flat black shoes, and a plain light brown suit. She said she had called her mother in Wisconsin to ask what she should wear in Canada. This was her first assignment out of Kenyon and Kenyon's New York office and she was obviously excited.

I gave her lunch while she kept asking questions about Rigglevake cookies and the ways of Old Order Mennonites, until unexpectedly a food-magazine editor from Toronto, and then several other friends, arrived separately and visited all afternoon. I felt that Anne Barschall, anxious to get on with her job, listened to our conversation with impatience.

My editor friend, when she was leaving, had a chance to speak to me privately. "Edna, be careful about getting involved in this Cookie War," she warned. "You think it's a lark having these bigshot city lawyers coming out here to Sunfish Lake, but it could eventually take more of your time than you want it to."

After the rest of my guests departed, Anne Barschall and I went to St. Jacobs for dinner. She kept quizzing me about cookies, Mennonites, and what the P&G lawyers had been after, in a way that made me feel I must be wary and not tell anything that might make me disloyal to the lawyers from Toronto.

Next morning Anne and I went to the Waterloo farmers' market where I introduced her to Ada, the granddaughter of Bevvy Martin. She had agreed to make the Rigglevake cookies for Nabisco. She was a pretty, shy, unmarried woman in her late twenties who came every Saturday to the market to sell vegetables, fruit, and flowers from her buggy after tying her horse in the market's horse shed. Anne was delighted with her first Mennonite.

Because I had told Anne apple molasses was used by the Mennonites in their cookies, we then drove to a cider mill on a country side road to buy some for her to take back to New York.

The Old Order women in the house of the cider mill owner were busily preparing dinner for a group of men who had helped with the threshing. Anne kept asking questions about Rigglevake cookies till they asked if we were staying for dinner. Though I said, "No, thank you, we must go now and not bother you any longer," Anne kept talking to an Old Mennonite guest named Malinda who said she had often made the cookies. The women of the house were putting dishes of mashed potatoes, country pork sausage, schnippled bean salad, pickled beets, and apple butter pies on the table. I finally said, "Anne, the men are waiting at the door for their dinner and it will be getting cold; we must not stay any longer." I walked out the door and she reluctantly followed me with her half-gallon jar of apple molasses.

At two in the afternoon we went to the farm of Bevvy Martin's daughter, Lyddy Ann, who lives in a tidy new doddy house attached to the sprawling brick farmhouse, with its woodwork painted bright red and yellow.

Lyddy Ann, a slim little woman with great dark eyes, greeted me joyously, "It's so long since you were here." She shook my hand with vigour, then shyly asked Anne to take a seat beside the kitchen sink.

We arranged for Lyddy and her daughter Ada to bake a batch of Rigglevake cookies in a couple of weeks. While Ada was showing Anne the rest of the doddy house, Lyddy asked me timidly, "Could we get into trouble if the cookies don't turn out right?" I assured her they couldn't and added, "Nor do you have to answer any questions you don't want to." She smiled with relief, because ever since we'd arrived Anne had been asking questions.

Next morning Anne called to ask me where she could buy jars and boxes to mail the apple molasses to New York, where it would be analyzed. "You can't buy things like that on Sunday," I told her, "but I have jars and boxes here that you can use." After she'd finished packing she called her boss in New York and came at me with more questions.

"Would the Mennonites be witnesses at the lawsuit when it comes up?"

I told her they would never go to court or take an oath.

"Of course you'll be called as a witness and you'll go," she said.

"Oh no, I wouldn't do that."

"In my country if you are called as a witness and don't appear you can be put in jail," she told me.

"Isn't it lucky that I don't live in your country?" (I didn't know then that the same thing could happen in Canada and that the Cookie War could be brought to court in Canada as well as in the USA.)

Anne said she thought I should seek advice from my own lawyer.

"Why should I? The business of Nabisco, and Procter and Gamble, is not my affair. If I choose not to answer any more questions or to have nothing more to do with lawyers representing either company I don't have to and nor do any of my Mennonite friends."

Anne called her boss again from the phone in my bedroom.

On Monday morning, on her own, Anne found the farm of Malinda, whom she had met at the cider mill. She came to my house the next day and told me Malinda had baked a batch of Rigglevake cookies for her.

"I thought Malinda might act as a witness for us but she refused," Anne told me. "I told her she could give the money to her church if she didn't think it was right to keep it, but she wouldn't even do that."

Anne called her boss again from my bedroom phone. Determined to get what he told her to get, she was frustrated.

"I don't understand you," she said to me. "You're always so polite I can't tell what you're thinking."

"Would you want me to get mad?"

"When people get mad you can tell what they think."

She kept trying to find out what had transpired between me and the P&G lawyers. She asked if I'd signed any papers for them. I said I had signed a statement and mentioned that I had a transcript in my P&G file.

"You have a file? May I see it?"

"Of course not."

Anne said she thought she was getting a stomach ulcer. When she left me to return to New York, she said she'd be back in a couple of weeks to pick up the cookies that Lyddy Ann and Ada were going to bake for her.

Next day, Anne called to tell me she'd arrived safely at the posh offices of her sixty-lawyer firm. She said, "I'm having a hard time explaining you folks up there to my colleagues here in New York. They just can't understand you."

She called again a week later to tell me the box of apple molasses had arrived in a sticky mess because one jar had broken in transit.

When Don and Gordon came in September to pick up more cookies, they asked no questions about the Nabisco lawyer's visit. They brought packages of Duncan Hines cookies that had recently been introduced to the Canadian market. Eva was delighted. "You know we've had so many Rigglevake cookies around here this summer that even little Harvey says he's getting tired of them."

A week later Anne arrived to watch Lyddy Ann and Ada bake cookies for her. We sat in the neat kitchen of Lyddy's doddy house, Anne making notes of everything the women were doing. They worked quickly and carefully, measuring all the ingredients, baking the cookies, and spreading them out on the table and counters.

Anne took samples of the sugar, flour, and molasses used in the baking and wondered if she should also take a sample of the well water that was used. (I wondered if she should also take an egg.)

Anne told us she had baked Rigglevake cookies in her Brooklyn apartment. Because she had never before done any baking they had come out of the oven black and brittle. She said her boss, too, had tried making them and all through the offices of the law firm there were samples of crisp and chewy cookies from Nabisco and Procter and Gamble. She had brought some packages with her for Lyddy, Ada, and me.

Before coming to my house the next morning Anne said she wanted to scout around a bit. She was determined to get a Mennonite somewhere who would consent to being a witness in court. She called the minister of a Mennonite church (not Old Order); he turned her over to his secretary who abruptly refused to have anything to do with a commercial endeavour that had no purpose other than making millions of dollars.

Anne then drove to Floradale to talk to some Old Order Mennonite women in the store there; of course they refused. She finally gave up and said goodbye to me. "I probably won't ever see you again," I said as she walked up my path.

"Maybe you will," she said, smiling. "I'd like to come back and bring my boyfriend."

When Anne called from New York to tell me she'd arrived safely, she said her boyfriend, a divinity student, had just told her he thought they were incompatible and he wouldn't be seeing her anymore.

"Don't worry, Anne, you'll find somebody else."

"Do you think so?" she said wistfully.

"Of course; there are lots of men in New York."

"But they're nearly all gay."

Sometimes I would get a handwritten letter from Anne's apartment. In one she wrote, "Somehow my trip up there made a very deep impression on me. I'm not exactly sure why. I think the warmth of all the people up there must have had a lot to do with it. The much more common reaction is to be very suspicious of strangers."

Anne also called me occasionally from her office to see how things were going here. She had had a trip to Mennonite country in Pennsylvania and Ohio, but she said she couldn't tell me anything about it.

Meantime I was told by a woman in St. Jacobs that two lawyers from Ottawa representing Nabisco had stayed in the area for two weeks; she said they had interviewed fifty Old Order Mennonites and had got some to bake Rigglevake cookies.

One day in November Anne called and asked me to get a transcript of Bevvy Martin's little handwritten cookbook that had the recipe for Rigglevake cookies.

I drove to Bevvy's house. She had been ill during the summer and looked very tiny and pale in her dark print dress and white head covering. She showed me pictures of her two latest great-grandchildren, named Marlin and Tiffany Dawn. She had heard about the Cookie War from Lyddy Ann, and Malinda, who had baked cookies for Anne. When I told her that Anne wanted me to have her book duplicated she said firmly, "I think the whole business is a lot of foolishness and I won't let them have it."

When Anne called me from New York and I told her Bevvy's reaction she almost shouted. "That's terrible. You're sure she can't be persuaded?" Then she added, "But I guess I know those people well enough to know that when they say no they mean no."

Before Christmas, Don and his two daughters came from Toronto, with gift-wrapped boxes containing Cuisinarts for Hannah and Eva— gifts from him, not Procter and Gamble. The young women were overwhelmed. "They'll come in so handy when we have company after church. Sometimes thirty-five or more come and we have to slice so many potatoes," Eva said, glowing. "Isn't it good we have the electric. Many of our people don't have it."

And Hannah, reading the brochure said, "I think it could even make butter, and it says here it can make bread."

One stormy morning in February, Gordon Zimmerman called to ask me to have Hannah and Eva do more baking.

Because he had to go on a business trip to Europe, it was weeks before Don Sim managed to come for the cookies. By that time Eva was busy canning maple syrup (from their own sugar bush) and taking it to the Kitchener market to sell. Don drove her there, then went enthusiastically from stall to stall buying asparagus, eggs, quilted place mats, sausages, cheeses, until—with the pies, buns, and cookies Eva had baked for him—the trunk of his car was filled.

While we had lunch at the nearby Brittany Restaurant, Don said, "You know, Edna, it's almost a metaphysical experience for me every time I am with the Mennonite ladies. When I go back to Toronto I feel a better man." He grinned. "For at least a day and a half."

In mid-May Anne called from New York to ask if she and a Nabisco lawyer from Ottawa might come to see me soon. She said he was one of the lawyers who had spent two weeks in the fall calling on Mennonites in the St. Jacobs area.

"Why do you want to come?"

"We want to explain Nabisco's side of the case to you."

"But why should I care? I'm on neither side. Besides on Sunday I'm leaving to visit friends in Paris and Brittany and I won't be back for three weeks."

A month later Anne called from Kitchener to tell me she had arrived. Next morning at ten she and a pleasant young man named Michael Manson came to my cottage. He was a lawyer and biochemist from the Ottawa legal firm of Smart and Biggar, which represented Nabisco in Canada. He brought me a pretty peach-coloured azalea.

They asked me what I thought of cookies being patented and gave me a copy of P&G's patent—twenty-six pages of incredible legalese with seven pages of diagrams!

"Most cookies," I read, "will reach their equilibrium textures via

processes which are either logarithmic or signoidal in their time progression." They were described as "organoleptically acceptable and
crumb-continuous, with a crunchy chewy mouth texture dichotomy."

I said, "Such gobbledegook I have never read. Does it have any meaning?"

Michael Manson smiled at my reaction. "Oh yes, for anyone with
training in that vocabulary it's quite simple."

We discussed the absurdity of patenting cookies. Then somehow the
subject of being a witness came up. Anne asked me again if I would
appear. "You'd get a trip to Delaware where the case would be held," she
enticed.

I said I had no desire to go there. One could never tell how soon a witness would be called and I had better things to do than sit in a hotel
room waiting weeks or months to be called to the witness stand.

Anne looked frustrated. Michael Manson said, "There is no way you
can get Edna to go to the States if she doesn't want to go."

"The only alternative then is a deposition. Would you agree to that?"

"What's a deposition?"

"You would have to answer questions of both P&G and Nabisco
lawyers in the presence of a court reporter and a video person."

"Where?"

"They'd all have to come here."

"That should be interesting. I don't think I'd mind that."

"You'd be wise to get your own lawyer to represent you," Anne said.

"Why?"

"Well, sometimes lawyers have different ways of interpreting what
you might say and it would be well for you to have counsel."

"My lawyer doesn't know a thing about baking cookies and I haven't
anything to tell except that Bevvy Martin loaned me her little black
handwritten cookbook and I put her recipe for Rigglevake cookies into
Food That Really Schmecks."

Anne looked at Michael as if she were gritting her teeth; he smiled and
didn't say anything.

We drove into town for lunch and on the way through Erbsville
Michael was pinched for speeding.

The whole summer passed without a visit from the lawyers. Don Sim
had told me he was going to China for a vacation. Anne called once to
say she was just pushing papers in her office.

In October Anne called again. She said, "Edna, my boss is very anxious to meet you but he can't spare the time to come up there and won-

ders if you would come to New York in November. We'd pay all your expenses, of course."

"Anne, I would love to meet your boss. But what would I do in New York?"

"We'd take you to the theatre and to some very nice restaurants."

"I'm sorry, Anne, but I don't have your passion for New York. I was there last in 1954 when I boarded the old Queen Elizabeth for my first trip to Europe. After I saw Paris and London I said I'd never go to New York again."

"I'm sure you'd find New York more interesting now."

"No doubt, but I couldn't leave here in November; when it's dark and cold and rainy I can't get anyone to stay with my cats."

I was afraid if I accepted the hospitality they offered I might feel obligated to sign some papers or say I would act as a witness. I didn't want to take any chances.

Anne called me back the next day. "Edna, my boss said I was to offer to come up to stay with your cats while you come to New York."

I didn't go. I wouldn't leave Cecily and Willie in the care of a New York City lawyer who knew nothing about cats.

Just before Christmas, Anne wrote me a letter; she said she had made a whirlwind trip to St. Jacobs but hadn't phoned me because she had been too busy calling on Mennonites and buying Christmas presents in St. Jacobs for her relatives and her new boyfriend.

Then Don Sim called to tell me that P & G wouldn't need any more Rigglevake cookies. But he said he wanted to keep in touch with the Mennonite ladies and me. That was the last time I spoke to him. Three weeks later, Gordon Zimmerman called to tell me that Don had died of a heart attack. Eva and Hannah and I felt we had lost a good friend.

In December *The New York Times* had a long article headed "Chewy Cookie Market Falters." The piece stated that, despite the many millions spent on promotion, the market for the crisp and chewy cookies was far below the expectation of the companies that were making them. The problem was that millions of cookie eaters just didn't believe that the cookies were as good as those baked at home.

One day at a luncheon in Toronto around this time I was entertaining friends with my adventures in the Cookie War. June Callwood, the author and journalist, said, "That would be a good story for my column," and asked me some questions.

On the same day her piece appeared in *The Globe and Mail*, Canadian Press called me and a CP story appeared across Canada.

A week later a neighbour who owns a banquet hall told me one of her waitresses had said, "Isn't it too bad Edna is being sued?"

"What for?" I asked.

"A headline in the *Kitchener Record* said, 'Sick of Cookies' and she thought it meant you had baked cookies for some lawyers and when they ate them they got sick and are suing you."

After Christmas, I was asked to go to Toronto to be interviewed about the Cookie War by Peter Gzowski on *Morningside*. Immediately there seemed to be a media explosion. Radio stations called me for interviews from Buffalo, New York; Toronto; Saskatoon; Memphis, Tennessee; and San Diego, California, where the program was syndicated to twenty-nine countries around the world. A TV crew came to my cottage from the Kitchener-Waterloo station. The *Ontario Lawyers Weekly* had a two-page spread. A reporter for the *Wall Street Journal* spent half a day with me at Sunfish. (His piece on the front page of the second section of the paper was headed "As Long As They Schmeck Who Cares If They're Patented?") A CBC producer came to arrange a filming for *The Fifth Estate*. *Harper's* and *Forbes* magazines in New York had long conversations with me on the phone.

With all these people questioning me, I kept trying to remember what I had told them. I think I said P & G and Nabisco are mythical giants who mean nothing to me. I have no stock in their companies and know no one who works for them except their lawyers, whom I have enjoyed and trusted.

In February 1986, Michael Manson called me from Ottawa and asked if I'd have lunch next day with him and a colleague. He picked me up in a Lincoln Continental that he'd rented at the airport and we drove to a restaurant where we waited for Don Phenix, the other Nabisco lawyer. He apologized for being late. "I went to see a wonderful old Mennonite woman, ninety-five years old and still making cookies and quilts." When Michael had called me I was afraid they'd be pressing me to be a witness for Nabisco but the word witness wasn't mentioned; we simply had a good lunch and fun talking about the Cookie War.

In the spring more reporters called me for stories. I said yes to all of them. But then I started to worry. All the lawyers who had come to see me had been adept at not explaining what was really going on in the Cookie War. Because I didn't care which large company won the case, I hadn't asked many questions. I confidently thought my Mennonite friends and I could withdraw any time we wanted to. But questions the media people asked now began to make me uneasy. Since P & G and

Nabisco were making cookies in Canada, what if the case would be tried in Canada as well as the U.S.? What if I inadvertently wrote or said something that might make it possible for the two conglomerates to sue me for millions of dollars—which of course I don't have.

I phoned Gordon Zimmerman who came promptly to Sunfish. He told me it was quite possible that I might be subpoenaed to appear in court in Toronto or Ottawa if the case were tried in Canada.

"And what about Hannah and Eva—could they be subpoenaed?"

Gordon looked uncomfortable. "I'm afraid they could be."

"Aren't Old Order Mennonites exempt? They won't go to court; they mayn't; their religion won't let them."

"I'm afraid the penalty is jail."

"Oh no, that's terrible," I exclaimed. "Hannah and Eva in jail! I got them into this; they trusted me; they'll think I've betrayed them."

He looked sympathetic. "Edna, I can assure you that P & G won't subpoena them."

"What about Nabisco?"

Gordon raised his shoulders. "I don't know. I hope they don't know who it was that baked the cookies for us."

"It wouldn't be hard to find out. The Old Order Community is like a family, they talk to each other and might know and tell without realizing the consequences. The Nabisco lawyers have been around here often, talking to dozens of Mennonites."

Now I really had something to worry about. If I were subpoenaed I would have to comply and probably even find the experience interesting.

But to have to face Hannah and Eva with the probability—I decided to try not to think about it until the case was called perhaps next year—perhaps never.

Early in September, the Nabisco lawyers phoned from Ottawa to see if I could have lunch with them. They brought me a beautiful red azalea. The first question I asked was if I would be subpoenaed. They both said an emphatic no. I wouldn't even be called as a witness.

"And what about the Mennonites?"

"Never. Nothing could be worse for the image of Nabisco—or P & G—than subjecting Mennonite ladies in white bonnets to a session in court. Can you imagine what the media would make of that?"

Mike Manson said, "You know, we've called on so many of those people and grown so fond of them that we've become thoroughly protective. We wouldn't want anything to disturb them."

"Great," I said, "I'll have a good sleep tonight."

Whenever I go to Hannah's or Eva's to drink tea and eat sticky buns or cookies mixed in their Cuisinarts, they ask if I've heard from the cookie lawyers. I say I haven't. The last time I saw them they told me Anne Barschall is no longer employed by Kenyon and Kenyon. Nabisco is no longer making the crisp and chewy cookies that were accused of infringing P&G's patent; Nabisco now has a formula of its own. When asked if the Cookie War will ever be fought in court the lawyers didn't seem to know. Or, if they did know, they weren't telling.

(When this story was published in the May 1987 issue of Saturday Night *magazine, the names Katie and Sarah were used to protect the anonymity of Hannah and Eva — at the request of* P&G.*)*

Notes

1 Nabisco owns 80 percent of the world's cookie market, including Christie's, Peak Frean's, Dad's and Béton in France. Duncan Hines was also involved.
   Staebler learned the Rigglevake (Pennsylvania Dutch for railroad) recipe from her Old Order Mennonite friend Bevvy Martin.
2 If a recipe has been published, it is in the public domain and cannot be patented. The smaller Procter and Gamble company had secured a patent and the larger Nabisco company was trying to prove that P&G did not have rights to the patent because the recipe was in the public domain, thanks to Staebler's book with its recipe for Rigglevake Cookies. The disagreement was eventually settled out of court.

the
1980s
*The Business of
Publishing*

THE SUCCESS OF *Schmecks* led to numerous honours and opportunities for Edna. She was named Kitchener-Waterloo Woman of the Year in 1980. McClelland and Stewart proposed publishing a selection of her magazine articles, and *Whatever Happened to Maggie* appeared in 1983.[1] Wilfrid Laurier University awarded her an honorary doctorate in 1984, the year of the Great Cookie War in which Staebler played a starring role. Her written account of the Cookie War, published in *Saturday Night* in 1987, won her a Canadian National Magazine Award. The same year, Edna's third cookbook, *Schmecks Appeal*, was published. Staebler closed out the decade with three more awards: the Waterloo-Wellington Hospitality Award (1988), the Kitchener-Waterloo Arts Award (1989), and a Province of Ontario Senior Achievement Award (1989). Not bad for a woman who was now in her eighties.

In her journals, Edna remained a harsh judge of how much and how well she was writing. With regard to publishing and promoting books, she was of two minds. "To hell with publishing," she pronounced January 11, 1983. "It's the writing that counts, not the publishing." A few months later, however, she demanded, "Why write unless one is read?" (June 4, 1983). She was annoyed at the lack of promotion for *Whatever Happened to Maggie* (June 10, 1983). At the same time, she recognized that she should write for her own sake. "That must be my life, my main enjoyment, my *goal*" (November 21, 1986). This was a goal that, almost in spite of herself, Staebler achieved through her journals. "I'd really like to do something with these," she recorded October 15, 1988. "I've read them over for the first time and was surprised to find that they are well written, straight from the heart and really fascinating" (October 15, 1988). As the 1980s drew to an end, Staebler was encouraged by her friend Judith Miller (May 11, 1989), a professor of English at the University of Waterloo, to consider more seriously the possibility of her journals appearing in print. But several more publication projects lay ahead in the 1990s.

Note

1 The book was later reissued by McGraw-Hill under the title *Places I've Been and People I've Known: Stories from across Canada* (1990).

~

December 31, 1985. Edna at Rose and Kent Murray's New Year's Eve Party.

top May, 1987. Edna and friends; *bottom left* 19 October 1987. Edna at the Blue Heron Bookstore, Comox, BC; *bottom right* Edna and the Rigglevake cookies of the Great Cookie War.

From the Diaries

January 11, 1983[1]

I must keep on recording, forever and ever, as long as I can hold a pen or type on my typewriter. To hell with publishing. Let it come if it will, but I must keep on writing and reading as long as I can see to read and write and live. I must do more and more and more. It's the writing that counts, not the publishing. Maybe it will never be read, so what? I will have done my share of keeping myself alive and aware and grateful. Amen.

January 18, 1983

When I write to Pierre [Berton], I want to thank him and ask if he'd mind my deleting the word "counsels" from his MS. He said I counsel the people I write about and I'm sure I don't. I have always tried to accept them and to write as objectively and incisively as I could without hurting their feelings. Now I must try to suggest changing my mentor's script without hurting him. I'll try.

Jennifer [Glossop] called me yesterday.[2] The book has gone to the printers. It will be *big*, 6 x 9, the shape of Pierre's *National Dream* books, but not as thick.[3] It will cost $18.95, which seems exorbitant and probably won't sell very well. The sketches for each piece, she said, are lovely and I'll have the proofs this week to approve. The jacket, she said, will be blue with other bright colours, very attractive. I hope so. M & S always produces good-looking books, so I'm excited and eager to see it.

June 4, 1983

Every morning I wake before 4 AM and I stew about the Kitchener *Record* not putting anything in the paper about *Whatever Happened to Maggie*. I wish I didn't do this but it makes me so *mad*. The book is *not* being sold in my home town. Martha says it's doing well, but where? In Ottawa last week I did seven interviews and Liz Waddell said the book will sell well there, the *Citizen* published the lousy piece Judy Creighton did for the CP of the book and a front about me.[4] [Illegible] said he sold 500 books in London after I spoke there. But the Kitchener stores have one or two copies or *none*. The Kitchener library has one copy; it is *out*. Waterloo has *none*. Dammit. Why is this? Must I go out and sell it myself? I don't want to do that. The book should be in all the schools, but it isn't there. Why am I so upset about this? I don't need the money. I've told myself that all I want is to have the articles published. Now that is done and done well. I want it to sell. That is normal, I suppose. Why write unless one is read? I'm sure the book would sell if it was sold. I've done five radio interviews in Toronto, three interviews in London, seven in Ottawa, two in Kitchener (total seventeen) but it needs more. Martha has now put off the Halifax trip and the Toronto interviews, [Peter] Gzowski and Sheila C., September she says.[5] But will she? I'll hound her. She believes in the book, loves it, then why does she not get me on the shows that will sell it? Like Liz Waddell in Ottawa. She was great and enthusiastic and worked hard but the two stores I went into had only one or two copies. What should I do? Forget it and let it languish as I did CBH? Sell less than 5,000 copies in eleven years? And all who have read that book say they *love* it. But people didn't even find out about it. No promotion, great reviews. Why don't good books sell? I suppose every author feels that way.

June 10, 1983
I've got to write or do something to get rid of my obsession about the fact that the KW *Record* has not written a word about my new book. I wake up in the night almost every night and don't sleep again because I'm composing anonymous letters to the editor, asking why, why, why? One night I started a letter to *Maclean's* magazine asking why they have refused to do a review. They told Martha they don't write about their own writers. Not even Peter Newman's books are reviewed there. Damn stupid policy.

Damn stupid me to let this thing *get* me. Why do I care so much? I don't need the money, that is the last reason. That is no reason at all. I have more money than I need. It's just that I want *Maggie* to be *read*. I know it is good and is being enjoyed by all the people who have read it and I want new people to know about it because I am fond of it myself. I go into the bookstores, see it obscurely hiding, singly on a shelf some- where, instead of being prominently displayed with *Schmecks* and *More Schmecks* so people will notice it, and that annoys me too. What can I do? I don't want to be a pest and make the *Record* and the booksellers mad at me.

October 4, 1983[6]
One step at a time. One day at a time. Relax and love and be grateful for what I have, my home, Sunfish Lake, my wonderful friends and family, books to read, my health, my cats, my rich, eventful life. Perhaps I should write my memoirs. It could take up *volumes*. No one would publish it and if they did, I don't think I'd want to be around to get the reaction. Not if I told the whole truth. How could I tell the *whole* truth? What is it? So many contradictions, rationalizations, and explanations and introspections and *action*. What a wonderful life I've had and now I can add V to my memoirs.[7] Perhaps he realized that and didn't want to be added.

October 8, 1983
Is this popularity a fleeting thing that has no substance or lasting quality but the joy of the moment? It inflates my ego which seems to never get enough praise. I love it. I bask in it. I'm probably fatuous and sappy when people give it to me, as they constantly do. Please, God, don't let me blow it by my conceit and craving for more and more and more. Watch it, Cress, watch it. Why do you need it? There's much more out there in the world to talk about and think about than Edna Staebler. Who the hell does she think she is? But surely I don't talk about myself all the time? I tell about Tony's ducks and the French people or my trip to Alaska and Belle and anything or anyone that has recently happened.[8] I'm enthusiastic. I love things and people and like to pass on my experiences or to talk to other writers, or would-be writers, about writing, mostly my writing, which they seem to want to hear about.

October 20, 1983
My book *Maggie* is a good book and should be selling very well, but its promotion has been poor. The sheet of information that was sent to reviewers and producers of interview shows was so banal and stupid and lacking in guts that I'm sure no one would have read more than four lines before they'd say *no*. It didn't even tell what the book is about, started by saying I was educated at U of T, as have a million other people, no wonder the media balked at interviews. Jack [McClelland] offered to have the blurb reprinted. I'd like to rewrite it myself. Hope I'll *do* it— at least make some suggestions.

November 19, 1983
Because I had to work at my writing, my Mother always said to me, "of course you're not a *real* writer." She thought writing was some sort of

magic. I once thought that too, that one shouldn't have to work at it, it would just come by some sort of magic. Bill said, "There is no magic," and I agreed. There's only hard work.

But we were wrong. There is magic. That is why one wants to write, to capture the magic that is in the idea, the thing, the passion, the sense, the beauty, or whatever. Because the magic is there, one is eager and willing to work and work hard to put it in words.

March 10, 1984

I must write. The passion is not spent. It is still there and I must make it vivid in my writing. I've written nothing this winter, only wasting time. But I've learned something surely and I must use what I've learned to *good* advantage. Not by carrying on this ridiculous, unnatural affair with V, but by using the passion in my work. Thank God it's still there. I still have it. Please, God, make me *use* it. Make me *write*, every day.

July 15, 1984[9]

A writer must have many, many hours of solitude and silence when ideas can be incubated. I find it hard to think of the past because I am always so involved with the present. My past is so much longer than my future. If I am ever going to do anything about it I should start now. But damn it all, I'm still living, learning, experiencing, and having fun. There isn't time for the past. It's over. Still, it has been so interesting, exciting, and wonderful. I'd really like to write about it. There have been so many fascinating people in my life, so many places and stories. Every day has had something in it that I should have recorded. Maybe it was only a new bird at my feeder, maybe a great revelation.

October 29, 1984

It's all over; I'm now Edna Staebler, BA, LLD, Doctor of Letters. Dr. Staebler!! I'll no doubt be riding high and insufferable for awhile, till the glow wears off and I see that glazed look in people's eyes when I boast. The Lt. Gov. (John Aird), who has been the Chancellor for eight years, and the President (John Weir), and many members of the faculty, told me that never in the history of WLU has a speaker at convocation been given a standing ovation! And I didn't even realize it. I heard the thunderous applause; there were thousands of people filling the arena. I just stood there, the applause kept on, and I finally sat down. They told me the rising started in the student body, thru the faculty, and all the people in the seats and the faculty and those on the platform. Amazing! And Pierre

[Berton] said it was a very moving speech and Janet [Berton] said he wiped tears from his eyes. Pierre said it was moving and charming and witty and clever. Addressed to the graduates, they could relate to it and they all said it was a speech that they would never forget. Amazing! I did work hard and long at it but I wasn't at all sure it was what was right. I was still typing the ending between phone calls yesterday morning. So many people had said, "Don't worry, just be yourself," whatever that means. I couldn't just get up and grin. I was really concerned. The speech could be only ten minutes long and it had to be good. I talked about myself all the way through it. I hoped in a way that the graduates could relate to my experiences of pride in my accomplishments, despair in not getting a job in hard times, taking anything I could get, wanting to write but lacking the skill and the confidence, then finally writing and working, filling thousands of pages. I put in a few quotes that have helped me through the years, quotes from English courses, to show how what I had learned in university had stayed with me. Milton—"The mind is its own place and [in itself], can make a heaven of hell, a hell of heaven."[10] Shakespeare—"The fault, dear Brutus, lies not in our stars but in ourselves that we are underlings."[11] And finally, at the end when I wished they would wake up every morning with a feeling of eagerness to learn something new, Plato—"Only this is to be feared, the closed mind, the sleeping imagination."[12] And may all your dreams come true. Amen.

November 21, 1986 [13]
All my life I have talked about writing and kept scribbling in my note-book as if that makes me a writer. I've managed to write a little bit, five books, to prove I can really do it and do it well and enjoyably and with pleasure for many other people, and more shame to me if I don't do more and *give more*. I'm letting myself vegetate. I read a book and I think I'd like to write one, a novel, to see if I could, just for fun, for the hell of it, and I know I should write another cookbook. I know all these recipes and I should tell about Fred [Kruger] and Philip [Knowling], or George [Dowse] and my own life with Keith and how I came through it. And I should work on Ruby's letters and have them published, and Dr. Robins's letters too. All that I should do, enough to keep me alive and busy for another ten years or longer, and why not? If I'd stop being lazy and *do* it, all I have to do is *sit* as I have always done and get words down on paper, stop wasting my time reading, knitting, listening to the radio or tv and the phone. Now I'm talking myself into martyrdom. If I'd *write*

just a few hours every day, I'd soon have some accomplishments. I'd feel wonderful, as if life could go on enjoyably and profitably for once. What motivation have I? I don't need the money. I have enough now to be a burden. I spend time taking care of it and wondering what to do with it. I should settle that fast, with a will, and arrange to give it away.

I should write for the sake of writing because I feel I have something to tell. And I have. People always listen to me when I talk. They say they could listen to me for hours, forever.

So, when I'm home alone, as I am all winter, I should get it all down on paper. Every morning, or in the middle of the night, instead of this self-indulgence. I should get it all down, a first, careless, rapturous draft. Then I'd have something to work at during the day at my typewriter. It would be good to do, to publish books when I'm over eighty. That should inspire other people my age. I should do it for them. Is that enough motivation? Or am I too selfish? Probably. Do I really care about all those old senior citizens out there who are running around the country in buses? Or the lonely ones in nursing homes with senility patients, or those who are still alone and struggling in their own little rooms, subsidized apartments, or lonely in their own big empty houses? Do I really care enough about them to write *for* them or to inspire them? Would what I write have any effect on them? Probably not. They wouldn't even know I had done it. Would anyone else, except perhaps a few? *No*, forget about a *public*. I'd have to do it for *me*, because it would relieve me, make me feel better. Admit my selfishness and do the best I can for my own sake, because I could enjoy doing it, as I enjoy knitting mice and watching birds, mindless occupations, wasting time, and letting my brain atrophy. I must *write or work* for my own sake. That must be my life, my main enjoyment, my *goal*. Whatever else comes along that is fun could be an extra bonus, a plus. A surprise or insight.

But even as I write this I wonder if I'll have the *guts* to do it. I've always been *bone lazy*. And I probably always will be, even though I know it is self-destructive. Why am I? Why are we, mankind, self-destructive?

December 13, 1986

Kit and V[McDermott, Edna's friends from Brantford] came after lunch irate over June Callwood's attack in the *Globe and Mail* yesterday about the Cookie War and my involvement in it.[14] They resented her patronizing description of me as a "pleasant Canadian woman who writes cookbooks." And Kit said so on her radio show. I love their loyalty. The minute they came through the door they were like a couple of ruffled hens. "Doesn't she *know* who you are, what you've written?" They were really mad at her and I'm afraid I feel, too, that her description was a put-down. She and Mavis Gallant were runners up when I won The Woman's Press Club award [1950], and she has never been given an honourary degree by a university, though I think she deserves one for all her energetic work in many welfare fields, as well as her books and her journalism.[15] It must rankle with her and she probably feels my honours have been undeserved. And compared with all her achievements they were undeserved.

Otherwise, her piece was very good despite several errors. Judy Creighton called me and wants to do a piece for the Canadian Press and someone from a radio station in Toronto called and asked questions. I wonder what Don Sim thinks of it all.[16]

October 15, 1988[17]

There is so much amongst my papers that should be written about. My journals, kept sporadically since I was fifteen years old, could be a fascinating autobiography. Pierre said it would have great reader identification and I know it would be interesting to read how I struggled thro' the twenty-eight years with K's alcoholism, thro' Helen's betrayal and overcoming my resentment and making a new and wonderful life for myself here at Sunfish.

[…]

I'd like to publish the book of quotations I've been writing in my old university notebook. Ever since those days, whenever I read something that inspired me, or moved me, or taught me, I'd copy it there and now there are over three hundred pages single-spaced. I'm going to have Laura Gateman put it all in her computer.[18] She's so crippled with arthritis that she's in a wheelchair all the time and needs help even to make meals, but she can still type and I think it would be good for her to have a project. She's eager to get at this and I must have it duplicated before I let her have it. She lives with her Elmer on their farm near Chelsea and will someday come and get the book.

My journals, I'd really like to do something with these. I've read them over for the first time and was surprised to find that they are well written, straight from the heart and really fascinating. I've had such an exciting life, full of so many people and action, travel, adventure, love affairs, agony and bewilderment and ecstacy and joy and fun.

This winter, or until last week, I read a few pages every night in bed of L.M. Montgomery's journal Vol 11.[19] She was such a sniveller! I realize that she wrote out her woes in her journals, as I have, but her life was very dull compared with mine.

October 17, 1988

Doug Gibson called me today to see what I had in mind to write.[20] I told him about the cookbook series and he was really excited about it, could hardly wait to get it. He said they'd publish three books in a year. There are fifteen chapters in each book and combined there should be fifteen books in the series.

Wow. I called Mike Manson and he's going to find out what my rights are for the recipes in *Schmecks*.[21] I don't want to do more writing if I can avoid it, except introductions. I'd like to think the whole project is one of organization.

Also, I told him about Fred [Kruger]. He said Harold Horwood had told him about Fred and when Kit called I asked if she and Vern would let me tell them the story while it was being typed.

Also, Doug is going to see about reprinting *Cape Breton Harbour* and *Sauerkraut and Enterprise*. I told him about my book of quotations and Dr. R's letters and the possibility of doing something with my journals.

I was such an idealist, wanting the impossible, believing in the impossible.

October 23, 1988

Fifty-six years ago today Daddy died, after long agonizing weeks in bed in the front room he and Mother shared. I can't remember where Mother slept during those last weeks of his life. She always said she couldn't stand being with sick people. Norm and Ruby and I each had our own bedrooms and she didn't sleep with us. I must ask Norm if she remembers, not that it matters.

I was the one that Daddy seemed to prefer to have look after him and sometimes a nurse, Miss Ferry. He said Norm walked too heavily and Ruby was skittish and undependable. I know I often sat with him and brought John D. Scottish whisky he needed to stop the awful spasm of hiccoughs. He ate almost nothing during the last six weeks and was just a skeleton when he died.

I was with him, holding his hand. Ruby was there too. Daddy said something about The House. He and mother often quarrelled because she wanted to build a house on a lot at the corner of King and John Streets in Waterloo and he wouldn't do it. The last word Daddy spoke was my name, then he collapsed, closed his eyes, and was gone. We called Miss Ferry who came and looked after him alone in the room. Then the undertaker took him away.

October 25, 1988

I hate all this business part of publishing, but it is very tricky and important that I be alert and firm and demanding. The series could be a bonanza because of my reputation and the quality and popularity of the work. Mike also told me, not to be retold, that Nabisco is now going to press to have the Cookie War brought to court in Canada—because P[rocter] and G[amble]'s lawyers are not doing anything....

November 19, 1988

Edith Fowke has said my cookbooks are not just collections of good recipes, they are folk literature.[22] They are described as Canadian classics. *Schmecks* after twenty years is still making royalties of almost $8,000 a year, something of a record for a hardcover Cdn book available in Canada, though it has been sold in the U.S., Kenya, S. Africa, England— until I withdrew the rights, always intending to get an agent who would sell it, but I never bothered, though I should and hope to get one this year. And that man has declared that my lifetime accumulation of literary papers is worth only $20,000! To hell with him.

November 20, 1988

The Staebler Award [for Creative Non-fiction] could be administered by WLU and give them prestige, $50,000 should give an award of $5,000 a year, not a bad sum to encourage a serious writer.[23]

I don't want it to go to a student in creative writing who idly thinks he might be a writer, but may never have anything published. I want it to go to someone who is really seriously working at writing and shows promise of going on with it. Winning the award would give the writer confidence, stature, and a feeling of professionalism, encouragement, and perhaps a needed monetary boost.

December 16, 1988

This morning in bed I've been thinking of Dr. Robins and his influence on me. I have always said, "he was the wisest man I knew." Is that still true? I have also known Pierre Berton for forty years. I've been privileged to know him as an editor, friend, and mentor, and as the great public figure who is constantly quoted and listened to. I have also known him with his family, where, like many husbands and fathers, I have seen him when he was angry and irritable, but more often tender, sensitive, and caring.

May 11, 1989

Judith Miller came out at ten yesterday morning to talk about the possible publication of my journal, written from the time I was fifteen.[24] I haven't read back that far but I think it was probably pretty silly and restrained, scared someone might read it and find out if someone had kissed me. I would never have admitted that.

Perhaps the most interesting and uninhibited part begins in 1945 after my visit to Neil's Harbour and my determination to write about it. Soon after that I met Philip and Dr. Robins, learned about K's affair with Lib, my best friend, K's growing alcoholism, my agonizing over my writing, my guilt and fear and rationalizing.

Judith asked if I'd be concerned about revealing all that and I said, "No, I don't think I would. I don't give a damn now what people say about me. I feel quite secure." But what about K, who is now eighty-seven and playing tennis three times a week, and Lib and Gerry who are not well? She is in a wheelchair, he is often ill, and they have a homemaker looking after them.

Judith took with her the part of the journal written from '45 to '50. A friend of hers will transcribe it, make it readable and workable. Judith would like to spend much of the summer working on it and she's sure WLU press would publish it in several volumes.

May 14, 1989

The journals also show my struggle with my writing. Had a wife a right to spend her time indulging herself or should I be a proper wife who plays bridge in the afternoons and does all the entertaining and petty things that other men's wives seem to enjoy? Live K's life—I tried to do that. I entertained his friends, always his, always going with him to parties where I'd watch him play the piano and get too drunk to drive home.

[...]

Also in the journals there is revealed my determination to keep up my spirits, to not let K destroy me, to keep loving and appreciating the world around me, the beauty and the joy in the neighbour's children and Barbie and Jim, in my reading, visiting true friends, and my dreams.[25] I was up and down, down when K was down and angry and keeping me up late or staying out till all hours of the night while I worried about him and lost sleep and felt awful and angry thro' most days and couldn't work at my writing.

Frustration with myself because I didn't write. I really had plenty of time to do all I needed to and to write as well but I didn't write except in my journal. I couldn't write and I felt so guilty about that and longed so desperately to write until I went to Neil's Harbour and at last had something I really *had* to write about, and I did it.

August 5, 1989[26]

Why should I bother with any more promotion or business dealings, like having my books sold to the USA, having CBH reprinted, publishing Dr. R's correspondence, and publishing my journal? I could say I'm too old, tire more easily, and I don't need the money. But if I say that to myself, rest on my laurels, vegetate, then I'm ready for the boneyard. If I don't fuss and worry and work at my writing, publishing, I'd probably become like so many older people, start fussing and worrying about my arthritis and relative other ailments that might turn up. I'd no longer be a writer. I'd be a has-been. I'm not ready for that yet. I want to keep giving and working and promoting as long as I can.

Notes

1 Box R3–3. Diary September 2, 1982–June 11, 1983.

2 Jennifer Glossop, an editor at McClelland and Stewart.

3 Berton's impressive two-volume history of the Canadian Pacific Railway: *The National Dream: The Great Railway 1971–1881* (1970) and *The Last Spike: The Great Railway 1881–1885* (1971).

4 Liz Waddell, Ottawa journalist. Judy Creighton, Canadian Press journalist. She and Edna met in the 1970s following the publication of *More Food That Really Schmecks*. Creighton has written several articles about Staebler.

5 Possible reference to Shelagh Rogers, Peter Gzowski's co-host on the popular CBC radio program *Morningside*.

6 Box R3–3. Journal September 23–March 1984.

7 "V," of whom Edna wrote on a slip of paper folded in between the pages of this diary, "my obsession with V my last love affair."

8 Ducks belonging to Tony Vandepol, a neighbour at Sunfish Lake. Staebler travelled to Alaska in 1952.

9 Box R3–4. Diary May 29, 1984–October 29.

10 John Milton (1608–74), *Paradise Lost* (1667).

11 William Shakespeare (1564–1616), *Julius Caesar* I, ii, 140–41.

12 Plato (c.428/7–c.348/7 BC), Greek philosopher. The correct quote is: "This alone is to be feared—the closed mind, the sleeping imagination, the death of spirit."

13 Box R3-3. Oct.–Nov. 1986 and 1987 Diary [page 88]. There is some inconsistency in archiving of journal titles here.

14 June Callwood, "Companies Wait to See How Legal Cookie Crumbles," *Globe and Mail* December 11, 1985.

15 Mavis Gallant (1922–), Montreal-born writer, renowned for her short stories, left Canada for Europe in 1950 and still lives in Paris.

16 Don Sim, legal representative for Procter and Gamble in the "Great Cookie War."

17 Edna's Journal October 15, 1988–May 24, 1989. Lent by the author.

18 Writer for the Clinton, Ontario, newspaper, and member of the Canadian Authors Association.

19 Mary Rubio and Elizabeth Waterston, eds. *The Selected Journals of L.M. Montgomery* (Toronto: Oxford UP, 1985). The final volume, 2: 1935–1942, published 2005.

20 Douglas Gibson, McClelland and Stewart publisher.

21 Mike Manson, lawyer for Nabisco in the Great Cookie War. He and Edna later became friends and Manson visited Sunfish Lake whenever he was in the region.

22 Edith Fowke, *Canadian Folklore* (Toronto: Oxford, 1988), 100, 110.

23 As mentioned in the introduction, Staebler established this award in recognition of a genre that she enjoyed and admired and had practised herself with *Cape Breton Harbour*. It has become a prestigious annual prize that has been won by such notables as Wayson Choy, Elizabeth Hay, Charlotte Gray, and Denise Chong, among others.

24 Judith Miller, professor of English at University of Waterloo. Miller contributed an excerpt from Staebler's diaries to the collection *The Small Details of Life: Twenty Diaries by Women in Canada, 1830–1996*, edited by Kathryn Carter (2002).

25 Edna's niece and nephew, Barbie and Jim Hodgson—Norma's children.

26 Box R3-5. Diaries August 1989–September 1989.

the
1990s
Must Do

S TAEBLER'S HIGHLY ESTEEMED FRIEND and mentor, Dr. John
Robins, had described her book about Neil's Harbour as "creative
non-fiction" ("My Writing Life"). The term had stuck with Edna
and eventually became the inspiration for the book award that she created in her name. Conceived toward the end of the 1980s, the Edna Staebler Book Award was formally established in 1990. Staebler wanted to
recognize and encourage the efforts of writers who were as yet unestablished, as she herself had been.[1] And she had the funds to do so.[2] The cre-
ation of this award became for Edna one of her most rewarding acts
(October 17, 2000) though its development was not without its irritants.
The press release was dull, she felt (September 10, 1991), and university
spokespersons seemed slow to grasp her intentions and stipulations for
the award (March 15, 1995). But eventually terms and conditions were
settled and the award went on to become one of the premier prizes for
non-fiction writing. Some recent winners include Linda Jones, Denise
Chong, Elizabeth Hay, Wayson Choy, and Charlotte Gray, all of whom
Edna has befriended and with whom she has stayed in touch.

Staebler's unflagging passion for writing (March 10, 1984) found its
outlet in a number of new projects. She conceived the "Schmecks
Appeal" series as an affordable alternative to the successful *Company's
Coming* cookbooks that were attracting reader attention. The plan for
twelve short *Schmecks* books did not develop as Staebler hoped and
expected, however, and several diary entries record her annoyance, once
again, with publisher distribution, marketing, and promotion (December 24, 1991 and March 15, 1995).[3]

Another sore point for Edna centred on the sale of her papers. She was unhappy with the original offer of $20,000 and, perhaps more importantly, offended by the inference that the sum reflected her status as "merely" a cookbook writer (November 10, 1992).[4]

On the other hand, Edna's initiative to publish letters written by her sister Ruby met with great success. *Haven't Any News: Ruby's Letters from the '50s*, a title Edna did not care for, was published by Wilfrid Laurier University Press in 1995, with Edna as editor.[5] The collection was the first book in the Press's new Life Writing series, edited by Marlene Kadar. The book elicited favourable response. Jocelyn Laurence wrote a positive review for the *Globe and Mail*.[6]

The 1990s was a decade of awards and accolades for Edna, beginning with the Silver Ladle Award for Outstanding Contribution to the Culinary Arts (1991). Kitchener mayor Dom Cardillo declared April 28, 1991, "Edna Staebler Day." In 1993, Staebler was presented the Governor General's Commemorative Medal, and the following year she received the Regional Municipality of Waterloo Volunteer Award. Joseph Schneider Haus, a Kitchener museum and gallery dedicated to the region's heritage, established the Edna Staebler Research Fellowship. Two years later, in January 1996, she received the Order of Canada. The same year, it was determined that the Lifetime Achievement Award of Cuisine Canada would be called "The Edna" in perpetuity. Meanwhile, Edna had decided to endow the Edna Staebler Writer-in-Residence position at the Kitchener Public Library. In 1997, she was honoured to be asked to address the Writers' Union of Canada at its annual meeting, which took place in May, in Kingston, Ontario. Rounding out the honours for the decade, Edna was inducted into the Waterloo Region Hall of Fame in 1998.

People had started to call Edna Staebler a role model, a function with which she was not entirely comfortable. "I'm no saint," she stated (November 1, 1991). She was slowing down (December 2, 1994), she knew, though she was not about to give up the independence of her life at Sunfish Lake.

> I can't bear to leave Sunfish and my life here. I drove into town yesterday afternoon and I noticed that my driving was rather erratic. I may not be able to do it more often. I'd have to find someone who would drive me wherever I wanted to go, which means I'd have to stay home most of the time. But what if I did? I love it here. I'd have to have someone to buy food for me and anything else I might need. And in the winter there might be times when the roads are impassa-

ble, but I could keep my freezer and cupboard well stocked and my back bedroom.... I'm so comfortable here. Everything is where I want it." (October 18, 1997)

It would be another six years before Staebler would have to consider leaving Sunfish Lake, after she suffered a mild stroke in May 2003.

Notes

1 "Giving confidence and recognition as it was meant to do, unlike the big awards which go to well-established writers who have perhaps already won other awards" (January 6, 2001).
2 "My books have earned for me over $400,000, which when invested in blue chips stocks, has made me a millionaire" (December 16, 1988).
3 "The series could be a bonanza because of my reputation and the quality and popularity of the work" (October 25, 1988).
4 "That man has declared that my lifetime accumulation of literary papers is worth only $20,000! To hell with him" (November 19, 1988).
5 Her preference was for "Ruby's Letters of the 1950s."
6 Jocelyn Laurence, "Sparkling Bulletins from the '50s Homefront," *Globe and Mail* August 3, 1995.

September 1, 1992. Edna Staebler Collection. (Archival and Special Collections, University of Guelph Library)

top left Edna delivering the "Margaret Laurence Lecture" at the Writers' Union Annual General Meeting, May 23–25, 1997; *bottom left* Plaque honouring Edna as a member of the Order of Canada, May 1996; *bottom right* Edna with niece Barbie Wurtele on the occasion of being honoured for her Order of Canada award, May 1996.

 *top* September 1, 1992. Edna at Sunfish Lake; *bottom* 1990s Edna at Sunfish Lake.

From the Diaries

June 7, 1990[1]
I enjoyed so much working on the books. I should now start working on another one—Dr. R's letters, my journal, or Fred [Kruger], Philip [Knowling], and George [Dowse]. What is there to stop me? I still wake up early and could write here in bed, as I am doing now, get a first draft written, think about a new book instead of letting the [*Schmecks*] series fester. That's what it is now, it's festering, a horrible, painful condition. I must end it, forget about it by filling my mind with something new. I must do it. I can do it. I've done it before, perhaps not consciously, just letting it come naturally, not forcing it, being tense and determined about it. Be relaxed and casual and loving about it, as I am and can be so easily in all my relations with people, and especially my cats. Now again I persevere. I amend the three Ls to four: *Looking, Listening, Learning, and Loving.*

September 6, 1990
Promotion for the *Schmecks* series has begun and I'm saving myself for it. Hope I can go through with all that is planned. I did it and enjoyed it three years ago when *Schmecks Appeal* was published. I know that now I need more rest. I'm nervous about the tic coming back. It's much better than it was but still hurts morning and night. I went to Toronto on Tuesday and did three interviews with Vicky Gabereau in Vancouver on coast-to-coast CBC *National*, a really important show, and I wasn't good.[2] Vicky gave me plenty of scope and I talked but didn't tell the right thing, missed the real core, and was silly and egotistical, I'm afraid. Damn it. I can't remember all I said but I think I put myself down instead of telling what prompted the series, how I did twelve books through the winter, writing at five every morning, etc. I hope I improve as I go along. I should plan what I must say.

June 21, 1991[3]
Last time Judith [Miller] and Linda [Kenyon] were here, they said they thought I should start writing my journal again. At eighty-five, it should be unusual and interesting. The last of my journal they are transcribing was written between 1945–52 and is largely introspective. I no longer

seem to agonize about myself. Now I just live and enjoy life. When I lived with K, I spent most of my time trying to justify my right to have some life of my own. Since I've been on my own, I can do as I please, and I love it.

July 5, 1991

I'm mad. Four books published this year and I've not been invited to the CBA [Canadian Booksellers Association] convention ... I've not been invited. I always enjoy it. If they don't want to sell my books, why should I worry? I've worked darn hard doing interviews, talking, autographing, and now I'm ignored. Blast them anyway.

I was given the Culinary Guild Award, the Library party, Rogers Cable TV, *90 minutes* four times. I'm speaking tomorrow afternoon at the Schneider Haus symposium, but my publishers are ignoring me.

These may be my last books, certainly my last cookbooks. They should be selling really well, but are they? They were supposed to be sold in gift shops across the country, like the *Company's Coming* Series, which has sold millions of copies.[4] But they are only in a few local gift shops. My recipes, my books, are far better than *Company's Coming* but they're not being given the exposure. Also, the price is higher. I've worked so hard on those books, writing them and promoting them and if they aren't selling really well, it's my publishers' fault, the marketing dep't. Hell, why should I care? But I do, I'm mad.

July 16, 1991

Judith Miller is coming out this morning with books for me to read, autobiographical ones by May Sarton.[5] She's hoping they'll inspire me to write my biography. But how could I? I've had such a long and wonderful life, full of many adventures and people and problems and concerns. My journal is thousands of pages long and it doesn't tell half of it. It could make interesting reading if it were done well. Judith and Linda said there would be much that people would identify with and be helped by. I guess so. I was so sappy some of the time and I hope I'm not sappy now. I had so much growing to do, so much changing and it was often painful. But now I'm eighty-five and more serious, much of the time, than I have ever been and really excited about living. Ill health is my only real fear. I don't want that—ever.

[...]

Not that I really regret the cookbooks, they've been fun to do. They've given pleasure and help to many thousands of people (half a million sold) but I should somehow have managed to do much more creative writing as well.

Pierre [Berton] keeps saying I'm really a novelist, though I've never written a novel. Harold [Horwood], too, and Bill Mitchell call me a creative writer, because of my style, I suppose. I've always written about real people, real things, and made them come alive for readers. They tell me they *know* the people I've written about, not just in CBH and the magazine articles, but Bevvy Martin, Mother, Norm, and Ruby, and my friends in the cookbooks. I must, I must write more about so many people who have come into my life.

July 17, 1991
Tonight it occurred to me, when I had dinner with Mike Manson at Rundle's, last summer I was eighty-four then. I told him I was almost twenty-eight years old when I was married. Twenty-eight years I was married and twenty-eight years on my own. The first twenty-eight were difficult, searching years, trying to find who I was, not at all sure of my identity. The twenty-eight married years were more difficult, trying to live Keith's life and cope with his alcoholism and both our insecurities. The last twenty-eight years I've been living my own way and loving it and being creative, having fun and many friends and readers who love my books.

Perhaps I could do a trilogy!!! I feel excited when I think of the life I've been privileged to live. I've recorded much of it in my journal, mostly the early years of trial and error but great times of discovery and travel. I regret none of it, though while I was learning I was frequently baffled and sometimes despairing, but determined always to get through it. Working really hard to keep up my spirit, to survive and love and live attentively, if a bit recklessly and fearlessly.

September 10, 1991[6]
I'm in a tizzy, have a feeling I won't sleep as soon as I turn out my light. I've just read the press release sent out by WLU about the result of the Edna Staebler Award for Creative Non-Fiction. Instead of calling it that, they've called it the University Writing Contest, which makes it sound like a class exercise and it will probably get no notice at all. The young woman who won the award [Susan Mayes for *Ginger*] will get $3,000, and little else and that is not at all what I hoped the award would do. When I won the Canadian Women's Press Club award of $200 in 1950, the Canadian Press printed my picture and the story and I got letters and wires from people I didn't even know. The press release WLU has sent

out probably won't even be published, it is so dull. They should have sent the winner's picture—she's very pretty—and told more about her. What duds these academics are, though I guess this was handled by the people in the office who looked after the award.

September 24, 1991

Instead of writing here I should be writing a book. One of the best winters of my life was the one when I was working on the *Schmecks* series. M & S called a meeting in their boardroom on Sept. 18, 1989. I was given deadlines to meet. Every morning from there on until March 31, I would work in bed when I woke at 4:00 or 4:30. From there for two or three hours I'd go through the recipes, write in my notebook, do whatever I needed to do. I'd turn on my radio if I was sleepy again, sleep or rest until about eight or nine, then get up and work at my typewriter the rest of the morning. It gave me a great sense of accomplishment, no guilty feelings, and the whole series was done by March 31, except the last book which I enjoyed working on and lingered over until it was time to send it off to Jennifer [Glossop], who kept it and read it until its date was due, late in the fall of 1990.

For years, ever since I met him in 1940, I've been wanting to write about Fred. I've talked about him and people have said they were fascinated by his story, but I've always worked on something else that a publisher wanted. If I'm ever going to write about Fred, and Philip and George, I should do it now. But I probably won't. Why do I have this negative approach to the books? The longer I put it off the farther it fades from my memory. Am I just being lazy? Afraid of all the organization it would require? Would anyone publish it? Would it serve any purpose? Must it? (209)

September 27, 1991

Would I have written more, better, if I hadn't had to agonize over living with K's aberration? It was hell most of the time. But my best literary writing was done during that time. I had to think my way out of it. But it was damn hard to do, and I produced only one good book and a few magazine articles. Would I have done more, or better, if I'd been free and unworried? No use wondering, no use regretting. My life since K and I separated has been so much more productive and fun and *my own*. (223)

(undated) [7]
I remember years ago, fifty years ago, when I was having so many problems with K and trying to be a writer, looking for answers from Dr. Robins, whom I revered, the wisest man I knew. He seemed to know everything, but he said he no longer ponders, he just lives, I might add, grows like a tree. He said introspection should end at age twenty.

November 1, 1991 [8]
Perhaps we don't need to talk intimately with people we love. We just love them, feel for them. They perhaps instinctively know they can count on us, like my cats. We don't talk, but we know. I feel affection and awareness for many people and they respond, but I don't have time to be friends with all of them. Judith [Miller] experiences this with many of her students. They'd like to keep coming to her, she's a caring, generous person, but she has her own life to live, her priorities. We all do.

And there are people Judith calls sappers. They would cling if they were given a chance. I think I have many of those. I perhaps let them come here once, then I discourage them and sometimes I feel guilty about that. But people must find their own way. And yet would I have found mine if Dr. Robins hadn't loved me and given me so much encouragement though his real thinking about me, my work?

Quite often people tell me I am their role model and they admire me and want to emulate me in some way. Well, I'm glad they think I'm OK, but a role model? They don't really know me. They know I'm old and still working, enjoying my life, my cats, my friends, my lake, my books, my freedom, my independence, my knitting—that is my life and I love it. I guess I'm not a bad person, but I'm no saint. I'm selfish. I have my intolerances, my resentments, impatience. I love attention, I talk too much, and am often bored with other people's inconsequential conversations. How could I be a role model with all those faults? I'm a good storyteller and they like to listen to me. I make myself sound pretty good, fairly fearless, and funny. People like that, they seem to like being with me. But only for a while. I couldn't have them around more, couldn't live with anyone. I need my space, my solitude, my aloneness. I'm never lonely. I love having people here, invite them, welcome them, give them tea and muffins. I talk a lot and entertain them, make them laugh and they like that, they like me but what do I really give them? I get their attention, their adulation. I like that, and I like them. They go away from here feeling good, they tell me, feeling inspired, confident. Why is that?

But why wonder? That's the way it is, the way I am. So why think about it? It seems to be good. It pleases me and if it pleases whoever comes here, I'm very glad. That word *glad*, I like that. I must think of it more often. I must more often be *glad*. And show it. (414–16)

November 2, 1991
I don't like that word—work. I don't like sitting at my typewriter. I haven't touched it for weeks. Except for a couple of business-type letters I haven't used it for months.

I love to sit in my big chair with Cecily [Edna's cat] in my lap and where I can swivel round to look at the lake and the sky, the trees. And maybe some ducks are just swimming by and birds checking out the feeder at the corner of the patio. And maybe a chat on the phone with whoever calls me, and a drink of chocolate milk or fresh cider. And so a day goes by and I've done nothing that makes me feel that I've *accomplished*.

I've had so many of these fallow periods in my life. I tell myself what I should do, but I don't do it. Then I begin to hate myself for my laziness, my lack of will, my constant procrastination. I make lists and strike off the odd thing, maybe one thing a day, one inconsequential thing, and though there is much I should do, I don't do it. (424)

December 24, 1991[9]
Awake since 2:37. Have just finished reading my contract for my *Schmecks* series. The Cornerstone Books people have been offered the sale of the whole remaining series at a price that sounds like remaindering. I'm sure there is a violation of the contract in this. The series should have been a great success if it had been marketed as I suggested when we first envisioned the project. It should have been sold to gift shops and drug stores, at a price of $5 or $6 instead of $9.95 + GST = $10.65.

When I'm autographing books in stores, I've seen people look at the books with enthusiasm but put them down when they were told the selling price. Books of comparable size are all priced at $5 or $6.

The *Company's Coming* books, selling at $9.95 and GST, are twice as thick and have coloured pictures. No writing except recipes which are not as good as *Schmecks*, and the books are on sale everywhere in their own metal serial racks in supermarkets, gift shops, drug stores, airports. They have sold over five million.

The books have no anecdotes, which has made my books so popular, and the recipes are not as good. Jean Paré's name is not known as well as E.S., whose books are considered Cdn classics because they present the cuisine of a region. In *Fodor's* large travel book on Canada they mention E.S.'s famous contribution to the Mennonite heritage of southwestern Ontario.

I am very disappointed that the series has been badly marketed. It should have been a great success. People who have them love my books and I'm sure would have bought the series if the books had cost less and been made available in more outlets. Many people who buy cookbooks never go into a bookstore. They buy books in gift shops etc.

The airport in Montreal [Smith Books] had a whole shelf of *Company's Coming*, no *Schmecks* books at all. Wordsworth Books in Waterloo doesn't sell C.C. [*Company's Coming*]. People don't buy it.

Anyway, why can't I get this out of my mind? Why should I care? Because I worked hard at the series, I believe in it, I want people to have and to enjoy my books, and I am mad because the marketing has failed to make it successful. The series was well promoted. It has excellent reviews and good newspaper coverage, but the price and non-availability in gift outlets defeated it. (500–501)

January 26–27, 1992

Why do I write all of this? No one will ever read it. I'll never read it. But I always feel better having written—as if a day hasn't passed unrecorded into oblivion.

I can't stand the feeling I have of not doing anything. I'm working on nothing, no project, no deadline. Of course, I must do the piece for the *Farmer's Almanac*, I forget, I must do that. Perhaps today, anything to get over this malaise. I can't stand purposelessness, is that a word?

Working on a book seems useless now. I'm sure no one would publish what I wrote, not just because of the failure of the series, which was the marketing's fault, not mine, but because of the recession and cutting down of publishing of books that have a low print run. Publishers want only blockbusters, not my style. They can't stay in business unless they make money and costs are so high now that small print runs are too expensive, even though books may be very good.

In the news right now is the story of a book commissioned by Macmillan about a large Cdn conglomerate which wrote a letter threatening a libel suit if the book is published. That is blackmail, libel chill, they call it. The publisher is backing off because he can't afford to get involved in the legalities. Avie Bennett of M & S last year spent over $100,000 defending a book that had a slightly derogatory sentence in it about Conrad

Black. He demanded that the book be taken off the market. The case has not yet come to court and already Avie has had to spend all that money in legal fees.

Of course nothing I write would be controversial, but it might not be popular and saleable either. Why not? Am I losing my enthusiasm? If so I should be ready to die. Should I be getting my affairs in order for that? (574)

February 21, 1992

Now I sit in my Lazyboy chair by the window of my cottage and look at the birds at the feeders and the squirrels and the frozen lake and I'm not lonely or discontented. Days pass; I do nothing of any importance. I accomplish nothing and I don't like that, but I keep on doing nothing and that makes me so sad.

There are so many thoughts I've had, so many experiences, so many ideas for books to write and now I know no one would publish them. They wouldn't make any money for a publisher, no matter how good they might be, so why bother to write them? But if I don't write, I am dead.

So, I write here, and that eases me a bit in these early morning hours when I can't sleep any longer.

There are always things I should be doing. I have priorities. I keep putting them off, or slowly getting them done in spurts. Like the *Almanac* piece. Next I'll do income tax figures. Then I must answer letters. I have a whole pile in my window sill.

Then what? Dr. Robins's letters—no one will publish them. Should I do it myself, a very limited edition? For whom? I'd have no distribution, so why bother?

Also, my book of quotations, it's wonderful, could give much inspiration, as it has to me through the years. I sent it to Doug Gibson; he returned it months later without even a covering letter of rejection.

Fred [Kruger]'s story—fascinating—but who would be interested in it now when so many young people are going to jails, coming out, and going back in again? My involvement with Fred was unusual and gave me much to think about, changed me as well as him. But who would care to read about this?

But I must do something. I can't let myself vegetate. I've always put off writing about the past, always too eagerly living in the present and wanting to write about it. But now my present is mostly self-aggrandizement and that's nothing to write about, basking in past glory, my books, the Cookie War, awards, fan mail, talk. Always I talk, and people seem to like to listen. They come to see me, to listen, and they invite me for dinner and I'm pleased about that and I *talk*.

But during these long winter days and nights I have lots of time to write. I haven't been anywhere for almost three weeks and all I've accomplished was a rehash of *Schmecks* for a piece on Mennonite cooking and recipes for the *Old Farmer's Almanac*.

I waste all of my evenings watching TV and, except for the Olympics, it's pretty damn poor, a complete waste of time. At my age time is precious and should be treasured and used in a fulfilling way, not wasted on TV and [knitting] mice and long phone conversations with Norm and Lorna about nothing consequential.[10] I'm thinking this, writing this, but will I do anything to change my slothfulness? And it isn't old age. I've gone through these fallow periods of time-wasting all my life. By now one would think I'd have learned to stop having them, a long build-up of habit. I should keep on working, never stop the momentum. It's so hard to get a new habit started. But it is the only way to go, the only way for me to live. Why do I resist it? (621–24)

March 6, 1992

And that's that, another wasted day. Watched two short days passing without any accomplishment. And no reason why that should be so. I have so much I should do instead of just sitting and reading. But I do enjoy reading and haven't indulged myself for a long time, not while I was writing all of my *Schmecks* books.

At eighty-six, have I not earned the right to do whatever it pleases me to do, instead of working at writing? Just take it easy? Read, knit mice, watch TV, talk on the phone, accept invitations, give my friends tea, muffins? Why not?

I remember long ago Dr. Robins saying, "Edna girl, do the thing that only you can do. Use your talent. You have much to tell; you have the ability to tell it." And I certainly have much more to tell. I've told it in my journals, but I should retell it, amplify it, fill in the gaps. (662)

May 8, 1992 [11]

Toronto is no longer The Good peaceful city it once was, nor is it a smallish comfortable city of single homes. Now two ? million people live in high-rise apartments and townhomes, crowded together and many have no homes at all, just live on the streets or in shelters. It's hard for me to conceive of it, I who live at beautiful Sunfish, with my cozy cottage,

Cecily, sky full of birds, no noise, the lake, the wooded hills. It is Paradise, and I thank God for it every day of my life. (819)

June 12, 1992
All this year I've written nothing for publication except a piece about Mennonite cooking for the *Old Farmer's Almanac 1993*. But I've been writing here in my journal almost every day, early in the morning, and why? Because Judith Miller suggested that an eighty-five-year-old woman's life might be interesting to read. But I don't think I've written anything worth publishing, my journal has become mundane, more like a diary, a mere recording of events—I did this, I went there, etc. No ideas or growth, no advancements. It gives me a sense of guilt because the time I've spent writing here might have produced a book that could have given pleasure or information, the story of Fred and George, Philip, the Molly book I started years ago, Dr. R's letters and mine.[12] Judith suggested that I should write autobiographical books and last time she was here she said she'd like to read about the men in my life. Now, if she only knew. I wouldn't dare write about all of them. (924–25)
[…]
What am I now? I don't want to speculate, don't want to be introspective, don't want to be perfect. I just live each day and each moment as it comes along and I don't worry about myself.

September 1, 1992[13]
I read more of my '54 and '55 this morning and in the afternoon typed, on typewriter, about ten pages. It took over two hours; the writing is sometimes hard to read. I made many mistakes. In the evening I read more. Such soul searching, such melodrama and agony and fear and guilt and longing for love and wisdom. I wonder if anyone else would relate to it and perhaps be encouraged by it. It might scare anyone from marriage. (1,128)

September 4, 1992
But why perpetuate the years now? People in similar circumstances might relate to them, tho' now there are support groups for people with problems and they talk about them more freely and are not stigmatized. I do find my old journal fascinating. Not much fun, too serious and searching and scared. I was really in a bad state during those times and had to fight hard to keep sane and productive. But I did survive and maybe it would be helpful to read about that. But I'm sure no publisher

would take a chance during these recession days. Maybe when I'm dead. Anyway it won't hurt me to type them out and make them readable. I'm not doing any writing now. (1,138)

September 7, 1992
My journals are much more dramatic, so many awful things kept happening or threatening to happen because of K's drinking, my trying to cope and to find a way to be loving and alive. I was always philosophizing, figuring ways to keep happy and loving and alive to overcome my resentment and anger. I remember that I used to envy people who seemed to be naturally loving, they didn't have to work at it as I did.

Now I don't think or write about that sort of thing at all. Does that mean I've finally achieved natural lovingness, or that I don't give a damn and if I'm angry I say so?

I doubt it. I seldom show anger, except with my publisher for not selling my books and politicians for doing a poor job and threatening our country.

As for loving naturally, I don't know. I find most people I meet interesting, or do I? I do most of the talking when I'm with people who come here. Maybe I feel loving because I love myself more, don't worry about myself, no longer try to be perfect. I accept myself. If I'm loving, fine, if not, so what? I can't love everybody.

I'm seldom bored. If I find people dull I do the talking. Of course, I find that always interesting, if repetitious. I'm no longer introspective. I just do and say what comes naturally and I have fun and love to make people laugh, tho' I don't try to. And I am constantly grateful: for life, for health, for Sunfish, for Cecily, for friends, for having enough money, for books, beauty in the universe, and because people seem to like me and seek me out. I am a very lovely lady and keep thinking so. (1,143–44)

October 7, 1992
There is a certain magic about telling a good story, a gift I am grateful for, and I have had so many things happen to me that I can tell stories about. But I know I'd be better if I organized my talks ahead of time. (1,200)

November 10, 1992
He [Nelson Ball] said, guessing, the papers were probably about $20 000,

same as the previous calculation, even tho' I have four more cartons to add.[14]

Apparently I am not considered a major writer because I haven't written a novel. I told him about CBH, which he didn't know about, and he thought because it is literary it might make a difference.

Last night he called me again and said it was only a guess but he thought that the whole collection might be valued from $30–50 thousand. Incredible—when I think of the hours and hours of writing it contains. I guess Harold was right when he said I shouldn't write a second cookbook or I'll be known as a cookbook writer instead of the creative writer that I am. (1,269)

December 20, 1992[15]

Of course, university libraries now have machines that quickly duplicate manuscripts but my journals are probably millions of pages and I have more than thirty cartons of papers. If they're not easily accessible to whoever is interested in them, they'd probably never be used. But why should I care? I'll be dead. But if anyone worked on my papers, used them and perhaps had the journals published, I'd live forever. Or would I? But I hope in that way my life would not have been in vain. That is a silly statement, no life is in vain and mine in my lifetime has touched many people thro' my books and articles and my contacts with people. Influence goes on forever, ad infinitum, from person to person. Spirit never dies. It is the resurrection and the life for eternity. (1,266–67)

January 9, 1993[16]

Since Mother died in 1972, CBH was published, then *More Schmecks, Maggie, Schmecks Appeal* and the series. I was given an LLD and got involved in the Cookie War, was given a number of awards and went to New Zealand, France, and a couple of cruises. I've had many visitors and made some great new young friends. The past twenty years have been the most productive of my life and the most fun and interesting. I've been very happy here alone in my cottage with Willie and Cecily [Edna's cats] and people who have come to see me. Almost every day I've had a wonderful life this past twenty years and I'm still having it. I have much to do to keep me very busy and enthusiastic for many years to come, however many there may be. Ralph [Hodgson, Edna's brother-in-law] keeps saying I'll live to be a hundred and I mentally squirm when he says it. Common sense tells me I can't be healthy and competent forever. I don't want to wear down, become less able to do things here and alone. I don't even want to have to be taken care of and be a burden to other people, especially to me. As soon as I am no longer able to carry on in my usual way, without pain or disablement, I want to be finished. It's hard to imagine being gone, leaving this house that I love, and all my books and Cecily and the lake. I'm sure my spirit will haunt this place forever. It could never be gone, never die. My books, my papers, my journals are my immortality, and my friends and relations. I've had such a wonderful life. I'd like it to go on forever, as long as I am healthy and curious and loving. (1,330)

February 8, 1993
And here I am, eighty-seven and still healthy, mobile, and able to do anything I like, but lazy and wasting precious time. But I have knitted over 24,000 mice now and written eighteen books and some people consider that an accomplishment. I would too, if I didn't feel guilty about not doing a great deal more. (1,383)

March 3, 1993[17]
I couldn't believe what I was told in K's church—Christian Science. We alternated between it and my Presbyterian church every Sunday. After being dissatisfied with cs doctrine I began questioning what I heard.

Dr. Munro preached and I came away always arguing mentally with him. He was an educated man. So, I thought, was I. Why must I believe and do what he tells me and his congregation? Shouldn't I be thinking for myself? What did I really believe? That was a worrisome thought. I started to read and to think of these things and I found it very disturbing. I could no longer go to church, it made me unhappy. I became almost obsessed with finding an answer that satisfied me. What was God? What was loving? What was the afterlife? All the orthodox answers were no longer satisfying. Many of the books I read were obscure, too complicated, theoretical, obscure. Only a highly educated person could find a way thro' their labyrinths. I must believe in something simple, that any child could understand. How else could simple people find their way? The Answer had to be easy to follow, consciously or unconsciously, simple, continuously repeated, lived by, practised daily until it became such a habit of living that one was no longer conscious of it, of oneself. I paid attention to people—some had it. They are so naturally gentle, loving. I envied them. I was so self-conscious and anxious. Sometimes I'd think I had found the Answer and I'd be ecstatic but then it would evade me

and I was lost again. I kept trying and agonizing and reading and thinking. It was a very worrisome time. I talked sometimes about it but got
little help. K was drinking too much, running around with women. I
felt I must find a way that could change him, but I've written about all
this in my journal of that time and it took years of living to change me
and give me peace of mind until I could simply love without fear or
constant questioning. K's sojourn into AA for his alcoholism taught me
the art of living one day at a time, living it fully and joyously and lovingly, conscious of every minute, outside oneself. That is ideal. I haven't
achieved it. I still get mad about things and some people, and I become
temporarily obsessed about them—things concerned with my books,
why they aren't marketed properly, or now I'm concerned about the
new jacket for *Schmecks*. Things like that bother me until I resolve them
or let them peter out if I don't do something about them—like writing
a letter or making a phone call, which would be unpleasant. I avoid
unpleasantness. I procrastinate. I get mad at myself.

So maybe I haven't yet learned the Answer. Maybe as long as one
lives one must keep searching, trying. For perfection, no. I used to try for
that and it always disturbed me. I tried too hard. I could never achieve
it. Now I don't try any more to be perfect, I know I can't be it. I'll just keep
reading, making mistakes, getting mad, sometimes negative, but still
hoping for understanding and tolerance and unself-consciousness. I'm
seldom now introspective. I just live and love my little cat and many
people and my house and my lake and wherever I am and with people
I meet, constant awareness of life around me. Every day, every precious
minute. And what of an afterlife? Do I believe I'll go on forever as an individual? It's hard to conceive of obliteration. Complete nothingness, no
longer me. That's why I believe that now is the important time. Everything I do or say or write has influence and goes on forever, negatively
or positively, it affects someone, somehow. So an unborn child lives forever as it affects, influences those who are concerned with it. Can I make
that claim? I seldom try to explain it. When I'm asked by someone I try,
but I don't think I'm successful. So what? It satisfies me. It's a sort of
deep knowledge inside me. I can't explain it, yet it's so simple, really. At
this moment Cecily lying on my bed, licking her paw. It gives me pleasure to watch her. I hope that loving in me is somehow transmitted, like
radio waves or air waves into the other part of the unconscious, to go on
forever and ever. For me afterlife is that spiritual transmittance, starting
in the present in my brain, or even if I had some little brain, like a cen-
tipede or a mourning dove, it could have its place, its influence, its life,

its process—is that simple? Is it too complicated to explain, to grasp? It shouldn't be. It's simply oneself consciously living. (1,440)

September 29, 1993[18]

Why do I persist in reading these things [diary entries], in living in the past? What a life I have had, what a struggle until my later years, which have been serene, friendly and interesting, rewarding, until now when I seem to be having bit-by-bit problems—fleas, cats, teeth, and my thyroid. What next? At eighty-seven I can't expect rejuvenation. But if I can keep my sense of humour alive I can still enjoy life and make my friends enjoy being with me. If I can no longer make them laugh, I want to go *quick*. (1,948)

February 15, 1994

Every morning I lie awake and think of what I *must* do that day. Sometimes I do a little bit but most of the time I procrastinate as I have done all my life.

There were so many books I was going to write. They have not been written. Now I think, "so what?" It might have been helpful to someone or interesting if I'd written Fred's story. I've told it verbally so many times to fascinated listeners. Amongst my literary papers are Fred's "books" about his life, but no researcher could put it together and tell of Fred's friendship with K and me, especially with me.

Last year I was going to transcribe more of my journal but because my typewriter broke and I got the electronic one I've not yet learned to use, I did nothing but read.

May 16, 1994[19]

The WLU Press committee met on Wednesday and they approved the publication. Sandra W. told me one of those people said he'd learned more about the '50s from reading a few of Ruby's letters than he had from a whole book he'd read earlier.[20] I'm really excited about this project. Anything could happen. It might be a bestseller and Ruby could at last be famous and have lots of money. At the Murrays' luncheon yesterday I spoke to Elizabeth Baird, food editor of *Canadian Living*, about publishing the letters individually in the magazine. She said to send her a copy of them and she'll present it to their executive team!

May 19, 1994

Ruby went back to Peterborough yesterday morning. No unpleasantness during her visit. She's excited about the publicity of her letters being published. She'll be an author! A dream come true. She asked me if she'd get fan mail. I told her she'd probably have to have her picture taken for the back cover of the book and she looked nervous. I hope we both live long enough to experience the book's launching. It takes so long for a book to be processed.

June 30, 1994

In my talk to the CAA [Canadian Authors Association] I said I had always wanted to be a writer because I thought it could bring me Fame, Fortune, Freedom, but I didn't follow that through in the talk. I don't think I ever had enough confidence in myself to aspire to Fame. I did hope I could earn enough money to give me freedom to travel and do as I pleased. I should have said Faith instead of Fame, not faith in myself, tho' I needed and still need that, but I learned that I needed faith in the importance or interest of whatever I was writing about. I know when I started writing about Neil's Hbr, I was so nervous of my own inability to write, but I had to keep telling myself that Neil's Hbr and the sea and the people were wonderful and I must learn to write well enough to share them as I had experienced them. And I did have faith in them, and enthusiasm for them, which, with much strength and hard work and rewriting for seven years, did come through. And so it was with all my writing after that. I had faith in my subject and enthusiasm for it, I never thought of fortune when I was writing. It was merely a byproduct. I never expected it—magazine articles didn't pay much. $300 was my highest pay for a piece that might have taken me a couple of months to write. I always thought only of making it the best I could possibly do it and fortunately didn't need to make a living with my writing until after K left and my income was less than $8,000 a year, tho' I could manage on that.

It wasn't until I wrote *Schmecks* and it became a bestseller that I earned more, and then more and more as my broker increased my savings. My lifestyle, as always, was simple and satisfying and beautiful here at the lake, where friends love to come and I have my cats and I am and hope to be constantly and forever grateful. (2,305–307)

December 2, 1994

It seems old age is finally catching up with me. It is inevitable, I suppose, but what now? Must we be taken care of? I fell on Wednesday when I took out the garbage. Three major errors on driving. I went very slowly up the steps at the party, and when I walk I'm aware of my hips. They don't hurt but I'm aware of them, a bad sign. I should walk more to limber them up but with winter coming, ice and snow, I might fall. Can I keep living here alone? I don't want *help*. If people have to come out here and pick me up they'll soon stop inviting me. I'd have to make arrangements about getting food—*Hell*. (2,524–25)

February 9, 1995 [21]
In 1968 I had to battle to get the *Schmecks* title for my first cookbook and it was certainly successful.
WLU wants: Haven't Any News
The Letters of a Fifties Housewife
At the bottom of the cover—Edna Staebler, Editor
Afterword by Marlene Kadar

I want: Ruby's Letters of the 1950s
Edited by her sister
Edna Staebler
Afterword by Marlene Kadar

That connects my name with Ruby's, otherwise I'm sure people would wonder why in hell Edna Staebler, the writer, would become an editor of letters by an anonymous housewife.
I shall stand firm, and they'd damn well better give in.

March 15, 1995
I'm mad as hell. A letter today from Lorna Marsden giving me the results of the meeting with "the experts" to which I was not invited.[22] It negates most of the rules I had stipulated and the definition of creative non-fiction produced to be sent out to the publishers is a paragraph of academic jargon that I do not understand and doubt if many writers of creative non-fiction could recognize, or publishers, or their promotion staff who send in the books to be judged.
There's no mention of the purpose of the award, as I gave it for the recognition and encouragement of an unestablished writer. As it is in this new set of rules, the award could be won by anyone who has a first or second book in the genre: Margaret Atwood, Alice Munro, Tim[othy] Findley or Pierre Berton could win it. No way! They don't need it. I want my award to go to someone who does need it. (2,725)

January 5, 1996 [23]
The announcement has been made—I am a member of the Order of

Canada. Margaret Tyrol, a reporter from the *Record*, called me last night and told me the announcement had been made to the media. We talked for about an hour. Over the years, I have done so many things…. I've made a list of the people I must phone today to tell about my membership in the Order of Canada.

January 6, 1996

Thirty-five people congratulated me yesterday about the Order of Canada. The correspondence I had with the governor general's secretary was addressed to me with CM, BA, LLD after my name. The piece in the *Record*, headed, "Order of Canada Awarded to Two Locals," was brief but well done.

January 14, 1996

People at the concert hall greeted me enthusiastically and congratulated me on my ninetieth [birthday] and the Order of Canada…. The governor general called me a remarkable woman. What is remarkable about me? My old age—or just that I've done what I've done because I wanted to do it and had to, like deadlines for my books and knowing many people who became my friends.

May 30, 1996 [24]

On Monday I was pleased to get a letter from Romeo LeBlanc, the governor general, thanking me for my books, saying he enjoyed meeting me. He said he liked reading books about people in Canada—Indians, Mennonites, and Maritimers. I think he had read the books…. ¯

September 21, 1997 [25]

I'm sure no one would publish my journal entries but there is much good writing and feeling and philosophizing there that it seems a waste. Transcribing is difficult. I'd like to pay someone to do it but it costs a lot and would take a very long time because it's so hard to read my writing. Linda Kenyon did some for me six years ago. I paid her $3,000 and she did only a part of '52, not worth it to put in a filing cabinet then Guelph U forever.

Maybe I should work on Dr. R's letters. I think they are worth publishing, perhaps with my letters to him. But who would publish them? And if I paid for publication myself who would distribute the books? I couldn't. It seems I've left things too late. But I must work on something for the winter in the apartment. I hope I don't fall into the pattern of all my friends who are there, putter in the AM, then go to their hairdresser once a week. They dress for lunch, then rest, have a cup of tea with somebody in the aft, dress again for dinner, watch TV at night alone. Sometimes they aren't well and go to a doctor. (4,168)

October 18, 1997
I think I've changed my mind about moving into town. I can't bear to leave Sunfish and my life here.

[...]

The apartment at Waterloo Heights is being prepared for me, floors done over, walls are painted. Chris Cameron, the administrator, is supplying the drapes, a floor lamp, chesterfield, bed, and two dining-room chairs. She said they are looking forward to having me there.

But, I don't want to go. Preparing to move is an almost insurmountable chore. I've been making lists for weeks of things I couldn't do without.

And what about living there? I can't bear the thought of it. I'm so comfortable here. Everything is where I want it.

There I'd be confined to those rooms, almost empty and without lamps wherever I might choose to sit or lie down. And what about Mally? She'd have nothing to do or to see from the windows on the sixth floor, her litter box on the floor of the linen cupboard! I know she'd be very unhappy. And I know I would be too. (4,208)

December 29, 1997
Jim [Edna's nephew] came out yesterday morning to put the plastic over my windows to keep out the drafts/draughts? Which is it? He said Ruby is still mad at me for not correcting her poor spelling in *Ruby's Letters*. She blames me for the fact that her grandchildren don't come to see her and didn't want a copy of the book when she offered it to them. *And* she still hasn't read the book, says she lived it and knows what's in it.

The book has given pleasure and insight to thousands of people who have bought it and they love the quaint spelling and they love Ruby. She thinks because the spelling in the book wasn't corrected, people will think she's *stupid*. There's no explaining anything to her. She has a fixation. (4,165)

January 23, 1998
I was very introspective when I was married to K but now I don't know myself much. I always have too much to do: letters to answer, visitors almost every day. I like my life. When people come here, I talk a lot but people tell me that's why they come, they want to hear my stories. They ask me questions, tell me I'm their role model, etc. And I know I have a happy time with them and they seem to enjoy coming and want to come again. I don't want to think about me and I used to be a good listener— now I do most of the talking. (4,194)

February 4, 1998
Can't sleep—my mind has been racing around composing letters to Doug Gibson about the new edition of *More Schmecks*, which is lovely to look at but has been bound so it snaps shut and didn't lie flat so the recipes can be used. I wrote him a letter early in November and told him to be sure to have the right binding and I urged the editor to be sure of it and in spite of my warnings they did it wrong. Why? Probably a couple of cents *cheaper*.

Then my mind got started on the local hall of fame, which seems to be composed mostly of athletes, the arts almost completely ignored. And tho' ten or eleven local people have been given Canada's highest honour, The Order of Canada, Mabel Krug and I are the only ones recognized.[26] Who decides these things? Don't they know anything about priorities? I'd like to tell them what I think when I make my speech at the induction.

I'm supposed to be grateful, or flattered at finally being accepted. I think I've been given more honours and awards than anyone in the hall. I thought they were waiting for me to die before they acknowledged that. Tennis players, rugby, badminton, cattle breeders, 4-H clubs, none of any national distinction in there. Is it a sports hall of fame or a rural one? Should I refuse to be one of them? Because the arts have been ignored? Or should I smile and say how grateful I am to be so honoured? Should I be a hypocrite? Or should I say what I think? The bio they sent me which is to be hung on a wall with my picture is ridiculous, saying I had a brief career as a teacher. I had one year teaching and fifty years writing. The bio said I'd written six books, not twenty-one,[27] and did not mention honours and awards, except the CM and D. Lett. I think I'll set that straight. I had Kevin fax my bio in *Cdn Who's Who* and I'll send them that.[28] They'll no doubt say *it's too long*.

Don't they want to be proud of local achievement? (4,205)

April 9, 1998[29]
In my memorial to Lillian [Snyder, a friend of Edna's], I said, "She was fun to be with." I think that is probably the greatest compliment I could give her, or anyone. I'd like it to be said about me. Some people have said it to me, but most say I am their role model, which makes me nervous. How could I live up to their aspirations? (4,287)

April 26, 1998
Today I am the only living author in this hall of fame. Because I am ninety-two years old I thought I didn't qualify until I was dead. I think fifteen people in Waterloo Region have been honoured by being given membership in the Order of Canada but only three have made it to the local. Because I consider it a special occasion I am wearing the medal that was pinned on me by the Gov. Gen. two years ago today. On that very impressive day at Rideau Hall, after the elegant dinner, I said to a woman who had congratulated me, "The medal is so beautiful. I hate to put it in a safety deposit box where it will not be seen again. I'd like to wear it on a silver chain around my neck."

The woman said, "Why don't you, it's yours. You can do with it what you like." But all the recipients had to go to a table to pick up the leather case for their medal from an official in uniform. I asked him if it would be OK to wear the medal on a chain round my neck.

He looked shocked and said, "Madam, it is not costume jewelry. It represents Canada's highest honour and must be worn above all other medals and only on special occasions. I'm sure the Queen would object." (4,308)

May 7, 1998
Also a letter from Paul Knowles who would like to publish my correspondence with Dr. Robins.[30] Wthout any promotion or distribution costs it would cost me over $8,000, which I suppose I could deduct from my income tax, but what would I do with over 2,000 books? How could I promote them? Where? The project, tho' long dear to my heart, would take much time and energy, editing, re-typing over two hundred pages. And this morning Kathryn [Wardropper] is bringing out the books I must read for my award.[31] That could take all summer.

I must speak to Sandra [Woolfrey] about all this. I wish Doug Gibson would be interested. I'm afraid I don't have much faith in Paul Knowles's self-publishing company. I've never had to self-publish. Paul has much enthusiasm and energy but no reputation in the literary world. Would

I lose mine too if I self-published a book? I've never tried to have it done by a *real* publisher. I've never had to be aggressive because M & S and MHR [McGraw-Hill Ryerson] have always *asked* for my books and wanted more. But I've asked Doug to come here to talk about more of my writing and he's ignored me. All he's been interested in is my *cookbooks*, because they have sold phenomenally. (4,325-26)

June 8, 1998
I finished reading the transcribed part of my 1953 and '54 journal yesterday AM. What a life and some good writing wasted. What can I do with it? Probably nothing. (4,368)

June 9, 1998
Now it is 4:42. Why do I bother to write all this? A record of my old age. Thousands of pages which no one will read. I can hardly read it myself. And what interest is in it for anyone? None. Writing here is just a habit, a compulsion. (4,372)

July 1, 1998
Radio telling us we are Canadians. I get tired of hearing our constant search for a Cdn identity, but our family has been here in Canada almost two hundred years, the eighth generation. We have always felt we're Canadian, a mixture of Swiss, German, French, Irish, and Scotch in equal proportions. (4,410)

July 12, 1998
I'm not satisfied with what I write here every morning in bed. It's like a diary, I did this, I did that, not at all thoughtful. I miss so much, like a Thursday night when I was in the sunroom alone with Mally and the moon came up over the hills at the south end of the lake, a huge, bright, golden orb, lovely to see. I watched it rise and become bright white and high in the sky.

Also, the tranquil stillness of the lake every morning as I sit on the chesterfield and eat my bran flakes and watch the still and sparkling water and the reflections near the shore. I love these precious moments. (4,419)

August 30, 1998
I called Jean Williams and had a good talk about Neil's Harbour and all her family, all doing well. Lily is in The Manor, a convalescent home

for seniors. Lil is now fifty-four and can't walk but is happy in her new place. Jean is seventy-four. Owen retires and is making boat models. There is no fishing except lobster and crab. Jean's grandchildren have university degrees and her son Freddie has retired and is working on his book about Neil's Hbr. She was very glad to hear from me, urged me to come down for a visit, but how could I? Most of my friends there are dead. I could no longer walk up the hills and along the sea to the Lighthouse Point. The lighthouse now has a balcony across it and the lower part now is an ice cream parlour! Jean said they all have cars now and could drive me wherever I wanted to go. (4,473)

December 31, 1998
Tonight is New Year's Eve and I'm invited, as usual, to the Murrays'.[32] I can't enjoy parties as I once did because I can't hear conversations, only snatches, and I can't take part. I wouldn't mind staying home. I'm alone here every other night. It would just be another night. But if I don't go I won't be invited any more and I don't want to give up. I invite small groups here and I do most of the talking. I don't have to listen and keep asking people to repeat things for me. How long can I keep that up? People tell me they come here to listen to me and I always seem to have stories to tell them. I'm not aware of a problem. They keep coming and I'm happy to have them. (4,673)

January 25, 1999[33]
This morning I wrote five letters. In one to Gerry, in Florida for six months, I wrote answering his "Silent witnessing." I like that. I guess that's the initiation of the creative process. Then comes the compulsion to tell or show, the excitement. For me, writing has never been trying to achieve an ambition. It has been an enthusiasm for something that had to be expressed and the need to learn how best to express it, as in CBH: seven years of writing and rewriting, a carton full of various drafts as I kept trying to tell it better, give it better form. That was my beginning, my apprenticeship.

Simplify, simplify, make it clearer, easier to read, to visualize, to feel. I wanted my Mennonite friends to be able to enjoy it. I had to overcome an earlier thought that I should write for the *Atlantic Monthly*, that I should be more intellectual, but took a long time to realize my limitations. Writing about people, I had to learn how to let them speak for themselves in their own way. (4,697)

March 9, 1999
"To Youth," by John V.A. Weaver, a poem I have always loved since I
found it in a book sent to me by Tom Glover.[34]

> This I say to you.
> Be arrogant! Be true!
> True to April lust that sings
> Through your veins. These sharp springs
> Matter most.... Afteryears
> Will be time enough for sleep....
> Carefulness ... and tears...
>
> Now while life is raw and new,
> Drink it clear, drink it deep!
> Let the moonlight's lunacy
> Tear away your cautions. Be
> Proud, and mad, and young, and free!
> Grasp a comet! Kick at stars
> Laughingly! Fight! Dare!
> Arms are soft, breasts are white,
> Magic's in the April night—
>
> Never fear. Age will catch you,
> Slow you down, ere it dispatch you
> To your long and solemn quiet....
>
> What will matter then the riot
> Of the lilacs in the wind?
> What will mean—then—the crush
> Of lips at hours when birds hush?
>
> Purple, green and flame will end
> In a calm, grey blend.
> Only... graven in your soul
> After all the rest is gone
> There will be the ecstacies ....
> Those alone ....

I told Joan I didn't find life yet a calm, gray blend, as long as I can see.[35]
Calm perhaps, but not gray. (4,748)

April 6, 1999
Today? A man is coming to talk to me about giving a talk to two-hun-

dred secondary school students who have won awards for their writing. They will pay me "an honorarium of $500," which is a lot so I must be *good* and inspiring. The man told me on the phone that he heard me speak to Gerry [Noonan]'s creative writing class at WLU many years ago and he has never forgotten it. I hope I can do it again. He'll tell me when he comes today what he wants, my life as a writer, or how to do it over and over again. First believing that what I have to tell is important or beautiful or interesting or exciting, and *I must believe it* and *be willing to work at it until I feel I have brought it to life on the page.* I must watch every word to be sure it is exactly right and true, not trite, not repeated, unless needed.

I must never give up—*Ruby's Letters*, Dr R's, six years for *More Schmecks*, months for an article, rearranging, rewriting sentences, the order is so important, for emphasis. (4,771)

April 15, 1999

But the club where I've been a member for seventy years and contributed much won't acknowledge me until I'm *dead*. Well, I won't commit suicide. (4,781)

July 28, 1999

Judith Miller came out at ten to interview me about my award for a community radio show. We talked about our winner. She favours *Crybaby*, that book about incest written by an Edmonton English professor which is to me so obscurely written that I can't understand it but which she thinks is the most sophisticated and experimental of all the books sent in.[36] She feels very strongly about this, being the only one of our judges who teaches creative writing, is herself a poet, and has written and recently published a book that I, and others, don't understand. I don't have a PhD. I don't know the words, the rules, the descriptions of ways of writing. She has called me a "postmodernist." What's that? I try always to write as simply and clearly as I can, as I might talk, only more carefully. Like modern abstract painting, I don't understand magic realism and experimental writing. I guess I'm obsolete. Have I a right to refuse it as a winner of my award? Should it go to a university professor writing about incest, her own by her father? Why would she want to reveal all that to the public? Judith said at our time these things were never revealed but now, thanks to women's lib, they can be talked about. (4,903)

July 29, 1999

In my own writing I have always tried to write as clearly, simply and honorably and universally as I can and for as many readers as I could reach, aware of my audience as readers who are interested and seeking and could be aware and appreciative. I remember as I worked on CBH, how I struggled to forsake facts for the honest and universal, the artistic, to show what I had experienced and been excited about as honestly as I could, in the best words I could find. I wanted to *share*, to give my understanding and love of the people, the landscape, the community I was writing about.

For my award, I would like it to go to the person who has given all that, not glibly, not just cleverly, but thoughtfully, clearly, so any reader could experience what I had been privileged to feel.

I've just looked up and read on page 146 of CBH my description of a glorious sunrise which had exalted me. I wanted to waken the whole village to see it, and as it faded I wondered how I could share it and write it. I spent hours thinking about that sunrise and trying to capture it in words. Did I succeed? As I read it this morning I remembered it. I remembered the ecstacy I felt, but have I communicated that to my reader? I tried. (4,906)

August 9, 1999

I've been thinking about living with cats, or any pets, always in an atmosphere of affection on my part. It is truly unconditional, uncritical love, allowing a cat to be a natural cat and loving its every action, its earnest, pleading, green eyes, and its faith in me as a supplier of food. I must think more of this and expand on it when I speak to the evening meeting of the Pet Helpers fundraising. Also, I think I must somehow give a home to that dear little pregnant stray cat. I love her and can't bear the thought of her being out in the cold and afraid of all the predators that threaten her. (4,924)

December 22, 1999

I woke this morning just as I dreamed that Mary Lou [(Dimma) Cuff, Ruby's daughter and Edna's niece] was asking me, "what do you think about dying?" And I kept thinking about that. What do I think? I must think about that now and try to put it into words. A long time ago when death for me was not imminent as it should be for me when I am ninety-four, I believed firmly that life was eternal for everyone and everything because everything that has had life, has life, has had an influence, an effect, on someone, something else, and that has gone on and on forever.

So, even an unborn child has had its influence, its effect, its life, its love which is undying, eternal. But impersonal. Is the influence, effect, only alive as long as there is memory of it in the minds of those who have been influenced, often without acknowledging or realizing it? Dr. Robins and I sometimes discussed these ideas. He understood them and agreed with me, did not believe in a personal afterlife, but later he told me he had changed his mind and did believe there was a lasting personal life. I wish we'd talked more about that. He never explained his change of mind, and then he died. But for me he would live forever in my thoughts. His influence on me was profound. He was the wisest man I knew and in the many years since we talked together I have not met anyone I've revered and believed as I have him. I depended on him. I trusted him implicitly. He was my mentor, my example of how I wanted to be, how I must search always to learn more, to find wisdom, and to express it in the best words that I could use to share clearly and simply for other people to read and feel as I have felt. Have I succeeded? In part I have, in the books I have written, I think I have, even in the cookbooks because so many people have written to me and have told me my books have meant so much to them, have changed their lives. I am so grateful for that. They were written with love I felt for the people I wrote about, even the food I enjoyed.

[...]

So many lovely things have been happening for me this week, cards from old friends and new ones. They make me feel bursting with joy and they make me feel humble. How can I live up to the wonderful things people have said or written about me? (5,046)

Notes

1 Box R3–5. Diaries June–Sept 1990.
2 Vicky Gabereau, former host of one of CBC's afternoon radio programs.
3 Box R3–5. Diaries June 1, 1991–August 10, 1991.
4 Jean Paré's hugely successful *Company's Coming* cookbook series, launched in April 1981, sold over twenty million copies by 2003. The aim of this series was to simplify cooking for Canadians.
5 May Sarton (1912–1993) Belgium-born American writer, author of over fifty titles, including novels, poetry, memoirs, and journals. Sarton's interest in

the everyday and in ordinary subjects such as animals and flowers presented parallels with Staebler's interests.

6 Box R3–5. Diaries August 12, 1991–October 3, 1991.

7 Box R3–5. Diaries August 12, 1991–October 3, 1991.

8 Box R3–5. Diaries October 4, 1991–December 23, 1991.

9 Box R3–5. Diaries December 24, 1991–March 8, 1992.

10 This is a reference to small, knitted catnip mice that Staebler makes and gives to friends who have cats.

11 Box R3–5. Diaries May 8, 1992–July 9, 1992.

12 In the mid-1950s, Staebler undertook a novel fictionalizing her experiences in Europe. The protagonist, Molly, is a naive young woman from "Inglenook," Ontario, whose travels abroad in search of culture become an education in matters of the opposite sex. The book was never published.

13 Box R3–7. Diaries September 1, 1992–November 9, 1992.

14 This was the initial assessment of Staebler's papers.

15 Box R3–7. Diaries November 10, 1992–January 4, 1993.

16 Box R3–7. Diaries January 5, 1993–March 1, 1993.

17 Box R3–7. Diaries March 2, 1993–May 7, 1993.

18 Box 4 File 6. Edna's Journal September 1993–May 1994. Box 4 does contains archive files.

19 Box 4 File 7. Edna's Journal May 1994–February 1995.

20 Sandra Woolfrey, former director of Wilfrid Laurier University Press and close friend of Edna.

21 Box 4 File 8. Edna's Journal February 1995–April 1995.

22 Wilfrid Laurier University president, 1992–97.

23 Box 3 File 2.

24 Edna's Journal February 14–August 7, 1996.

25 Edna's Journal December 20, 1997–November 22, 1997. Lent by author.

26 Longtime Kitchener-Waterloo citizen Mabel Krug was awarded an Order of Canada for her tireless efforts in support of community programs.

27 Edna is including the *Schmecks Appeal* cookbook series of twelve here.

28 Kevin Thomason, Edna's neighbour at Sunfish Lake. Thomason maintains regular contact with Edna and often drives her to events or appointments.

29 Edna's Journal March 6, 1988–January 3, 1999. Lent by author.

30 Paul Knowles, then associate editor of the local business magazine *Exchange*.

31 Kathryn Wardropper of Wilfrid Laurier University Bookstore administers the Edna Staebler Award for Creative Non-Fiction.

32 Rose Murray, a friend and, like Edna, a successful cookbook author. Murray has also acted as a consultant and recipe developer for government ministries and food companies.

33 Edna's Journal January 1, 1999–December 31, 1999. Lent by the author.

34 John Van Alstyne Weaver, "To Youth," *In American, The Collected Poems of John V.A. Weaver* (New York: Alfred A. Knopf, 1939), 175–76. The ellipses in the poem are correct. On several occasions Weaver uses a set of four periods.

35 Joan Mackenzie, a writer friend in Ottawa.

36 Janice Williamson, *Crybaby!* (Edmonton: NeWest Press, 1998). Williamson did not win the award, which went to Michael Poole for *Romancing Mary Jane: A Year in the Life of a Failed Marijuana Grower* (Vancouver: Greystone Books, 1998).

13

2000 〜

Still Interested
and Interesting

IN HER NINETIES, STAEBLER BEGAN to think more and more about
telling her life story. Friends were passing on (February 7, 2000;
May 3, 2001) and she herself had endured some health complications (June 15, 2000).[1] Once again, the question of literary form arose. Several friends and admirers encouraged her to consider autobiography.
Others expressed eagerness to tackle her biography (September 20,
2000). A few suggested that her story was already written—in her journals, which only needed editing and some work from her (August 10,
2000).

Notwithstanding her slowly increasing personal retreat, Staebler was
still in demand and still enjoyed the attention. She was an appreciative
and appreciated guest at a party given by the Bertons (July 16, 2000). She
enjoyed a huge party in honour of her ninety-fifth birthday in January
2001.[2] She was invited guest speaker at the International Women's Day
Breakfast at Kitchener City Hall, March 1, 2001.[3] In October 2002, she was
invited to appear on *The Tonight Show*, with host Jay Leno, in California.
Newspapers across the country and the USA headlined the story of the
woman who turned down Leno.[4] "I told [him] it was too far and I hope
I said 'Thank you very much'" (October 2, 2002). By April 2003, it was
hardly a surprise that when Edna Staebler was announced as the guest
of honour for the annual Mayors' Dinner, hundreds signed up. It was the
largest turnout the dinner event had ever drawn.

In May 2003, Edna suffered a stroke, and while she rebounded with
the fortitude of someone many years younger, doctors advised against

full-time return to Sunfish Lake. Staebler took up residence in town, making occasional day trips to Sunfish Lake with friends. She no longer writes, neither in her journal nor in other forms. But she does continue to "get on with life as it presents itself to every new day, giving attention to every passing minute, to every person, pet, book, to whatever one can do or see or hear, to all of life as it is given to us" (April 2, 2002).

Notes

1 Staebler was especially sad at the death of her friend Gerald Noonan, a professor of English at Wilfrid Laurier University. In his memory and honour, she established the Gerald Noonan Scholarship, the first recipient of which, Sally Heath, worked as a research assistant for this book.

2 Held at Luther Village, a Waterloo retirement home, the party attracted friends and fans from across the country.

3 An invitation she declined with regret (February 24, 2001).

4 "Staebler Says No to Leno" (*Record*, October 4, 2002); "Leno Is Toast" (October 7, 2002).

▨ *top* 2001, summer. Edna with portraits and paintings; *bottom* Edna and Pierre Berton (photograph courtesy of Lawrence McNaught).

top The "cottage" at Sunfish Lake in winter; *bottom* October 2000. Edna on the dock at Sunfish Lake.

From the Diaries

February 7, 2000[1]
Gerry is dying. My dearest friend. Trish, his stepdaughter, called me yesterday afternoon to tell me he won't be here long and he was concerned about how he could tell me and she said if I want to see him I should go to him in the next two weeks! Gerry who has always been there, or here, for me ever since he came to teach at Laurier thirty years ago.

We always had so much to talk about when he came here, or on the phone, almost every week, often for over an hour, about books and people and my problems, never his. He was always so generous and thoughtful and kind. He did so much for me, nominated me for the honourary degree at WLU and wrote a beautiful citation, took me to the ceremony. He nominated me for the Order of Canada and helped plan the celebration of it at Castle Kilbride for Wilmot Township.

My house has so many gifts he has given me. Wherever I look there is something to remind me of Gerry. The bird clock on the wall which I glance at a dozen times a day, the light switch on my kitchen wall, the cow mug in my kitchen cupboard. There have been many other things given every Christmas and birthday for years and years.

And Gerry was always there. I could and did phone him whenever I needed, or wanted to ask his advice, or discuss things or people, or to just talk about books or cats or finances or our houses or travels, about anything.

He was so dependable. He'd take me wherever and whenever I wanted to go. He was my escort when I needed one at Marilyn Short's wedding. When being introduced to her stepmother, he said, "Edna is my best friend—and I am hers." And I'm sure that was true. He had girlfriends, but never for long. He was married to Pam for nine years. He had a couple of friends but none lasted forever as his friendship with me.

[...]

Ours was a strange relationship, in a way, a true friendship, not an emotional attachment tho' truly loving. If I hadn't been twenty-six years older than Gerry there might have been complications. Gerry—I can't think of my world without him. He's been my friend for so long, thirty years. He's always been there for me. I shall miss him more than I'd miss anyone.

Maybe I could establish a fellowship or scholarship in his name at WLU. I think he'd like that. He should be honoured in some way. He touched so many lives and everyone liked him. He always thought about people and what he could do for them and even when he was very busy he'd give them time and thought and help people he didn't know well— not friends, just people he'd met or taught. (5,110)

April 10, 2000
Whenever I'm invited to go anywhere out of town overnight, I am reluctant to go, nervous about a "trip" and preferring to stay comfortably at Sunfish with Mally [Edna's cat]. I'm always secretly hoping something will turn up to prevent me leaving. (5,185)

June 15, 2000
How can I forget this?[2] Pretend it doesn't exist? Look out at the world and people and love them and forget about *me*. That is what I'd have to do and how could I when I'd know people would be reluctant to look at me? I feel as if this can't be real. If I'd no longer look like myself how could I be me, sought after for my joy in many things, my humour, enthusiasm, and whatever it is that makes so many people say I am their role model? I am so *grateful* for all the friends and even strangers who make my life so remarkable and beautiful. I keep saying, "I am so lucky." I am constantly grateful for so many people, so many things, the whole world, my darling cat, Sunfish Lake and the hills and trees around it, the birds and chipmunks, and tho' I deplore them, the squirrels, raccoons. And my eyesight which allows me to read, see things, and drive my car, which gives me freedom to do my own shopping for food, to visit Eva, Nancy, anyone else I please. Meanwhile, until there is a change, I must keep loving those things. They are my life and they will be, or will they? It's all up to me. I must make myself concentrate on them and *forget about me, me, me*. (5,258)

July 16, 2000
Yesterday was the best Berton party yet. Of course, I have said that every year they had a Splash party. But there hasn't been one for five years. It was so wonderful to see so many old friends again, tho' most of them had changed a lot in those five years—fatter, frailer, older. The young ones had become middle-aged. Pierre said there were 182 and I'm sure more than half of them greeted me with a kiss and said how happy they were to see me and that I hadn't changed, tho' I was the oldest person there.

It was like a who's who of celebrities, even Adrienne Clarkson, our new governor general, wearing a short denim dress, said "Edna" and kissed me on both cheeks and introduced me to her husband John Ralston Saul, wearing a *pink* shirt and light trousers. We chatted until Margaret Atwood, wearing a black hat and dress, claimed Adrienne's attention. (5,292)

July 30, 2000[3]
I am so happily grateful for all these kind, caring, wonderful friends. How can I deserve them? It almost frightens me. They all seem so fond of me and do so much for me and I've done nothing for them, tho' they say I have, just by being me, an inspiration to all of them, a "role model." How can that be? Because I'm old? And still interested and interesting? (5,434)

August 6, 2000
The Dr. Robins MS [manuscript] was on my counter when I got home, rejected by Brian Henderson [director] at WLU Press. He thought they were "too formal," didn't say a word about mine, but that he was "quite excited" about my journal entries and would like to publish them. Would I? (5,448)

August 10, 2000
On Wednesday morning Stephen Notar [Edna's friend] came bringing me milk and a basket of peaches. He talked about my 1946 and 1953 journal entries which he'd read and was greatly impressed with. He said I don't need anyone to write my biography, it's been done in the journal. It's all there, needs editing only and some work from me. But do I want it done? Do I want people to know all the details about me and all the Staeblers? It would certainly be a juicy tale and sensational. What would my Mennonite friends think if they knew I'd had lovers? They'd be disillusioned, shocked, even tho' the affairs took place fifty years ago before I knew Eva and Nancy [Martin].

And what would my friends now think? They'd accept me as I am, perhaps have had lovers themselves. All the people who knew me long ago, except Marnie and Dottie, are dead.[4] Marnie knows me well and loves me. Dottie is no longer part of this world, is slipping away fast. What purpose would be served if my story were told? Ralph [Hodgson, Edna's brother-in-law] thinks it would be an inspiration, all my problems with K, how I kept my sanity and hope and finally triumphed and wrote the book I hoped to do and became what I am now. I'd probably be dead before a book could be written and printed, but do I now want to give my time to it or just drift along as I do now, enjoying visitors who come almost every day and getting no work done, not even keeping up with my correspondence. Am I vegetating? (5,450)

September 5, 2000
Horrid thought—what if I had a stroke and couldn't press my Lifeline button and no one would know and Mally would eat me! How horrid! (5,492)

September 18, 2000
Alistair McLeod, whose *No Great Mischief* has been on the bestseller list for forty-five weeks, told me that he still has the fan letter I wrote him years ago before he had a book, and with my literary papers in Guelph is his reply (I hope).[5] (5,512)

September 20, 2000
Talked on phone almost all yesterday. Over an hour with Veronica who wants to write my biography.[6] There is so much she doesn't know about me. I talked long with Kathryn [Wardropper] who thinks my journal is so exciting and well written that it should be published on its own. I seem to have had a public life and a private one. But hasn't one made the other? There is so much, it could require several volumes. Fascinating development of an insecure, uncertain, but striving person, being helped and given confidence and finally producing and giving and achieving many friends and an interesting, creative, and exciting life. I've been so lucky. (5,516)

October 17, 2000
Thinking about the speech I have to make tomorrow night when I present my award at WLU.[7] Establishing it is the most rewarding thing for me that I have done in the past ten years because it has brought so many wonderful people into my life. (5,544)

October 22, 2000
Unfortunately, so many things in my journal have been written but not finished, i.e., I told about K wanting to adopt a baby, but didn't tell that the Children's Aid refused to allow it because both K and Nort were alcoholics and Nort's daughter was in the Home in Orillia for the men-

tally disabled.[8] She had the age of a two year old until she died at thirty-five.

Actually, my biography could be several books, one alone on Fred [Kruger]. (5,550)

January 6, 2001[9]
Kathryn called me after dinner. She wants to have a tenth year celebration of my award here at Sunfish, about seventy-five people, media, publishers, award winners. She assured me I wouldn't have to do anything. There would be a tent, in case of rain, outdoor privies, a bar, catered food, a great literary event at my place which is a literary shrine. How could I cope with that? In the summer? Of course it could be wonderful, but in the summer when many people are on holiday?

I do think the tenth anniversary of the award should be recognized and publicized. An article should tell about the winners who have gone on to become bestsellers, perhaps have them tell what winning the award meant to them, giving confidence and recognition as it was meant to do, unlike the big awards which go to well-established writers who have perhaps already won other awards. (5,669)

January 16, 2001
It's hard to believe all this is happening to me. I think I said in my speech on Saturday I was just a skinny, shy little kid and now I'm ninety-five and all these lovely things are being done and said about me.[10] It's all so gratifying and unbelievable and undeserved. (5,798)

February 13, 2001
Wende [Gregory-Frei] went out for my three days of mail. Incredible letters. One made me cry as I read it, from a *Schmecks* fan who made the characters in *Schmecks* her family because her own parents abused her. And a letter from Joe Kleinsaser who was a little boy in the Hutterite colony I visited fifty years ago! Life never ceases to have these marvels. (5,831)

February 24, 2001
Now I wish I'd not refused to speak at the International Women's Day Breakfast at Kitchener City Hall on March 1. They expected me to do it and have sold out the space for two hundred and fifty, with TV coverage and media. I wrote that it would be too stressful for me to do it at 7:30 in the morning when I am normally still in bed.

I was asked to talk about myself, my achievements. That scared me. What would I say without seeming to boast? But this morning I thought I could and should talk about my creative non-fiction award and what it has meant to the people who have won it and the chance the occasion would give me to promote them and their books. Should I call and say I'd changed my mind and I will speak? (5,845)

May 3, 2001
In the past two years, I've lost eight friends thro' death and I miss them very much and need replacements.... I love my friends and I think they love me, tho' they don't need me as I need them. My cat Mally is the only one who couldn't live without me. I am number one in her life, in no one else's. My sisters depend on me in a way. They talk to me but we are not friends in the way my friends are. We have few interests in common. I've given them money and they like that, but they are critical of me and get mad at me for not doing whatever they would like. They resent my friendships and generosity now. (5,928)

June 5, 2001
When I was young, I didn't know I was beautiful. No one ever told me that, except Alph[onse] in Switzerland. Norm was the beauty in our family. I was self-conscious about my "buck teeth" and put my hand over my mouth to hide them. Posing for photographers I closed my mouth. It wasn't until I went to an orthodontist in Toronto when I was at U of T and he told me to forget about my teeth that I did and had freedom I hadn't known before. But it was many years before I became really me, years of introspection and struggle with my miserable marriage and inability to produce the writing I hoped to. It wasn't until after my divorce that I became really myself as I wanted to be and was able to work at my writing without agonizing over Keith. I had started writing magazine articles and *Cape Breton Harbour* during our last years together, from 1945–1961, when we separated. All my *Schmecks* books came after that. (5,970)

January 6, 2002[11]
Since I woke at 4:20 or so, I've been thinking about things to tell Veronica [Ross] about me. First, I dreamed I was a journalist whose first piece had been a success and two more reporters at the magazine where I worked were in love with me and I with them. One was a solid, pleas-

ant, unimaginative man who wanted me. The other was absorbed by his work, complex, complicated, in love with me but his work and life were more important to him and I knew that but was fascinated by him.

From all these thoughts, my mind wandered to my relationship with K, who was also complex, wonderful in many ways, but depressed unless he was actually engaged in a love affair with anyone else but me.

Enough of this, it could go on interminably. Veronica wants me to give her a list of the wise quotations of great writers that were helpful to me when I slid into introspection and fear.

[…]

"God has not given us the spirit of fear but of power and of love and of a sound mind." (II Timothy 1:7)

"Weeping may endure for a night but joy cometh in the morning." (Psalms 30:5)

"The fault, dear Brutus, is not in the stars

But in ourselves that we are underlings." (*Julius Caesar*)

"A little learning is a dangerous thing
Drink deep or taste not the Pierian spring
There shallow draughts intoxicate the brain
And drinking largely sobers us again." (Pope—*Essay on Criticism*)

"I want to be thoroughly used up when I die, for the harder I work, the more I live." (G.B. Shaw)

"The mind is its own place and in itself can make a hell of heaven and a heaven of hell." (John Milton) (6,230)

April 2, 2002 [12]
When I was a little girl, I thought the older one was, the wiser one would be. So now, at ninety-six, and the oldest person I know, I should be the wisest. Unfortunately, I know that I have much to learn. There is so much life has taught me but all along the way there have been unponderables which have made me wonder and given up trying to understand. There are, I'm sure, many mysteries which perhaps one can never solve, so one must let them go, accept them as eternal mysteries and get on with life as it presents itself to every new day, giving attention to every passing minute, to every person, pet, book, to whatever one can do or see or hear, to all of life as it is given to us. (6,228)

October 2, 2002

Then the phone rang, it was a woman from *The Tonight Show* in California asking me to come there to be on the show with Jay Leno! She'd read Nancy Silcox's *Record* story.[13] I told her it was too far and I hope I said "Thank you very much." I'd never seen *The Tonight Show* or heard of Jay Leno. Then Jim came in and was greatly impressed, could barely believe I'd been invited to be on the show, all expenses paid, as well as Kathryn Wardropper's who had been phoned and asked to come with me! Jim said it is the biggest U.S. show. One hour long with interviews with celebrities who give anything to be on it. He said it has two million viewers a night! *And I'd turned it down.*

[…]

The Tonight Show came on at 11:35 and Mally and I watched it. Thousands of viewers in a huge auditorium standing and *screaming* as soon as Jay Leno came out on the great stage where there was a full orchestra. He is tall, with grey-black hair, a long face with a big *chin* like Brian Mulroney's.[14] For the first half hour he stood and told smart-alec stories like a stand-up comic (I can't stand any of them and never listen to them). Then he had a coloured man who is the lead in *My Wife and the Kids* sit beside him and talk and laugh. But I didn't think he was funny, and fell asleep briefly, while another young TV celebrity came and talked and Jay Leno laughed and listened. And the audience did the same. And that was it. Mally had stayed in the wing chair all thro' the programme. I said to her, "We're quiet people. That show is not for us. All those Americans screaming at the sight of TV celebrities. We're not part of that. What could I possibly contribute to a show like that?" And we went to bed. (6,328)

Notes

1 Edna's Journal January 2000–July 23, 2000. Lent by author.

2 A scare with skin cancer was treated with success.

3 Edna's Journal July 2000–January 2001. Lent by author.

4 Friends Marnie Paisley and Dorothy (Dottie) Shoemaker.

5 Alistair Macleod, *No Great Mischief* (Toronto: McClelland and Stewart, 1999).

6 Veronica Ross published *To Experience Wonder: Edna Staebler, A Life* with Dundurn Press in autumn 2003.

7 The Edna Staebler Award for Creative Non-Fiction in 2000 was won by Wayson Choy for *Paper Shadows: A Chinatown Childhood.*

8 Linda was Norton Staebler's daughter by his first wife, Helen Waimel.

9 Edna's Journal January 1, 2001–December 31, 2001. Lent by the author.

10 The ninety-fifth birthday party celebration, held for Edna at Luther Village.
11 Edna's Journal January 2, 2002–March 25, 2002. Lent by the author. Pagination is irregular in this journal.
12 Edna's Journal March 26, 2002–November 2, 2002. Lent by the author.
13 Nancy Silcox, "Too Busy to Slow Down: At 96, Edna Staebler Is Writing Less, but Only because Other Passions Fill Her Time," *Record*, Saturday, August 31, 2002, G1.
14 Brian Mulroney was prime minister of Canada from 1984–1993.

Bibliography

Works by Edna Staebler

Journalism (Selected)

"Airline That Goes Almost Anywhere and Does Practically Everything." *Maclean's,* April 17, 1965.

"Boats That Sail a Warpath." *Maclean's,* July 1, 1951.

"Cooking the Evidence." *Saturday Night,* May 1987.

"Country Cooking Mennonite Style." *The Old Farmer's Almanac Canadian Edition,* no. 201, 176–79. Dublin, NH: Yankee, 1993.

"Duellists of the Deep." *Maclean's,* July 15, 1948.

"Happily Married Cities." *Maclean's,* October 1, 1952.

"How to Live without Wars and Wedding Rings." *Maclean's,* April 1, 1950.

"Isles of Codfish and Champagne." *Maclean's,* November 1, 1950.

"Italian Canadians." *Chatelaine,* March 1965.

"The Lord Will Take Care of Us." *Maclean's,* March 15, 1952.

"Maggie's Leaving Home." *Maclean's,* November 1, 1951.

"Market Day in Kitchener." *Maclean's,* September 4, 1965.

"Miner's Wife." *Chatelaine,* March 1962.

"School of Tomorrow in a Town of Tomorrow" [Wabush, Labrador]. *Maclean's,* January 23, 1965.

"Stratford's Dark Day." *Maclean's,* January 22, 1966.

"Those Mouth-watering Mennonite Meals." *Maclean's,* April 1, 1954.

"Unconquered Warriors of the Oshweken (Six Nations)." *Maclean's,* November 12, 1955.

"The Village That Lives One Day at a Time." *Chatelaine,* December 1961.

"We're Happy Being Slaves of Jehovah." *Toronto Star Weekly,* June 1963.

"Why the Amish Want No Part of Progress." *Maclean's,* September 17, 1958.
"Would You Change the Lives of These People?" *Maclean's,* May 12, 1956.

Books and Cookbooks

Cape Breton Harbour. Toronto: McClelland and Stewart, 1972; Toronto: McGraw-Hill Ryerson, 1990.
Food That Really Schmecks: Mennonite Country Cooking as Prepared by My Mennonite Friend, Bevvy Martin, My Mother, and Other Fine Cooks. Toronto: McGraw-Hill Ryerson, 1968.
Haven't Any News: Ruby's Letters from the '50s. Edited by Edna Staebler. Waterloo: Wilfrid Laurier UP, 1995.
More Food That Really Schmecks. 1967. Reprint, Toronto: McClelland and Stewart, 1979.
Sauerkraut and Enterprise. University Women's Club of Kitchener-Waterloo, 1967; Toronto: McClelland and Stewart, 1969.
Schmecks Appeal. More Mennonite Cooking. Toronto: McClelland and Stewart, 1987.
Schmecks Appeal cookbook series. Toronto: McClelland and Stewart, 1990.
Whatever Happened to Maggie and Other People I've Known. Toronto: McClelland and Stewart, 1983; reprinted as *Places I've Been and People I've Known: Stories from Across Canada* by McGraw-Hill Ryerson, 1990.

Unpublished Speeches/Addresses

"Convocation Address." Wilfrid Laurier University, October 28, 1984.
"My Writing Life." Margaret Laurence Lecture, Writers' Union Address, Kingston, Ontario, May 24, 1997.

Reference Works

Benstock, Shari, ed. *The Private Self: Theory and Practice of Women's Autobiographical Writings.* Chapel Hill: U of North Carolina P, 1988.
Bishop, Alan. Introduction to *Vera Brittain: War Diary, 1913–1917: Chronicles of Youth,* ed. Alan Bishop, 16–18. London: Victor Gollancz, 1981.
Blodgett, Harriet. *Centuries of Female Days: Englishwomen's Private Diaries.* New Brunswick, NJ: Rutgers UP, 1988.
Brande, Dorothea. *Becoming a Writer.* New York: Harcourt, Brace, 1934.
Brittain, Vera Foreword to *A Chronicle of Youth,* in *Vera Brittain: War Diary, 1913–1917: Chronicle of Youth,* ed. Alan Bishop, 13. London: Victor Gollancz, 1981.
———. *Testament of Youth: An Autobiographical Study of the Years 1900–1925.* London: Gollanz, 1933.
———. *Testament of Friendship: The Story of Winifred Holtby.* London: Macmillan, 1940.

Brownley, Martine Watson, and Allison B. Kimmich, eds. "Theorizing the Female Subject: Who Writes, How, and Why?" *Women and Autobiography*. 95–96. Wilmington, DE: Scholarly Resources, 1999.

Bunkers, Suzanne L., and Cynthia A. Huff, eds. *Inscribing the Daily: Critical Essays on Women's Diaries*. Amherst: U of Massachusetts P, 1996.

Buss, Helen M. *Mapping Our Selves: Canadian Women's Autoiography in English*. Montreal: McGill-Queen's, 1993.

Buss, Helen M. "Reading for the Doubled Discourse of American Women's Autobiography." *Women and Autobiography*, ed. Suzanne L. Bunkers and Cynthia A. Huff, 97–112. Wilmington, DE: Scholarly Resources, 1999.

Carter, Kathryn, ed. *The Small Details of Life: Twenty Diaries by Women in Canada, 1830–1996*. Toronto: U. of Toronto P, 2002.

Culley, Margo, ed. *A Day at a Time: The Diary Literature of American Women from 1764 to the Present*. New York: Feminist P at CUNY, 1985.

———. *American Women's Autobiography: Fea(s)ts of Memory*. Madison: U of Wisconsin P, 1992.

Egan, Susanna. *Mirror Talk: Genres of Crisis in Contemporary Autobiography*. Chapel Hill, NC: U of North Carolina P, 1999.

Egan, Susanna, and Gabriele Helms. "Introduction: Auto/biography? Yes. But Canadian?" *Canadian Literature* 172 (Spring 2002): 5–16.

Fothergill, Robert A. *Private Chronicles : A Study of English Diaries*. London: Oxford UP, 1974.

Freedman, Diane P. "Border Crossing as Method and Motif in Contemporary American Writing, or, How Freud Helped Me Case the Joint." *The Intimate Critique: Autobiographical Literary Criticism*, ed. Diane P. Freedman, Olivia Frey, and Frances Murphy Zauhar. 13–22. Durham: Duke UP, 1993.

Godwin, Gail. "A Diarist on Diarists." *Antaeus* 60–61 (Autumn 1988): 9–15.

Hamsten, Elizabeth. *"Read This Only to Yourself": The Private Writings of Midwestern Women, 1880–1910*. Bloomington: Indiana UP, 1982.

Heilbrun, Carolyn G. *Writing a Woman's Life*. New York: Norton, 1988.

Hogan, Rebecca. "Engendered Autobiographies: The Diary as a Feminine Form." *Prose Studies: Special Issue on Autobiography and Question of Gender* 14.5 (September 1991): 95–107.

Huff, Cynthia A. "Textual Boundaries: Space in Nineteenth-Century Women's Manuscript Diaries." *Inscribing the Daily: Critical Essays on Women's Diaries*, ed. Suzanne L. Bunkers and Cynthia A. Huff. 122–38. Amherst: U of Massachusetts P, 1996.

Jelinek, Estelle. *The Tradition of Women's Autobiography: From Antiquity to the Present*. Boston: Twayne, 1986.

Jelinek, Estelle, ed. *Women's Autobiography: Essays in Criticism*. Bloomington: Indiana UP, 1980.

Kadar, Marlene, ed. *Essays in Life Writing.* Toronto: York University, Robarts Centre for Canadian Studies, 1989.

————, ed. *Essays on Life Writing: From Genre to Critical Practice.* Toronto: U of Toronto P, 1992.

Lejeune, Philippe. *Le Moi des Demoiselles: Enquête sur le Journal de Jeune Fille.* Paris: Seuil, 1993.

————. *On Autobiography.* Ed. Paul John Eakin. Trans. Katherine Leary. Minneapolis: U of Minnesota P, 1989.

Lensink, Judy Nolte. "Expanding the Boundaries of Criticism: The Diary as Female Autobiography." *Women's Studies* 14 (1987): 39–53.

Mairs, Nancy. *Remembering the Bare House.* New York: Harper and Row, 1989.

Miller, Judith. "Edna Staebler. Diary, Ontario, 1996." *The Small Details of Life: Twenty Diaries by Women in Canada, 1830–1996,* ed. Kathryn Carter, 454–57. Toronto: U of Toronto P.

Miller, Nancy K. *Getting Personal: Feminist Occasions and Other Autobiographical Acts.* New York and London: Routledge, 1991.

Neuman, Shirley. "Introduction: Reading Canadian Autobiography." Special Issue "Reading Canadian Autobiography." *Essays on Canadian Writing* 60 (Winter 1996): 1–13.

Neuman, Shirley, ed. *Autobiography and Questions of Gender.* London: Frank Cass, 1991.

Olney, James, ed. *Studies in Autobiography.* New York: Oxford UP, 1988.

Podnieks, Elizabeth. *Daily Modernism: The Literary Diaries of Virgina Woolf, Antonia White, Elizabeth Smart, and Anaïs Nin.* Montreal and Kingston: McGill-Queen's UP, 2000.

Rafferty, Ann. "Edna Staebler." *Women of Waterloo County,* ed. Ruth Russell, 189–99. Kitchener-Waterloo: Canadian Federation of University Women, 2000.

Rhiel, Mary, and David Suchoff, eds. *The Seductions of Biography.* New York and London: Routledge, 1996.

Rosenwald, Lawrence. *Emerson and the Art of the Diary.* New York: Oxford UP, 1988.

Russell, Ruth, ed. *Women of Waterloo County.* Kitchener-Waterloo: Canadian Federation of University Women, 2000.

Simons, Judy. *Diaries and Journals of Literary Women from Fanny Burney to Virginia Woolf.* Iowa City: U of Iowa P, 1990.

Smith, Sidonie. *A Poetics of Women's Autobiography: Marginality and the Fictions of Self-Representation.* Bloomington: Indiana UP, 1987.

Smith, Sidonie, and Julia Watson, eds. *Women, Autobiography, Theory: A Reader.* Madison, WI: U of Wisconsin P, 1998.

Ueland, Brenda. *If You Want to Write.* New York: G.P. Putnam, 1938.

Verduyn, Christl. *Marian Engel's Notebooks: "Ah, mon cahier, écoute...."* Waterloo: Wilfrid Laurier UP, 1999.

Waxman, Barbara Frey. *To Live in the Center of the Moment: Literary Autobiographies of Aging.* Charlottesville: U of Virginia P, 1997.

Index

Life Writing Series

In the **Life Writing Series**, Wilfrid Laurier University Press publishes life writing and new life-writing criticism in order to promote autobiographical accounts, diaries, letters, and testimonials written and/or told by women and men whose political, literary, or philosophical purposes are central to their lives. **Life Writing** features the accounts of ordinary people, written in English, or translated into English from French or the languages of the First Nations or from any of the languages of immigration to Canada. Life Writing will also publish original theoretical investigations about life writing, as long as they are not limited to one author or text.

Priority is given to manuscripts that provide access to those voices that have not traditionally had access to the publication process.

Manuscripts of social, cultural, and historical interest that are considered for the series, but are not published, are maintained in the **Life Writing Archive** of Wilfrid Laurier University Library.

Series Editor
Marlene Kadar
Humanities Division, York University

Manuscripts to be sent to
Brian Henderson, Director
Wilfrid Laurier University Press
75 University Avenue West
Waterloo, Ontario, Canada N2L 3C5

Books in the Life Writing Series
Published by Wilfrid Laurier University Press